THE SANDSTORM

Also by David Kimche, with Jon Kimche

Both sides of the hill
The secret roads

THE SANDSTORM

The Arab-Israeli war of June 1967: prelude and aftermath

David Kimche and Dan Bawly

London: Secker & Warburg

First published in England 1968 by
Martin Secker and Warburg Limited
14 Carlisle Street, W1

Copyright © 1968 by David Kimche and Dan Bawly

SBN 436 23380 0

TO ILON AND RUTH

Printed in Great Britain by
Billing & Sons Limited, Guildford and London

Contents

Contents

List of Illustrations

Acknowledgments

In the course of collecting material for this book we received help from dozens of people. The majority would, we feel, prefer not to have their names mentioned. This is as true for those Israelis who divulged to us the behind-the-scenes conflicts in Government and party as for the many Arabs in Cis-Jordan who provided us with a wealth of detail regarding the situation in Jordan before and during the June War. As for the numerous army officers who helped us, courtesy to Israeli military regulations forbids us to mention their names. We prefer, therefore, to forgo the pleasure of name-dropping, and to thank all those who gave us assistance without divulging their identities. There are, however, two names we can mention without fear of unpleasant repercussions—those of our wives, Ruth and Ilon, without whose forbearance and encouragement this book would never have been written. And we would also like to thank Jon Kimche, whose advice throughout the writing of this book was invaluable.

March 1968   D. K.
                                                            D. B.

Part I : Prelude

CHAPTER 1

The Arabs March to the Brink

One of the key figures in the Middle East today, who must bear much of the responsibility for the events which led up to the Six-Day War, is a man whose name very few people have ever heard. He is a small, balding man, in his late thirties, hardly the type to draw attention. But those who know him worship him. They speak of his magnetic personality, and describe him as a born leader. His name is Yasir Arafat. He is the secret chief of the Fatah,* the Palestinian underground terrorist organization.

Several years ago, the Fatah leaders, with Yasir Arafat at their head, swore to do everything in their power to bring about a military confrontation between the Arab states and Israel. This was their avowed goal. And it was to achieve this objective that they organized terror strikes against Israel. Indeed, loss of life and property within Israel itself was only a secondary aim of the Fatah: their main purpose was to bring about an escalation of Israeli–Arab tension, to bring that tension to a breaking-point so that war would be the inevitable and logical outcome.

The Fatah leaders succeeded in achieving their design, though they could not have visualized the disastrous outcome for the Arab people. For it was largely because of the actions of the small band of Fatah, and similar Palestinian clandestine organizations, that the chain of events was set in motion which led inexorably to that final showdown on the sands of Sinai and in the hills of Judea, Samaria and Hauran.

* The full name of the organization is Harakat-Tahrir Falastin, Fatah being the inverted initials of this name.

It is for this reason that we decided to open our book with the birth of the Fatah movement. Others may choose different starting-points of the events which led to the Six-Day War. The Arabs, who like to view history in a broad sweep, unhesitatingly point to the establishment of the State of Israel in 1948, or even to the founding of the World Zionist Organization in the late nineteenth century, as the real cause for the June War. The Israelis, more pragmatic, claim that the concentration along Israel's southern border of nearly 100,000 Egyptian troops with 1000 tanks and all the paraphernalia of a modern army bent on war, set in train the events which led to the expulsion of the UN Emergency Force, the closing of the Gulf of Aqaba and, finally and inevitably, to war. The Russians declare that it all began because the Israelis were about to launch a massive attack on Syria on 18 May, while the Churchills* assert that it was this Soviet claim—and their warning to Egypt and to Syria—which led to the movement of armies and thus acted as the tinder which set the Middle East aflame.

The choice is largely an academic one. Any of these starting-points—except, perhaps, the false claim of the Russians—could be taken quite legitimately. But we prefer the Fatah, for it had been their prescribed intent to bring about the war which took place, though they naturally had hoped for and expected a very different result from the confrontation they had engineered.

One of the striking features of the Arab countries, and indeed of many other parts of the world, is that the extremists set the tone of political behaviour; the would-be moderates have, time and time again, been intimidated into silence by the bellicose attitude taken by what is often a fanatic minority. The extremists could be found in every Arab government, indeed in every Arab institution. But towards the end of the 1950s a new dimension was added to Arab extremism—the Palestinian underground terror organizations, whose leaders held the Arab moderates in

* Randolph and Winston Churchill: *The Six Day War*; Heinemann, London, 1967.

bitter contempt. Of these organizations, the most important was the Fatah.

We cannot point to any precise date, place or event to mark the birth of this movement. Its antecedents can be found among Palestinian university students and high-school pupils from Syria and to a lesser extent, the Lebanon, who, in the early 'fifties, were organized in a para-military youth movement which became very active in the refugee camps of these two countries. These youngsters were great enthusiasts. They were given training in the use of light arms and in fieldcraft, and, aided by financial contributions from the former Mufti* of Palestine and from the Syrian Government, they set up clubrooms in the refugee camps, organized social activities and initiated ideological sessions in which the glories of Arab nationalism and the wickedness of the Jews formed the two major themes. In the mid-'fifties some of these students left for Europe to continue their studies. Most of them went to Germany and Austria where there were many Arab students at the universities. A large number made their way to the University of Stuttgart, which was destined to become the centre of all Palestinian nationalist activity in Europe. The Arab students soon acclimatized themselves to their new surroundings, and within months of their arrival in Germany, were once more deeply absorbed in ideological discussions and political activity.

Similar discussions were at the same time being held by Palestinians in the universities of Cairo and Baghdad and at the American University of Beirut. The subject was always the same: how to eliminate Israel as a political entity, restore the lands of the Palestinians, and establish an independent Palestinian state in the territory held by Israel, on the one hand, and by Jordan, on the other. But when it came to translating their thoughts into action these young Palestinians displayed a marked lack of ingenuity. Political organizations were formed, some even in the form of underground movements, but they never lasted long.

---

* Haj Amin al-Husseini, who was appointed Mufti of Jerusalem by the first British High Commissioner for Palestine, Sir Herbert Samuel.

Indeed, the very profusion of such groupings demonstrated the lack of seriousness of these first efforts. In the last ten years between forty and fifty Palestinian clandestine organizations have made their appearance on the Arab scene.* Some of them were formed and dispersed within a matter of months; others were disbanded, only to appear again under a different name with the same leaders. There was a certain amoeba-like quality in this constant grouping and regrouping of the Palestinian intelligentsia during the 'fifties. Their one great weakness was that they depended for their existence on the Arab countries, in which the movements were created, but, since 1949, the Palestinians had by and large been as a plaything in the hands of the Arab states. Each state made use of them for its own purposes. Thus they were either suppressed or recruited into the services of one or the other Arab country. The Palestinians changed allegiances and switched ideologies in accordance with the support—or lack of it—given them by the Arab rulers. And, as the inter-Arab fighting increased throughout the 'fifties, so too did the Palestinian intelligentsia become increasingly divided among itself. There were those who set up organizations under the aegis of the Egyptians, there were others who came under the protection of the Syrians or the Iraqis, or even under the Jordanians, who set up their own puppet organizations to counter the activities of the others.

Some of these Palestinian clandestine movements became glorified mercenaries, employed by their benefactors to engage in subversive activity in rival Arab countries. It was not surprising, therefore, that those countries most subjected to sub-

---

* The most prominent were Ahmad Shuqairi's Palestine Liberation Organization based in Cairo, the Fatah, and the "Jab'at Tahrir Falastini" – the Palestinian Liberation Front. The Front was an extreme left-wing body, closely associated with the Ba'th of Syria, believing that the Palestinian problem could not be solved without first overthrowing the reactionary Arab régimes. Palestine itself must be liberated by revolutionary action. The leaders of the Front are Ali Bushnaq and Ahmad Jabvil, while its leading theoretician is Fadil Shrur. The Front's activities, like those of Fatah, have been based in Syria.

version and agitation—Jordan, the Lebanon, Saudi Arabia—put these Palestinian organizations at the head of their lists of "dangerous elements". At best they were kept under close surveillance, but in times of stress and tension their members were more often than not clapped into jail or put under house arrest.

With such conditions prevailing in the Arab countries, it is hardly surprising, therefore, that the first successful attempt at establishing an independent Palestinian underground movement should have been made, not on Arab soil, but in distant Germany.

We must now return to Stuttgart, where Palestinians from Syria had enrolled as students. Among them was Yasir Arafat, who quickly became known among his fellow Arab students for his uncompromising and fanatic views. Together with him were Hani al-Hassan and Khalil al-Wazir. Hani, who became head of the powerful Stuttgart section of the Fatah, was no youngster; in his late thirties, he typified a large number of the Arab students who would spend ten or even more years "studying" for a degree, but who in reality spent more time immersed in politics than in their textbooks. Khalil al-Wazir was to become a key figure in the Fatah, for it was he who linked the budding clandestine movement with a much more powerful Arab underground which at that time was operating with ever-increasing success: the Algerian FLN. Khalil was a good friend of the FLN leader Khaidar, and through him extracted promises of help, which the independent state of Algeria later fulfilled to the letter.

In the late 'fifties these three, together with colleagues in Stuttgart and the other German and Austrian universities, formally established the Fatah. In a series of lengthy meetings, they expounded the ideology of their new movement: all inter-Arab questions were secondary to the primary aim, the "liberation" of Palestine; no reliance could be placed on any of the Arab leaders; the Palestinians must themselves fight for the liberation of their country, but as the Palestinians have no chance of defeating the Israeli army on their own, it was their duty to force the Arab countries to war by a steady escalation of Arab–Israeli hostility; this could be brought about by constant terror strikes against Israel—for terror leads to retaliation, which in turn creates rising tension and eventually war.

Their first task, however, was to recruit members and to gain strength. The Palestinian students were organized in a Palestinian Students' Association whose headquarters was situated in Cairo and which was very effectively under Egyptian influence. Its largest section was in Germany.* The Fatah students set about capturing the section from within. They succeeded in winning over the leading personalities, and by 1964 had completely dominated the Palestinian Students' Association in Germany and Austria, making it virtually independent of its Egyptian parent organization. By that time they had enrolled many hundreds of students in Fatah. They set up Fatah cells in all the large universities of Germany and Austria, as well as in Italy, Spain and Yugoslavia. But most of these students were active in pseudo-clandestine activities only: they collected money, distributed propaganda material, and held indoctrination sessions among the students and among the Arab unskilled labourers who worked in Central Europe in their thousands. The real business of organizing terror and violence was left to the inner ring of hard-core veterans centred around Stuttgart and to their emissaries whom they sent to the Arab countries bordering Israel.

The task of running the Fatah in Germany was left to Hani al-Hassan. The Fatah chief, Yasir Arafat and his aide, Khalil al-Wazir, were concerned with bigger game. In the early 'sixties they set out on the road taken nowadays by so many revolutionary have-nots—they went to Peking, where they were given a cordial welcome, a promise of help, and a special crash course in the arts of guerrilla tactics and popular warfare.

But the Chinese were not the only ones willing to help. Khalil al-Wazir's contacts with the Algerian FLN paid off once Algeria became independent under Ben Bella and a mecca for struggling

* Austria is a sub-section of the German group.

clandestine movements. Camps were set up in which nationalists from Africa and the Persian Gulf underwent military training. The Fatah leaders were also invited to send would-be guerrilla fighters to these camps. At the same time a Palestinian Office was set up at Algiers and Khalil became its head. All Palestinians in Algeria had to register at the Office as a condition for obtaining work permits. In this manner the Fatah was able to exercise pressure on the many thousands of Palestinians residing in Algeria.* While Khalil was active in Algeria, Yasir was preparing the ground for Fatah activity in the other Arab countries. He had initial success in Kuwait, where Palestinians made up a significant proportion of the entire population. The Emir of Kuwait agreed to the establishment of training camps and to the recruitment of members, and Kuwait together with Algeria became in the early 'sixties the main Fatah bases.

But this was not enough for Yasir Arafat. Neither Kuwait nor Algeria bordered Israel. He was in need of a forward base, alongside Israel, from which he could launch his terrorist attacks. Yasir Arafat turned to the one country he knew would give haven to the Fatah terrorists, the country in which he and his colleagues had begun their activities in the mid-'fifties—to Syria. And the Syrians welcomed him with open arms.

At that stage at least the Fatah leaders still remained faithful to their vow to remain independent of the Arab countries. They needed Syrian help, but were not yet willing to compromise their independence in order to obtain it.

During this early stage of Fatah activities, the Syrians allowed them to maintain their independence and agreed to help them.

This help was very necessary to them, for their training programmes in Algeria and Kuwait were proving dismal failures. Many hundreds of Palestinians had indeed been sent to the training camps, especially in Algeria, but hardly any of them made their way to the Middle East after completion of training.

* Many of them were employed as Arabic teachers, of whom the Algerians were chronically short.

The Palestinian students, it appeared, had no stomach for violence. They preferred to return to their studies in Europe. They were not of the stuff that terrorists are made of. The Fatah leaders, therefore, had to fall back on an entirely different method of implementing their aims. They took to hiring professional smugglers, robbers and killers from the fringe society of the refugee camps in the Middle East, to carry out, on a strictly cash basis, the terror strikes against Israel. This great gap between the ideologists of the Fatah leadership and those putting this "ideology" into effect became the Achilles heel of the movement. Fatah emissaries scoured the camps hunting for recruits from among the criminals and the outcasts. They would offer them a monthly pay of £15 plus special bonuses for difficult "jobs". Thus Fatah terror, instead of becoming the highest expression of a nationalist Freedom Movement—a Palestinian Viet Cong or FLN—as its leaders had visualized, became in actual fact a highly remunerative business for a number of toughs and cut-throats. The result was mutual suspicion and lack of confidence between the leadership and the rank-and-file which, more often than not, was totally justified. The terrorists who were eventually to penetrate into Israel often preferred to sit the night out in a place of concealment, dump their explosives anywhere and then report back that their task had been successfully carried out, rather than risk capture by Israeli patrols. This was the reason for the large number of Fatah communiqués announcing actions successfully undertaken which, in fact, had never taken place at all. For the same reason, the first actions of the Fatah were pitifully ineffective. Moreover, any terrorists sent by the Fatah and caught by the Israelis hastened to tell their captors all they knew about the organization, for they had little or no ideological motivation for withholding information. The Fatah leaders were therefore forced to tighten security and intensify the clandestine nature of the movement. They now acted under aliases, and used cut-outs in their dealings with the rank-and-file. The Fatah chief, Yasir Arafat, took on the alias Abu Amar (but was more generally known simply as the Doctor); Khalil al-Wazir became known in the organization as Abu-Jihad.

This switch from the Palestinians of Germany, Algeria and Kuwait to the fringe element of refugee society in Jordan, Lebanon and Syria forced the Fatah to change their entire tactics. They could not handle the task of recruiting, arming and preparing the refugee terrorists on their own. The Syrians, who over the years had developed widespread networks of their own in the refugee camps, especially in northern Jordan and southern Lebanon, could help, and they did.

The Syrians had their own reasons for giving limited help to Arafat and his friends. On 28 September 1961 a group of Syrian army officers had arrested Field-Marshal abd al-Hakim Amer in Damascus, bundled him on a plane bound for Cairo, and announced Syria's secession from the United Arab Republic. For President Nasser the Syrian secession was a stunning blow, and he never forgave them. He refused to have anything to do with the leaders who now took over the reins of power in the newly restored independent "Syrian Arab Republic". The overthrow of the Syrian régime became a priority for Egypt's intelligence services. While the Egyptian propaganda machine poured scorn on the Syrian leaders, Egyptian agents stirred up trouble inside Syria, and President Nasser himself brought all his influence to bear within the Arab world in order to isolate the Syrian régime.

The right-wing civilian régime which had taken over in Syria was weak and uncertain of itself. Cabinets were reshuffled, ministers replaced, policies changed. It hardly needed the army coup on 8 March 1963 to bring about the final collapse of Syrian parliamentary rule, for it was on the verge of disintegration when the army struck. The army take-over, however, did not change the turbulent character of Syria's internal politics. Throughout the spring and summer of 1963 the various political elements in Syria, as reflected inside the Syrian army, jockeyed for power. There were the pro-Nasserists, represented by General Quytaini and his supporters, who wished to restore the union with Egypt, and there were, increasingly, the supporters of the Ba'th Socialist Party, and foremost among them, the colonel who had been brought back from his post as military attaché in Buenos Aires to become Minister of Interior—Amin al-Hafiz. On 18 July 1963 a bloody attempt by the Nasserists to gain control of the Government was foiled by the pro-Ba'th elements in the army, and Amin al-Hafiz took over as the effective ruler of the country. The Ba'th rule over Syria was now complete.

If there had been any hope of reaching a settlement between the previous government of Syria and Nasser, there was none now. In the words of Malcom Kerr, "There was blood between them (the Nasserites) and the Ba'th, and 'Abd al-Nasir himself had declared war".* Henceforth it was a fight with the gloves off, and the two régimes poured vituperation on each other. For the first few months, the Hafiz Government could draw comfort from the fact that a Ba'th régime ruled in neighbouring Iraq, where abd al-Karim Qasim had been assassinated and his régime overthrown in February 1963. And, indeed, the talks which were now being held between the Syrian and Iraqi Ba'th leaders on a possible union between their two countries increased Egyptian determination to bring about the downfall of the Ba'th régimes at all costs—a determination which was exacerbated by the failure of the union talks which the Ba'thists held with President Nasser in March 1963. But by November 1963 the Ba'th hold over Iraq had been eliminated by the Iraqis themselves, and their President, abd as-salam Aref, was once more drawing his country closer to Cairo.

The Ba'thists of Syria were now the odd men out in the Arab world. Baghdad and Cairo treated them as traitors to the cause of Arab unity,† and openly called on the Syrian people to revolt against them. The Ba'th had long been banned in Jordan, and the conservative régimes in Amman, Riadh, Rabat and else-

* M. Kerr *The Arab Cold War*, 1958–1964 *A Study of Ideology in Politics*, Chatham House Series, London, 1965, p. 121.

† The Egyptians effectively pointed their finger at them for having been responsible for breaking up the one practical attempt at Arab unity—the Egyptian–Syrian Union.

where in the Arab world looked askance at the upstarts of Damascus who preached socialist revolution for the entire Arab world. Isolated, devoid of friends and allies, the Syrian Ba'thists set out to demonstrate to the people of Syria and to the other Arab countries that they were the real defenders of Arab nationalism, and that their path was the correct one, to be followed by all Arabs whose aim was to restore the glory of the Arab people.

But this was not so easy to prove. It was Nasser, not the Ba'th, who was reaping the glories of Arab leadership. He, and not the Ba'th, symbolized the struggle for Arab unity; the Egyptians, far more than the Ba'th, had coined the term "Arab socialism" as their own, and were pointing the way for Arab progressives to follow. The Syrians were in a quandary. They were keenly aware of their isolation, and wished, above all, to win full recognition by the Arab countries. They were desperately anxious to prove their superiority over the Nasserists, who were their main rivals and constituted their greatest danger. The unspoken attitude of the Syrian Ba'th leaders towards Egypt could be summed up in the words of a popular song, "Anything you can do we can do better", but they were at a loss as to how to put this into practice. They could not outmatch the Egyptians in promoting Arab unity, nor in being more socialist than the socialist régime of Nasser. But there was a third domain, the struggle against Israel, and here it was that Yasir Arafat and his Fatah organization merged into the picture. By becoming the champions of Arab endeavours to "liberate" Palestine, the Syrians could demonstrate the purity of their Arab nationalism, and in this manner "buy" back a respected place in the Arab family of nations. Moreover, the Fatah ideology of forcing a war against Israel suited the Syrian belief in the need for a "revolutionary peoples' war", while serving at the same time as an excellent means of blackmail, particularly against Egypt, so as to attain the full recognition the Syrians so urgently sought.

For Nasser was not ready for such a war. He had said so time and time again and was doing his utmost to prevent a conflagration from breaking out. Not that Nasser was any more favourably inclined to Israel than other Arab leaders. Far from it. But he recognized his own weakness, and had categorically stated that until his army was powerful enough to crush Israel it would be madness to provoke Israel to combat. Nasser, therefore, exercised extreme caution on the Israeli question. He had years before disbanded the Fedayeen (commando units) whose raids into Israel in the early 'fifties had been one of the prime causes of Israel's attack in 1956. Indeed, since the Suez War, there had hardly been any incidents along the Israeli–Egyptian frontier.

The Syrians knew of Nasser's caution, and understood its motives. And they realized that here was the ideal stick with which they could beat the Egyptians. By leading the crusade against Israel, the Syrians would be manœuvring the Egyptians into an invidious position and might thus succeed in forcing the Egyptians to grant recognition to the Ba'th régime and end its isolation. Hence the welcome given to the Fatah leaders when they turned to the Syrian Government for help.

Towards the end of 1963 the Syrians were given a golden opportunity of putting their belligerent policy into practice. In December 1963 the Israelis announced the completion of their Jordan water project, whose aim was to divert water from the Sea of Galilee to the parched soil of the Negev in southern Israel. The Arabs had repeatedly declared that they considered the project to constitute an act of aggression which would be met by force. Nasser himself had once declared that the Arabs would oppose the Jordan diversion project, even if it would cost the Arabs a million casualties. Now Syria called on Nasser to cash his cheque. If he did not, they warned, Syria would go to war against Israel alone. And they deliberately provoked a series of border incidents in order to drive their point home.

The circumstances, linked with the Syrian threats, put Nasser in an awkward position. He could not sit idly by and allow the Israelis to put their project into operation without lifting a finger to stop them, especially after all that had been said on the subject of the Jordan waters in the past. Nor could he risk going to war, with half his army embroiled in the Yemen. But above all he could not afford to let the Syrians steal a march on him and place themselves at the head of an anti-Israel crusade, which, at best, would make the Syrians heroes in the Arab world at the expense of his own prestige, and, at worst, could involve the Arab countries in a war for which they were not ready.

Nasser was forced to compromise. Hitherto, he had refused to have anything to do with the Ba'thists of Syria, or with the "reactionary" régimes of Saudia and Jordan, for that matter. Now he had no more choice. In a speech in Port Said, he turned to the Arab leaders, and declared: "Let us try to forget all the stupidities and irritations which we have seen in the past few years; also the disputes that took place, the words that were spoken, and the treachery and so on." Nasser was proposing a summit conference of Arab heads of state to deal with the question of the Jordan waters, but he wanted to make his position clear from the outset—he would not embark on any military adventure. "We will tell you the truth . . . that we cannot use force today because our circumstances do not allow us; be patient with us, the battle of Palestine can continue and the battle of the Jordan is part of the battle of Palestine. . . . For I would lead you to disaster if I were to proclaim that I would fight at a time when I was unable to do so. I would not lead my country to disaster and would not gamble with its destiny." Three years later he was to do precisely that.

The Syrians were delighted. Extremism had paid off. Nasser—their arch-enemy—had been forced to invite the Syrian President to Cairo. The Syrians had, at gun-point, forced the Egyptians to accept them. At the summit meeting, the Syrians were the only ones to call for war against Israel. The other heads of state outvoted them, deciding instead on a plan to divert from Israel the Syrian, Jordanian and Lebanese tributaries of the Jordan River. This was far safer, from the Egyptian point of view, than the firebrand demands of the Syrians. Nasser had, therefore, every reason to be satisfied with the outcome of this experiment in his new diplomacy.*

A new era of Arab co-operation on the Israel issue now began, based on Nasser's gradualist approach. The Arab High Command would prepare the Arab armies for the final passage of arms with Israel, and the summits, under Nasser's dominant influence, would decide when and how this culminating battle with the enemy was to be fought.

But the Syrians did not let up on their pressure. They had had a taste of the success which extremism could bring, and they intended to continue to make full use of this weapon. For the Egyptians, although inviting them to Cairo, had not yet granted the Syrian régime diplomatic recognition. The reinstatement was not yet complete.

Yet the Syrians had, perforce, to accept the summit dictates which expressly forbade any Arab state to make moves against Israel which could lead to war. They could not openly defy all the other Arab heads of state. But the Fatah could. The value of this instrument which had been placed in Syrian hands now gradually dawned on the Ba'th leaders in Damascus, and as the months passed they increasingly curbed the Fatah's independence, strengthening their own hold over the organization.

The first large-scale Fatah operation against Israel was to have taken place on the last night of 1964. Four groups of Fatah terrorists were to have crossed into Israel from southern Lebanon to strike simultaneously at a number of targets along Israel's northern road. But the operation was foiled at the last moment by the Lebanese Government, which got wind of the coming attack and prevented the crossings. The first successful terror strike was made only two weeks later, on 14 January 1965, when a charge of explosives was detonated under the Jordan Water Carrier (along which the waters of the Jordan flowed southwards to the dry land of the Negev) near the Israeli–Arab

* Other decisions of the summit included the establishment of an Arab High Command under Egyptian leadership, and recognition for Shuqairi's Palestinian Liberation Front, an Egyptian–oriented body.

village of Eilabun. From that day onwards, Fatah terrorists crossed into Israel with increasing frequency, but they caused surprisingly little damage and hardly any loss of life.

On dark, moonless nights small groups of armed men would slip across the long border separating Israel from its Arab neighbours, and head for their objective, which, more often than not, was chosen at random. Their targets were of no strategic importance. Terror did not need to pick or choose. The important thing was to strike at the enemy, to create confusion, to invite retaliation, to keep the Arab–Israeli tension simmering. Once over the border the saboteurs would make their way to the nearest Jewish village, lay their explosives against the wall of the end house, and beat a hasty retreat back to safety across the border. Or sometimes they made do with blowing up a water pump in a kibbutz field, or a culvert in some secondary road. Some of the more daring saboteurs headed for the concrete channels of the National Water Carrier. The Israelis countered these incursions by throwing out a wide net of ambushes and patrols along the smugglers' paths and shepherds' tracks which criss-crossed the border.

These first raids were nearly all carried out from Jordan. The Syrians did not wish to implicate themselves, and it was an easy matter for the refugee-saboteurs, having completed their training and preparations in Syria, to pass into Jordan and operate from there. And gradually they became more daring. On 28 February 1965 the grain silo at Kfar Hess was destroyed by an explosive charge laid by Fatah saboteurs. Three days later another band struck at the desert town of Arad. A further attack was made on 4 March. At the same time tension increased along the Syrian border as repeated exchanges of artillery fire took place near the village of Almagor, as the Syrians sought to prevent the Israelis from cultivating fields in the demilitarized zone.

The Israelis waited five months before they finally retaliated. But after six Israelis had been wounded on 25 May by a Fatah raid on Ramat Hakovesh, a veteran kibbutz in the Sharon Valley, and a woman and two children badly wounded a day

later when their house in the town of Afula was blown up over
their heads, the Israelis decided to react. On the night of 27 May
Israeli soldiers crossed the border into Jordan, and destroyed
Fatah bases in the Jenin and Qalqiliah areas. The attack had
been the first reprisal raid carried out against Jordan by the
Israeli Army since the Suez War. It marked the end of a period
of unstated understanding between the Israeli and Jordanian
Governments that both would refrain from acts creating tension
between the two countries. The next day the Israeli Chief of
Staff, Major General Yitzhak Rabin, declared that the attack
had been in answer to nine terror attacks all emanating from
Jordan, and that the Israeli Army would take further action
unless the raids stopped.

This was all that the Fatah wanted to hear. It demonstrated to
the Fatah, and to the Syrians, that their policy was succeeding
and that terror was paying off. They were delighted. And they
immediately stepped up their campaign of violence. Three days
after General Rabin's statement, they blew up the water reservoir
at the village of Bet Govrin, to the south of Jerusalem. And on
the night of 1 June, Fatah marauders crossed into Israel for the
first time from the Lebanon since their first abortive attempt,
and dynamited a house in the Galilean kibbutz of Yiftah. The
Fatah had launched its war.

While violence was flaring along Israel's long border, the
Arab world was being subjected to a series of controversies
which left it more divided than it had ever been before. The
fanaticism of the Syrians formed one focal point of controversy.
The moderation of President Bourguiba formed another.

The Tunisian President had, in February 1965, set out on a
seven-week tour of the Mediterranean and Middle Eastern
countries. He had conferred with President Nasser in Cairo, met
King Faisal at Riadh, visited King Hussein in Jordan, and gone
on to the Lebanon, Kuwait, Iran, Turkey, Greece and Italy.*
Some time during that trip, the Tunisian President reached new

* He pointedly left Syria out of his itinerary and cut out Iraq at the last
moment.

and far-reaching conclusions regarding the tactics the Arabs should use to solve the Palestine problem. He gave some hints of his new ideas during his visit to Jordan, and on 21 April, eleven days after his return to Tunis, President Bourguiba spoke his mind fully and frankly to a group of Tunisian students. The time had come, he declared, to stop thinking in terms of war against Israel. Instead, he proposed a new formula for settling the problem. The Arabs should recognize Israel and make peace with her. Israel, in exchange, would withdraw to the borders originally proposed by the UN in 1947 and would repatriate the Arab refugees. Israel, he declared, would cede territory but would gain peace. He proposed direct negotiations between the Palestinians and the Israelis at a neutral capital. "We shall take steps to bring the two sides together. I shall discuss ways and means with President Nasser. No effort shall be spared to gain concrete results," the President concluded. In private conversations the Tunisian President stressed the fact that one of the reasons that he had reached these conslusions was that since 1962 President Nasser himself had been repeatedly declaring that he had no plan for the restoration of Palestine to the Arabs.

Bourguiba's proposal was totally unacceptable to the Israelis. They saw his peace plan as a Trojan horse carrying in it the means to eliminate Israel politically: the ceding of territory plus large-scale repatriation of refugees would kill any chances for the young state to become economically viable, and would transform it into a ghetto within the Arab world. Abba Eban, then the Deputy Prime Minister, declared that Israel could no more return to the 1947 formula than an egg which had been broken seventeen years previously, could be put together again. On 17 May Israel's Prime Minister, Levi Eshkol, countered President Bourguiba's proposals with a peace plan of his own, which he announced in the Knesset. He called for immediate negotiations between Israel and the Arab states based on the principle of "full respect for the independence, sovereignty and territorial integrity of all states in the region". But he warned that Israel would be ready to make minor territorial adjustments only; any solution based on the 1947 boundaries (which the Arab leaders opposed at the time) would be unthinkable.

Eshkol's offer was ignored by the Arabs. Not so Bourguiba's earlier proposal. This was the first time a responsible Arab leader had openly called for a peaceful settlement with and Arab recognition of Israel. It left the Arab world shocked and breathless. It mattered little that many responsible Arabs had come to think in terms similar to those pronounced by the Tunisian President. It was one thing to talk of a settlement with Israel in the seclusion of a palace chamber or in the privacy of an informal exchange of views, but it was quite another to make such views public. President Bourguiba had done much more than propose a new approach to the Palestine problem. He had challenged the very basis of Arab policy of the previous eighteen years, saying, in as many words, that the Arab rulers had been guiding the Arab peoples along a false path, leading nowhere, in a sterile search for a solution which could never be found along the lines adopted by the Arab leaders. This was an accusation which the Arab leaders could not ignore. They had to retaliate, and they did so with all the force and vigour they could muster. On 23 April the first reactions appeared in the Arab press. "Bourguiba has stabbed the Arab people in the back," declared Cairo's *al-Akhbar*, while the authoritative *al-Ahram* wrote that Bourguiba's statement was the most dangerous ever made by an Arab leader. "He was moving in accordance with a plan co-ordinated by the forces of Western imperialism," and, in order to make it quite clear who had done the co-ordinating, the editors of *al-Ahram* noted that the "Bourguibistic solutions" had emerged only after the visit of the Tunisian President to Riadh. The UAR, *al-Ahram* concluded, would not take part in the forthcoming Arab summit conference in Morocco if Tunisia was present.

In the rest of the Arab world official reaction, as reflected in the press, was similar to that in Egypt. Syria's *al-Ba'th* wrote that "the Arab people from the Ocean to the Gulf today hear the voice of treason . . ." while Lebanon's *al-Jarida* did some plain hinting between the lines when it urged that those "who rejected Bourguiba's proposals should put forward a sounder argument, and they will be supported by the entire Arab nation."

The storm against Bourguiba rapidly mounted in violence. Tunisian embassies were attacked, ambassadors were recalled,* diplomatic relations broken off. At a May Day rally in Egypt, Nasser made a vitriolic attack on Bourguiba. The Arabs would never accept a political solution of the Palestine problem. They had the manpower to impose a different solution. If need be, they could have an army of two or three millions, Nasser declared amidst wildly cheering crowds.

Bourguiba was unrepentant. He had gone to the town of Sfax to rest after his arduous tour. His health was giving him trouble. But he was as tough as ever when reporters asked him to comment on the attacks levelled against him. "It is unthinkable that a man, as I am, after having fought for thirty years to wrest Tunisian sovereignty from France, should agree to abdicate it into the hands of President Nasser," Bourguiba replied. He was referring not only to the furore over his statements on Palestine but also to the recent disagreements between him and President Nasser when he, together with the kings of Morocco and Libya, refused to break off relations with West Germany after the German Government had declared its intention to grant diplomatic recognition to Israel.

Thus Nasser was faced in mid-1965 with the challenge of pragmatic realism as embodied by Bourguiba† on the one hand, and by Syria's efforts to embroil him in a war with Israel on the other. Bourguiba's declarations did not seriously affect Nasser's standing. From the inter-Arab point of view they could be dismissed as a passing incident. Their importance lies within the context of the Arab/Israeli conflict, for this was the first time

---

* The UAR Ambassador was withdrawn from Tunisia on 27 April.

† In a lecture given on 8 March, President Bourguiba had defined Bourguibism as an outlook on life based on a method imposed by the course of events.

that a proposal for a political solution to the conflict had been made. But for Nasser the Syrian stand was far more dangerous, and it was given renewed expression during the second summit meeting, and its attendant Arab High Command sessions, which were held in Cairo at the end of May 1965. During the closed sessions of the Command, it became apparent that the Arab plan to divert the tributaries of the Jordan waters was being thwarted by Israeli military action. Tractors, bulldozers and other equipment employed by the diversion project had been repeatedly destroyed by Israeli artillery or by air strikes. The Israeli Chief of Staff, Major-General Rabin, had given an explicit warning on 2 May that Israeli troops would take action to prevent the diversion of the Jordan headwaters, which were vital to Israel. In the face of this threat the Arab leaders were powerless to act, and, once more, the Syrians were the first to underline this fact. The Syrian delegate at the Arab Defence Council, Colonel Fahd Shaar, complained bitterly of the Arab High Command's failure to come to Syria's aid during Israel's attacks on the Jordan diversionary works. His shafts were directed at the Egyptian commander of the Arab High Command General Ali Ali Amer, and, through him, at President Nasser himself.

It was this demonstration of Egypt's weakness that provoked President Nasser into one of his bitterest and frankest commentaries on the state of affairs in the Arab world. Addressing the Palestine Congress in Cairo on 31 May 1965, Nasser rounded on his Syrian critics and declared flatly that Egypt would not go to war for the sake of one Syrian tractor. The Arabs, he declared, would have to give up ideas of war against Israel for the time being. They might even have to postpone the Jordan diversion project. "If the defence of certain countries is not possible, we cannot speak of attack, and if we talk about it, we are simply bragging and deceiving," Nasser declared. And he admitted that the policy he had undertaken seventeen months before, of rallying the Arabs against Israel within the framework of the summit conferences, was on the verge of collapse.

Speaking in his most restrained manner, Nasser said that there were "contradictions, problems and lack of confidence between the Arab forces. . . . There are problems between Iraq and Syria, problems between Saudi Arabia and the United Arab Republic, and suspicion that Lebanon does not want to permit the stationing of Arab forces. Unified Arab action is an essential aspect of Arab action." Palestine, he continued, would not be liberated by conferences, in which "each state tries to cast the blame on the other". The solution to Palestine would be found in "revolutionary action", whose principal base was the UAR. The return to Palestine, he warned, would be paved with blood. "We have enough manpower. We can recruit two million people, three million or four million. We are 100 million people. But shall we fight in an improvised manner? We have to equip and prepare ourselves and then face Israel and its supporters." Turning once more to the Syrians, Nasser declared: "They say 'Drive out UNEF' [United Nations Emergency Force]. Suppose that we do, is it not essential that we have a plan? If Israeli aggression takes place against Syria, shall I attack Israel? Then Israel is the one which determines the battle for me. It hits a tractor or two to force me to move. Is this a wise way? . . . Is it conceivable that I should attack Israel while there are 50,000 Egyptian troops in the Yemen?"

This was bitter talk indeed. But Nasser, in the summer of 1965, had become a disillusioned man. The Arab world, as he himself had said, was divided among itself. The dream of a unified Arab people, under Egyptian hegemony, appeared more a mirage than ever. Far more serious, Nasser was facing ever-increasing difficulties at home. For he had got caught up in his own illusions that Egypt was on its way to becoming a major industrial power. He had built up Egypt's industry by using up all her reserves, by taking every loan he could obtain, and by nationalizing the greater part of Egypt's economy. But his investments were not self-generating. They did not even give back sufficient income to pay back the loans. By the summer of 1965 Nasser had discovered that he had used up all his local

B

and international credit on an economic policy that had failed. On 9 April the US Senate Foreign Relations Committee recommended a cut in aid to the UAR, and by the summer the Western countries had virtually stopped all further credit to Egypt. Already earlier in the year the Egyptian Government had been forced to sell to a bank in Switzerland 37 tons of gold in order to obtain hard currency for immediate needs. Now, with loans from the West cut off and with internal savings insufficient to meet growing current expenditures caused by the ever-increasing rate of population growth, Nasser was thrown back on support from the Eastern Bloc. But Communist aid was not able to cover the costs of the three main fields of Egyptian expenditure: defence, including the enormous drain of money involved in keeping a 50,000-man expeditionary force in the Yemen; development, and in particular the ambitious indus-trialization programme which had become the cornerstone of Nasser's plan for an Egyptian "Great Leap Forward"; and expenditure on current needs. Nasser flatly refused to cut his expenditure on the army, which by 1965, had reached the figure of £250 million or approximately 13% of the Gross National Product.* He therefore had no choice other than to curtail his development plans, and, at the same time, to throw some of the burden on the people in the form of higher prices, rationing of essential commodities, and heavier taxation. The second five-year plan, which should have begun in July 1965, was summarily postponed—and finally cancelled in favour of a temporary and much more modest three-year plan in 1967.

But as the months went by, the economic situation steadily worsened. Confiding to a visitor from abroad, Nasser admitted that he could see no solution, no glimmer of hope for Egypt's devastating social and economic problems. Egypt's population was increasing by nearly a million persons a year at an annual rate of 3%.† This increase was not only eating up the nation's

* In 1967 £300 million were earmarked for defence and armaments.

† Egypt's population in 1965 was just over 30 millions. In the census of 1960 it had been 26·1 millions. The rate of natural increase rose from

reserves, but it was also steadily increasing the country's labour force at a time when the pace of development was insufficient to provide jobs for the extra population. Even the Aswan Dam project would hardly add sufficient extra arable land to provide a livelihood for the added population; it certainly would do nothing to alleviate the conditions of the masses of agricultural labourers who made up the great majorityof Egypt's population, and whose standard of living was one of the lowest in the world. This pressure of an ever-growing labour force had created an enormous hidden unemployment problem: ten people were cultivating land which one person could have worked just as effectively; the other nine, therefore, were not adding to Egypt's national wealth and were sharing the income which could have been earned by one person alone. The same situation existed in industry and in the services, especially in the Civil Service. Government orders to factory managers or to government offices along lines such as "you take on another hundred workers, even if you have no work for them" were very common. For the Government insisted on full employment, to avoid social unrest. The result of exaggerated manpower figures in agriculture, industry and in the Government was inefficiency and inflation. The answer to these problems, as Nasser had seen it, was a crash industrialization programme, to increase the national wealth of the country and to create additional places of work for the rural unemployed and high-school graduates who were yearly swelling the ranks of the labour force in the towns. Industrialization became the hub of Egypt's hopes, and Egypt's entire ceonomic policy was geared to execute the industrial break-through as rapidly as possible.

But by 1965 the inherent weaknesses of the industrialization programme had become apparent: the home market, with 90% of Egypt's population existing at subsistence level where everything beyond the barest essentials was a luxury, could not absorb Egyptian industrial output; and in foreign markets

---

1·6% in 1936 to 2·9% in 1964. If this rate is upheld, Egypt's population will stand at 34 millions in 1970 and will reach 46 millions by 1980.

Egyptian production could not compete in quality or price with Western-made goods. The only way to ensure markets was by creating customs unions in the Arab countries of the Middle East and in Africa. Both these regions could provide the hinterland needed by the growing industry, but this could only be achieved by political, and not economic means. This was one of the causes for Nasser's ambitious political drive in the Middle East and in Africa in the late 'fifties and 'sixties, and for his growing frustration at Egypt's failure to assert her hegemony over the Arab world, let alone Africa. Egypt's search for markets was not the only motive for Nasser's aggressive foreign policy, but it certainly was a major consideration which weighed heavily on his political strategy.

The dearth of markets was not the only difficulty which impeded industrial development. Lack of capital was another. The new industrial concerns not only failed to pay their way, but incurred enormous losses and represented a continuous drain of hard currency on Egypt's economy. By the summer of 1965 reserves of hard currency had reached bottom, Western loans had been cut off, Communist aid was directed to the upkeep of the giant military apparatus which Nasser refused to reduce in size, and the Egyptian Government was faced with the problem of finding foreign currency to buy wheat which the Americans refused to continue to supply free of charge. In such circumstances, the prime sufferer was the programme of industrialization. Further development was halted. Existing production was curtailed as one factory after another became paralysed because of the Government's inability to provide foreign currency to purchase raw materials and spare parts.

Thus the bottom had fallen out of the grand policy on which Nasser had based Egypt's progress away from poverty and backwardness. Moreover, the over-emphasis on large and costly industrial schemes was placing new strains on the Egyptian economy. Inflation, that old enemy of over-ambitious development, became a dominant feature in Egypt's economy. Prices were spiralling to a 40% increase over those of the previous years. Consumer goods, including some essential foodstuffs, were increasingly scarce. The buying power of the Egyptian pound was sinking.* And all this was leading to growing discontent at home, which was being aggravated by the rumours of Egyptian set-backs and defeats which filtered through the censorship from the battlefields of the Yemen.

These, then, were the real causes for Nasser's bitterness and frustration as he made his speech to the Palestine National Congress that May day in 1965. It was a feeling which was to grow in the Egyptian President in the months to follow as the economic trends turned into hard facts and Egypt's position in the Arab world worsened. This growing frustration was to form the background for Nasser's actions in the latter days of May 1967, and very probably played a decisive role in moulding Nasser's ill-fated decisions. We shall see how the signs of frustration, even of desperation, were to show themselves. But other elements were also being woven into the tapestry of events which made up the backdrop to the violence of the June to come. One of these was the Great Power involvement in the Middle East, and in particular that of the Soviet Union. Another was the shifts of political power inside Israel as David Ben Gurion gave up, for the last time, the reins of power. It is to these elements that we must now turn.

* The Egyptian pound was equal in value to the pound sterling when King Farouk was deposed in 1952. In mid-1967 the E£ fetched only 8s 9d ($1.25) on the free market, while its official rate of exchange is E£1 to 16s ($2.30).

CHAPTER 2

The Great Power Involvement in the Middle East

The Six-Day War would certainly not have unfolded the way it
did, and might conceivably not have occurred at all, if it had
not been for the active involvement of both the Soviet Union
and the United States in the Israeli–Arab conflict. Neither wished
to be involved. Both, as we shall see, made efforts to disengage.
Their presence in the Middle East over the years, and their
interests in that region, made such a disengagement impossible.

Both the Soviet Union and the United States were compara-
tive newcomers to the Middle Eastern scene.* Both had moved
in to fill the vacuum left by the departure of the traditional
colonial powers, Great Britain and France. For both of them
the first years of Gamal abd al-Nasser's rule was to be a vital
period which set the pattern for their later involvement in the
region.

For the Russians, the first turning-point in their attitude to
the Middle East had nothing overtly to do with either Nasser,
the Arabs or Israel. In March 1953 Stalin died and a new era
began in the Soviet Union. Together with Stalin, some of the
most fundamental precepts shaping Soviet internal and foreign
policies passed away into history. One of these, whose disappearance was to have far-reaching consequences on Russia's
attitude to the Middle East and to the entire Afro-Asian world,
was that only Communists could lead true national liberation
struggles, while "bourgeoisie nationalists", whether Indian or

* Except in Turkey and in particular, Iran, where both had been active
long before their presence was felt in the Arab countries.

Egyptian, were agents of the imperialists, and should be treated as traitors to their peoples. In Stalin's eyes, there was not much to choose between Neguib, Nehru, or Chiang Kai Chek. He treated the Egyptian revolution with contempt and continued to pin his faith in the tiny Communist Party of Egypt. This attitude, obviously, had to be erased from official Soviet thinking before there could be any drawing together of the new régime in Egypt and the Soviet Union.

But there was no sudden switch after Stalin's death. The process of erosion was a gradual one. The final burial of the Stalinist theories occurred only in February 1956, when the twentieth Congress of the Communist Party of the Soviet Union finally laid Stalin's ghost. One of the most important points to emerge from that Congress was the official support the Party now expressed for national movements and leaders who had previously been anathema to the doctrinaires of Communism. One of these was Nasser. The Congress called for a strengthening of the bonds of friendship and co-operation with India, Egypt, Syria and other states "which take a positive stand on the question of peace".* This was notice served by the highest organ of the Communist movement for the communist countries to cultivate relations with the Afro-Asian countries, and foremost among them, India and the Arab countries.

Even before this ideological approval of the twentieth Congress, two events had occurred in 1955, both of which paved the way for the Soviet–Egyptian alignment which now was to become official Soviet policy. The first was the Afro-Asian Conference which took place in Bandung in April, 1955; the second was the so-called Czech arms deal with Egypt in September.† The Soviet Union had not been invited to Bandung. The Communist world was represented there by China. But for the young Egyptian ruler, for whom the journey to Indonesia had been his first outside the Arab world, Bandung represented a

---

* *Pravda*, 25 February 1956.

† This was popularly known as the Czech arms deal because the first consignments of arms came from Czechoslovakia.

profound turning-point in his political thinking. For the first time he came face to face with other heads of state who had rejected Western influence and who searched for an alternative. His fanatic hatred of the West, and in particular of Great Britain, received full legitimization at Bandung. The path of non-alignment, of steering between the two Great Powers, was pointed out to him and he became an ardent convert. Such was the impact of Bandung on Nasser that, on his way home, he confided to an Indian journalist, Dewan Bernidranath, that he appraised the Bandung conference "as one of the two most important events of modern history"—the other being the discovery of atomic energy.*

But Nasser was not yet ready to accept all the implications of militant non-alignment. When, shortly after his return from Bandung, the Soviet Ambassador to Cairo, Daniel Solod, proposed to Salah Salem an arms deal on convenient terms, Nasser procrastinated. For the Soviets, an arms deal did not necessarily imply ideological approval of the Nasser régime. It was simply a question of exerting Soviet influence in one more country which was taking an anti-Western turn. For the same reasons the Soviets had, through the Czechs, supplied arms in 1948 to the Jews of Palestine, whose struggle, in Soviet eyes, was weakening British influence in the Middle East. Now they made a similar offer to the Egyptians. But instead of accepting, Nasser turned to the United States with a long shopping list of arms. The American demand for payment on delivery, in dollars—more dollars than there were at the time in the Egyptian Treasury†—was the official reason given by the Egyptians for the failure of the arms deal. But there were more fundamental causes for the failure. The Americans, in 1955, were at the height of their military pact policy. In the Far East, the Southeast Asia Treaty Organization (SEATO) had been set up in September 1954. The Middle East was next in turn. A Turkish–

* Dewan Bernidranath in *Caravan*, New Delhi, November, 1957.
† *See* Charles D. Cremeans: *The Arabs and the World: Nasser's Arab Nationalist Policy*, New York, 1963, p. 145.

Pakistani Defence Pact had already been urged in April 1954, but this did not worry Nasser unduly. But his attitude changed entirely when Nuri as-Said, the Iraqi Premier, visited Istanbul and London in September and concluded a defence pact with Turkey in February 1955. The Northern Tiers Alliance policy of the Americans and British was now taking shape and it was plain that it would hinge on Baghdad. For the Egyptians, quite apart from the ideological overtures, such a policy represented a challenge to Egypt's leadership in Arab affairs, and imposed the danger of isolating Egypt in the Arab world, with Iraq taking the lead in organizing the Arab countries of the Fertile Crescent within the framework of the Alliance. Nasser, therefore, fought the Baghdad Pact tooth and nail. And his attacks on Dulles's military pact policy was conveniently in accordance with his Bandung conversion to non-alignment. Nasser's increasing swing to positive neutralism and non-alignment in 1955 increased American hostility towards him. John Foster Dulles's atttack on the neutralists in his speech on 26 August was countered by an equally strongly worded defence of neutralism by Nasser a month later. But by then Nasser had already decided to cross the Rubicon. At the end of August Solod renewed his offer of arms. With Dulles's speech still ringing in his ears, Nasser now agreed. A month later the arms deal was made public, and the era of Western monopoly over the Middle East came to an end. Nasser's decision had broken the traditional pattern which had linked the Arab world with the West. From that moment, he was free to play off one Great Power against another, a gambit which characterized Nasser's foreign policy until the early 'sixties when the Soviet hold over him became too strong for him to continue such tactics.

For the Russians, the "Czech" arms deal marked the first real break-through into the Middle East. It was followed up after the twentieth Congress of the Soviet Communist Party had given official approval, and from that time onwards they steadily increased their support for Egyptian foreign policy and their aid to the Egyptian economy. Nasser's neutralist foreign

policy suited the Russians admirably. For one thing, it was directed primarily against the West. For another, as Professor Kerr has put it, "Nasser judged that his optimum bargaining position toward the major aid-givers could be reached by cultivating harmony with the Soviet Union, while maintaining a certain level of tension with the US—a position that has naturally fitted with the ideology he has come to propound".*
But such a policy, as Professor Kerr has pointed out, involved of necessity substantial Egyptian adjustments to Soviet interests.

Soviet inroads into Egypt gathered momentum after the Suez War and the forthright stand of the Soviet Union in Egypt's favour. They increased even more when the Russians took over the construction of the Aswan Dam after the Americans had turned the offer down. At the same time, the Americans, who had emerged honourably from the Suez War in Egyptian eyes, rapidly lost that credit by their economic boycott of Egypt in 1957, by their intervention in Jordan and in the civil war in the Lebanon, and by the promulgation of the "Eisenhower Doctrine" in 1958.

Nasser was still bent on pursuing a flexible foreign policy. In 1958 he roundly condemned the US for its Eisenhower Doctrine. He visited Moscow. He signed the Aswan Dam agreement. Yet in 1959 he was once more making friendly gestures towards the Americans. For the Americans themselves had decided on an important policy switch. The Dulles concept that neutralism was counter to American interests was finally jettisoned. The campaign against the Arab neutralists was called off. Foreign bases, in the new era of inter-continental missiles, were waning in importance. So was the "containment" policy on which US policy had been based. Nasser, for his part, was sorely in need of increased foreign aid and jumped at the opportunities which the American policy switch offered.

Thus began an interlude in Egyptian foreign policy of closer

* Malcolm Kerr: "Egyptian Foreign Policy and the Revolution", School of Oriental and Asian Studies, University of London, Conference on "Egypt since 1952", 14–16 September 1966.

relations with the US on the one hand, marked by an ideological dispute between Egypt and the Soviet Union on the other, which was sparked off by President Nasser's drive against the Communists of Egypt and Syria. Hard words were exchanged, but these did not detract from the continued Soviet–Egyptian alliance as reflected, for example, in their joint actions in the Congo. The improvement of relations with the US was characterized by the exchange of letters between President Nasser and President Kennedy, in which Kennedy expounded his belief that Nasser's nationalism was legitimate, and should be supported. This softening of relations with the West did not, however, lessen Soviet inroads into Egypt. Indeed, by 1960 Egypt had assumed a new importance for the Russians. Previously Egypt had been viewed by them as the gateway through which they might gain influence in the Arab world. Now they saw Egypt as a vital stepping-stone towards attaining a hold in Africa, and in the Afro-Asian world as a whole. For Egypt was becoming increasingly active in the Afro-Asian movement. And as one of the most advanced of the independent African countries, she was playing a leading role in the affairs of emergent Africa. Cairo was becoming, to an ever-increasing extent, the capital of Afro-Asia. The Afro-Asian Peoples' Solidarity Organization had its headquarters there. Its Secretary-General was Egyptian, and the Egyptians, together with the Russians and the Chinese, covered its budget and guided its policy, and organized the large number of Afro-Asian gatherings which were held in the early 'sixties, the majority in Cairo. Moreover, under the aegis of "The African Association" and "The African League", two bodies connected with the Bureau for African Affairs of the Presidency and with the Egyptian Foreign Ministry, the Egyptians encouraged African nationalists and exiles to set up national "Bureaux" in Cairo from where they could engage in political and subversive activity against the powers ruling their countries. In the early 'sixties there were thirteen such Bureaux situated in Cairo,* and through them a great number of contacts were

* There were Bureaux representing Kenya, Uganda, South Africa,

made not only between African nationalists and Eygptians but also with the Soviet and Chinese diplomats in Cairo, who made a special point of cultivating them.

Moreover, Nasser was an example to be followed, and the fact that he now steered his country into ever-closer contact with the Soviet Union was a fact which was not lost on a host of other countries in Africa and Asia. In the Arab League, in the "Casablanca Group", the Afro-Asian group at the UN, in African and Afro-Asian bodies the Egyptians could bring their influence to bear. Their support for the Soviet Union, therefore, was a matter of extreme importance for the Russians. It became doubly important after the Sino-Soviet conflict had come into the open in 1961. The Russians were keenly concerned to demonstrate to the Communist world the advantages of their moderate policies in contrast to Chinese intransigence. And nowhere were these policies of wooing nationalist, non-Communist, non-aligned régimes put to the test more than in the Middle East. The fact that Egypt and other "progressive" Arab régimes were shifting from non-alignment toward open support of the Soviet camp was a dearly-won feather in the Russian cap, sorely needed in view of Chinese inroads into the liberation movements of the Far East.

Hence the all-out efforts of the Russians to deepen their influence in Egypt. In February 1964 Khrushchev paid a state visit to Egypt and was royally received. For the Egyptians the efforts they put in making that visit a success were well repaid. Soviet aid was increased considerably in 1964 and 1965. Credits to the tune of E£100 million were placed at the disposal of the Egyptian Treasury for the implementation of the Second Development Plan. Heavy agricultural equipment, valued at millions of pounds, was sent to Egypt as a gift from the Soviet people. Credits amounting to $165 million were given for the purchase of goods and raw materials. Trade between the two

South-West Africa, Southern Rhodesia, Northern Rhodesia, Basutoland, Zanzibar, Nigeria, Cameroons, Equatorial Africa, Ruanda-Urundi, and Eritrea.

was widened. In 1965 the Russians supplied Egypt with 300,000 tons of wheat at favourable terms, and in 1966 they sent another 350,000 tons. And, above all, they stepped up their military aid, supplying the latest MiG-21 and Suchoy 7 planes, T-54 and later even the new T-55 tanks, and SAM-2 missiles. By June 1966, Eastern Bloc credits to Egypt amounted to $986 million, as compared to $133 million of the rest of the world.* This figure does not include credits for military equipment, which amounted to many hundred million dollars more.

This enormous surge forward in the scope of Soviet aid to Egypt was not halted by Khrushchev's removal from power in October 1964. Kosygin, who had criticized a number of Khrushchev's ventures, followed this one unhesitatingly. After his return from a visit to Egypt in May 1966, he declared in an election speech in Moscow that "the UAR is an important supporting base for national liberation and progressive development in the whole wide region of the Near East and Africa. . . . We and they have the same interests as regards the struggle for peace and against interference in the internal affairs of other countries, in strengthening the common anti-imperialist front. . . ." Support for Egypt meant support for many other peoples "who are fighting for freedom and independence", he declared.†

This aid made Egypt increasingly dependent on the Soviet Union. And the Russians themselves gradually became more assertive regarding their own interests. In December 1965 a high-ranking Soviet military delegation visited Cairo. It included Marshal Grechko, the Deputy Minister of Defence, General Rodenkov of the Soviet Air Force, and Admiral Sergeyev. The talks they conducted were, understandably enough, shrouded in secrecy. But a year later a Saudi newspaper‡ carried sensational revelations of the talks in what appeared to

* This figure does not include American aid under the surplus food agreements (PL.480 commodities). According to C. Tansky, American aid in this form amounted to $980 million from 1947 to 1965. *See* his *U.S. and U.S.S.R. Aid to New Countries*, New York, 1967, p. 145.

† *Pravda*, 9 June 1966. *See also* Kerr, op. cit., p. 11.

‡ *Nadwa*, 3 January 1967.

be an American-inspired report. According to the *Nadwa* the Defence Agreement reached between the Soviet Union and Egypt in December 1965 represented a new climax of Soviet activity in the Arab world. The Russians agreed to supply large quantities of modern military equipment—on the condition of Egyptian collusion with Russia which would enable the Soviet Union to fill the gap in Southern Arabia created by the withdrawal of Great Britain. The relations between the UAR and the Soviet Union "have subjected Nasser to Soviet neo-colonialism to a degree that was deemed impossible by most Western experts", lamented the Saudi paper.

Whether the Saudi leak was reliable or not, there could be no doubt that Soviet motives for the massive aid they were now pouring into Egypt extended far beyond Egypt's borders, and were focusing ever more sharply on the struggle in southern Arabia, and the neighbouring Horn of Africa. And this was something which the Americans could not ignore. "The areas of Africa of most immediate concern to the United States", declared Mr McNamara, the Secretary for Defence, in his report to a Senate hearing on defence on 23 January 1967, "are North Africa on the southern flank of NATO, and the Horn at the approaches to the Red Sea." He might have added that one of the areas of direct concern in Western Asia was the Yemen and Southern Arabia, also at the approaches to the Red Sea. Egypt, or so it appeared in 1966 and until the Six-Day War—held the key to the Yemen and Southern Arabia, while over the 25-mile expanse of water at the mouth of the Red Sea, both the Egyptians and the Russians were well entrenched in Somalia.* Thus the Soviet–Egyptian axis could hold some very tangible strategic implications for both the Soviet Union and the United States.

But Soviet objectives in the Middle East were not confined to Egypt and Southern Arabia. They were aimed at maximum

---

* According to *The Economist* of 25 March 1967, the Russians had supplied the Somalis with 150 MiGs, 20 helicopters and enough T-34 tanks to make up an armoured brigade. These figures seem quite fantastic for so poor and underpopulated a country as Somalia.

penetration on a broad front, stretching from Algeria on the extreme western flank of the Arab world to Iraq and the Persian Gulf in the east. In this wide range of Soviet activity, the Syrians held a special place. Soviet aid to Syria was of a comparatively recent nature. Until October 1964 the Ba'th party, led by Salah ed-din el-Bitar and Michel Aflaq, was anathema to the Communist doctrinaires in the Soviet Union. The Ba'th was slandered and vilified with almost the identical epithets which were later to be poured on the heads of Zionists and Israelis. But when Amin al-Hafiz took over the régime in October 1964 their attitude changed overnight. The Ba'th, far from being the renegades and traitors they had been before, now took their place in the forefront of the movements struggling against imperialism and for "true" national independence, and the Russians translated this ideological whitewashing into immediate economic and military aid. By the end of 1966 Soviet economic aid amounted to $250 million,* while the rest of the Eastern Bloc had given another $178 million in aid. Western aid was virtually non-existent, while nearly all the large development projects were being implemented with active Communist aid in funds, equipment and expert manpower. Hundreds of Russians, Czechs, Bulgarians, Hungarians and other East Europeans crowded the hotels in Damascus, Aleppo, Homs, Hama and Latakia as Russians and Bulgarians supervised work on the Latakia-Kamishli railway, Russians and Czechs constructed a fertilizer plant at Homs, Czechs helped out at the Homs oil refinery and Russians built its oil storage tanks, Poles prepared to build a steel-rolling mill at Hama and the Czechs a sugar factory, the Bulgarians drilled for water, the Rumanians supplied tractors and the East Germans gave expert advice on running the radio and television. The takeover by the Communist countries of all Syria's development projects was almost complete. The close relations were not confined to the economic sphere only. From 1967 Russian was taught in Syrian schools,

* Of this sum $132 million was earmarked for the first stage of the construction of a dam across the Euphrates River.

while a cultural agreement with the Soviet Union provided for certain textbooks used in Russia to be translated into Arabic for use in Syrian schools. The Soviet Union was solidly entrenching itself in Syrian society.

The extreme left-wing coup which took place in Syria in February 1966 surprised the Russians as much as any. They were still solidly backing the Hafiz régime, and were apprehensive that the new Ba'th ultras under General Jadid might "go Chinese". Moreover, the Russians had for some time been making strenuous efforts to unite the "progressive forces" of the Middle East, and first and foremost to draw the Syrians and the Egyptians closer together.* They had obtained some measure of success in these efforts; Nasser and Hafiz had publicly displayed their new friendship at the third Arab summit conference in Casablanca in September 1965. Now Hafiz had been overthrown, largely because of that rapprochement with Nasser. For nearly a month after the coup the Soviet press refrained from any comments on the situation in Damascus. Only after the Syrian Premier, Yusuf Ze'ayen, had granted a lengthy interview to *Pravda* correspondent Yu. Primakov, in which he stated that the new régime considered the UAR ("one of the chief progressive forces") its principal ally in the Arab world and the Soviet Union its ally in the international arena,† did the Russians voice their whole-hearted approval of the new Syrian Government.

The new régime did not disappoint Soviet hopes. Ideologically, Syria moved closer to the Soviet Union than any other country outside the Eastern Bloc, with the exception, perhaps, of Cuba and Yugoslavia. This shift to the Soviet camp reached its height when General Jadid arrived in Moscow with a thirty-man

---

* There were frequent allusions in the Soviet press to the need for such unity. See also Mr Kosygin's address to the Egyptian National Assembly on 17 May 1966 when he said "The joining of the efforts of such countries as the UAR, Algeria, Iraq and others would have great significance for strengthening the common anti-imperialist front." See also *Pravda* 2 June: there were more factors that united than divided Egypt and Syria, *Pravda* wrote, in particular "their common aim in the anti-imperialist struggle against the aggressive sallies of extremist circles in Israel, Arab reaction and imperialism".   † *Pravda*, 6 March 1966.

Ba'th delegation in January 1967. The Syrians now considered themselves to be in the vanguard of Arab progressives, and could not desist from crowing at Cairo. "Egypt," wrote the Syrian paper, *Jadid*, "while giving little or no publicity to General Jadid's visit to Moscow, cannot ignore Syria's endeavours to transfer the centre of the 'Arab revolution' from Cairo to Damascus. Nor can Cairo ignore the special sympathy enjoyed by Damascus in Moscow and the capitals of the Eastern Bloc, in addition to the Communist Parties of the region, whereas these capitals are still suspicious of Cairo. Further, it is hard for Cairo and her supporters to be reconciled to the holding of ideological talks between Salah Jadid's Ba'th and the Soviet Communist Party."* The old slogan, "anything you can do I can do better", was still operating as strongly as ever.

Yet the all-important Jadid visit to Moscow was not entirely successful from the Syrian point of view. The four major items high on their list of demands were SAM-2 missiles, increased supply of modern military equipment, a hastening of the Euphrates agreement, and a clarification on the Soviet view on Israel. Hitherto the Russians had refuted Israel's "aggressive policies", but the Syrians were now pressing for Soviet support of the popular liberation of Palestine and for the elimination by force of the State of Israel.† The Russian reply on the supply of planes and tanks, as well as regarding the Euphrates, was positive. But they refused to supply missiles because, as a member of the Ba'th delegation later pointed out,‡ they did not want "to participate in creating new unrest in the Middle East". The Russians also refused to go along with the extremist demand regarding Israel,§ but they promised full political support for

* *Jadid*, 27 January 1967.

† See a well-informed report on Jadid's visit to Moscow in *Sayyad*, 2 February 1967.

‡ Quoted in *Jadid*, 10 February 1967.

§ This attitude was criticized by the Palestine Liberation Organization leader in Beirut, Shafiq al-Haut, within days of Jadid's return to Moscow. He attacked the Soviet Union for taking a legal stand on Israel only, and not taking a stand on the elimination of the Jewish state. See *New York Herald Tribune*, 4–5 February 1967, p. 2.

Syria. The *Sayyad* report* on the visit commented cryptically: "The next weeks should demonstrate the fruits of the delegation." They did.

After the visit, the Russians emphasized the protective attitude they had adopted a year earlier towards Syria. Both in the UN and in the Soviet press Israel was condemned for creating tension on her borders. They accused Israel, the West, and Arab reaction of seeking to overthrow the Syrian régime because of its progressive character.

But in reality it was not so much Israel that the Syrians feared; they were far more apprehensive of hostile moves emanating from Jordan, where a large group of Syrian exiles, led by the Druze Colonel Hatoum was concentrated. Their "imperialist plan" aimed at Syria was given great publicity in the Syrian and Soviet press, and even in Cairo's *al-Ahram*. Saudi Arabia and Jordan were said to have concluded an agreement according to which the Saudis would finance a Jordanian attack on Syria. The plan of attack had been prepared in conjunction with British and American Intelligence officers, and predicated the establishment of a Syrian émigré government in Jordan which was to be installed in Damascus after the Jadid régime had been overthrown. The British and American plan, according to the Syrians, was that Israel was to provoke war with Syria; on the pretext of defending Syria, Jordanian troops were to occupy the country and install a new government in Damascus.

This Syrian-Soviet preoccupation with hostile intentions of the "reactionary Arab governments" continued until the outbreak of the Six-Day War. Jordan was repeatedly warned by the Soviet press not to embark on hostile measures against Syria.

As Syrian-sponsored raids against Israel increased, and as artillery duels repeatedly broke the peace along Israel's northern border, both the Soviet Union and the United States were forced to pay increasing attention to the deteriorating situation between Syria and Israel. On 7 April 1967, the Syrians opened

* *Sayyad*, 2 February 1967.

fire and pounded a number of Israeli border settlements with a heavy artillery barrage. Israel sent up her Mirage fighter planes to silence the Syrian artillery and in the ensuing air battle, six Syrian MiG aircraft which had been supplied by the Soviet Union were destroyed. The Israeli planes returned safely home. This was drawing dangerously close to the brink. In a strongly worded note to Tel-Aviv, the Russians warned Israel about "risky playing with fire in an area in direct proximity to the Soviet Union's frontier".*

For the Russians the April incident acted as a danger signal. The Damascus régime could be in real danger; its overthrow would entail a grave set-back for Soviet interests in the Arab world. Already by the end of March the Russians had become perturbed by the growing restlessness of the Israelis. Speaking in Tel-Aviv on 24 March, the Israeli Chief of Staff, Major General Yitzhak Rabin, had declared that Israel would "have to react against the country encouraging incursions into Israel". And he added: "Israel has the ability to deter the Arab countries from war. But in the eventuality of war the Israel Defence Forces will win."

At the end of March the Soviet Foreign Minister, Alexei Gromyko, paid a surprise visit to Cairo. The talks he held there were shrouded in unusual secrecy. Most commentators assumed that the major subject discussed was the tense situation in Southern Arabia. But the usually well-informed Yugoslavs had this to say on the visit: "Official quarters are reticent as seldom before. . . . The only concrete detail leaked out in the Cairo press is that Gromyko will also discuss the problems of the UN peacekeeping force in Gaza."†

This is the only indication we have that a possible move of the Egyptian army into Sinai, with its obvious implications regarding the UN force, was discussed by the Russians and the Egyptians as early as the first week of April 1967. But this

---

* Moscow Radio in Arabic, 12 April 1967 (quoted in *Mizan*, vol. 9, no. 8, May/June 1967, p. 100).

† *Tanyug in English*, 29 March 1967.

assumption is reasonable. There existed a community of interests between the two. Neither wanted to see a flare-up on Israel's northern border. It would appear only natural, therefore, that, on the occasion of a visit of the Soviet Foreign Minister to Cairo, this question was thoroughly discussed.

We do not know the outcome of these discussions. There exists only the hint from the Yugoslavs. But within a month of these talks the Russians had supplied the information about the massing of Israeli troops on the Syrian border needed for the Egyptians to enter Sinai and test the deterrent strength of its army. From the Russian point of view, both they and the Egyptians should have emerged from this move with their reputations considerably enhanced, and the Syrians with their régime intact. That, as far as the Russians were concerned, was all they intended. The fact that the manœuvre misfired took them as much by surprise as anybody else.

For in the spring of 1967 both the Russians and the Americans were becoming increasingly reluctant to become too involved in the Middle East. The Russians saw two danger points: Syria and Southern Arabia. They clearly sought to restrain the Syrians and there are indications that they also discouraged the Egyptians from pushing too hard with their policy of challenging Britain and Saudi Arabia in Aden and the Yemen.

The Americans had similar aims. They too exerted their influence to prevent the tension in the Israel–Syria and Red Sea areas from getting out of hand. They had persuaded Israel's Prime Minister Eshkol, after a terror attack on the outskirts of Jerusalem in October 1966, to take Israel's case to the Security Council instead of a military retaliation against Syria. They believed they could come to an arrangement with the Russians to curb violence by means of joint action. But the Russians had become prisoners of their commitments to the Syrians. They could not abandon them. They vetoed all Security Council intervention which favoured Israel. This was a severe rebuff for the Americans. They told the Israelis that they would not intervene again, but would let matters take their course if there was a recurrence of terror. They let the Arabs and the Russians know of this decision.

But the Americans were viewing their Middle East policy in a much wider context than the Arab–Israeli conflict. They too were becoming alarmed at the prospect of a showdown in the Arabian peninsula. They had taken note of an increasing recklessness in Egyptian foreign policy which heightened the danger of a conflict with Saudi Arabia. The Americans were as heavily committed to Saudi Arabia as the Russians were to Egypt. The possibility that these two client states might go to war over the Yemen or Southern Arabia projected hair-raising possibilities of a Vietnam situation in the Middle East, with the Great Powers drawn into a conflict which was none of their doing. Opinion in the State Department was sharply divided regarding the role the Russians were playing. There were those who saw a sinister Russian design aimed at gaining Soviet preponderance in the triangle stretching from Iran to Morocco and back to Saudi Arabia and Aden. The focal point of this Soviet offensive was, in their opinion, the Red Sea area, where, with the help of the Egyptians, the Russians were seeking to open up the back door to Africa and the Middle East and thus outflank the Western military line that sweeps down from Western Europe through Greece and Turkey to Iran. But there was another school of thought in the State Department that viewed the situation very differently. This considered the growing Soviet presence to be a natural corollary to the slackening Western control in the region. And they believed that this situation need not create undue alarm, for the Soviet Union was just as concerned as the Americans to prevent violent conflict. This would, in turn, create for the Russians the same difficulties as those experienced by the British and the Americans before them—for neither Nasser nor the Syrians would take kindly to the restraining Soviet hand. Moreover, these State Department officials were convinced that the Soviet Union would be neither able nor willing to meet all Nasser's coming demands for economic and military aid, and that Nasser would eventually have to turn once again to Washington. The conclusion of these officials was that the United States need therefore play no active role in countering Soviet initiative. They could safely cut American commitments in the Middle East and concentrate on the more urgent problems facing them in South-East Asia and the Far East as a whole.

This latter view gained the upper hand in the United States in the spring of 1967. The consensus of opinion was stated very clearly by Lucian D. Battle, the recently installed Assistant Secretary of State for Near East and South Asia Affairs. He told the Senate Foreign Relations Committee on 4 April 1967: "The Soviets have shown an increasing interest in the Middle East over the last few months and they will have to be watched carefully." He stressed, however, that it was up to the United Nations to "keep this very explosive situation from getting worse" in Aden, so that a larger US role in the area would not be required. The region should be closely watched, but there should be no dramatic US intervention, and no attempt to play the global policeman.

This had become the official policy of Washington, and called for a withdrawal of commitments. In order to implement this policy a number of high-level policy-making teams, comprising representatives of the State Department, the CIA and the Pentagon, were established to study the principal American involvements and prepare recommendations for future policy in this regard. Foremost among these teams was a group led by Julius C. Holmes, a senior State Department diplomat, whose special study covered the region within the triangle of Iran, Somalia and Morocco. The overall conclusion reached by this group was that the US must not intervene in local conflicts in order to avoid counter-pressures from the Soviet Union that could rapidly force such conflicts out of control. The Americans clearly meant to play it cool. They did not want another Vietnam on their hands. Whereas in the past the US had impressed on their friends that they could rely on American guarantees, they would now have to depend on their own forces with the Americans giving tacit support in the background.*

Thus we find that as the Middle East slipped towards its crisis in mid-May, both the major world powers were anxious to avoid becoming involved. And when the crisis erupted, both, as we shall see, drew back from the dangers which their full commitment might involve. But when it came to the crunch, the Great Powers were able neither to disengage completely, nor to prevent the war which neither of them had wanted.

* The approach in Israel, as reflected by General Dayan, had become similar. This was expressed at the General's press conference on the eve of the war, when he declared "In case of war I would not like American or British boys to be killed here for our sakes."

CHAPTER 3
The post-Ben Gurion Israel

Israel on the eve of the June war was a country in the throes of a deep ideological, social and economic crisis. Many factors contributed to this darkening of Israel's horizons, but underlying them all was the fact that Israeli society had entered a dangerous stage of transition. The "heroic" age of classic Zionist ideals and of the pioneering spirit was disappearing, but there were no signs yet of it being replaced by a period of normalization. The Israelis were witnessing the end of an era, but had yet to see the crystallization of a new one.

Reflected in this period of transition was the inexorable decline of the two greatest institutions in Israel's society, which, since the twenties, had borne the brunt of the creation of the Jewish state. One was the Histadrut, the General Federation of Labour, and the other was Mapai, the labour party which had ruled over Israel's destinies since the state was established. Both these bodies had been to a large extent synonymous with Israel's "heroic age". They had created the state, they led it, they gave it their own special brand of Socialist Zionism. The love of Zion, the cult of physical labour, the conquest of the soil, the creation of the underground defence organization, Haganah, illegal immigration, the establishment of the state—all these were milestones of that glorious period in Israel's history in which both Mapai and the Histadrut set the tone.

But that era was passing. The old values were disappearing. The familiar tenets of faith were losing their meaning. The old élite—the Zionists who had immigrated to Palestine from the

East European countries in the first years of the twentieth century—was now a small minority in the country. The new dominant elements were the "Sabra" (Israeli-born) youth whose knowledge of the Zionist heroic period sprang largely from history books, and the more inarticulate mass of immigrants, from both Oriental and European countries, for whom Zionist ideals and aspirations had formed virtually no part in their lives before arriving in Israel. While a considerable number of the 650,000 Jews in Palestine in 1948 had settled in the country for idealistic reasons, a great many of the million Jews who immigrated during the following twenty years had been brought there as survivors from the Nazi death camps or as refugees from Arab persecution. Entire Jewish communities had been transferred to Israel: 220,000 had been brought from Rumania, 125,000 from Iraq, 45,000 from the Yemen, and many more from Poland, Morocco, Iran, Hungary and every other country in which Jews were living in difficulties. The population of this new Israel was thus composed of a heterogeneous mass, whose character was vastly different from the hard core of idealists who had created the Zionist state. Whereas in 1948, 55% of the Jewish population of Israel had been born in Europe, and less than 10% in North African or Asian countries, by 1962 the European-born Jews had dropped to 33·5%, the Orientals had risen to 28% and there were now 38·5% Israeli-born Sabras. This demographic regrouping was a continuing process. It changed the face of Israeli society. Yet the élite remained in power. The standards and values of the pioneers from Eastern Europe continued to direct its actions. But between them and the greater part of the population—including their own children—there grew an ever-widening gap of comprehension and communication.

This growing gulf between élite and rank-and-file was particularly felt in the political institutions. For to a large extent the entire political edifice in Israel rested on foundations which had been built in the days when the in-fighting took place in Zionist Congresses, and not in a sovereign state, and when political practices were derived almost exclusively from the prevailing East European patterns. The narrow ideological differences between some of the parties, the fierce personal antipathies caused by clashes on issues long ago forgotten, were unintelligible, particularly to Sabra youth.

Yet the reputation of the old-time leadership was such that they still enjoyed a huge credit in the eyes of the people. There was dissatisfaction, but not open revolt. There remained a tremendous feeling of respect for the deeds done by the Zionist pioneering leaders. They were, in many respects, the "sacred cows" of Israel. The old-timers maintained complete control of Mapai, and of most other Zionist political institutions. When, a few years ago, Bebe Idelson,a septuagenarian who ruled with an iron hand over the women's section of Mapai, said excitedly to a friend that "the youngsters are trying to push us out", the "youngsters" she was referring to were Moshe Dayan, who had turned fifty, and his friends of the same age group.

These old-timers felt they held power by right. They had suffered the vicissitudes of war, malaria and poverty. Many of their colleagues had fallen by the wayside; others had emigrated to lusher, greener pastures in the United States, or in Europe. Those who remained were the toughest of their group. And, having gained power, they felt it was theirs to keep, that only through the inevitability of the biological process would a new middle-aged group eventually take over.

Thus, despite the deep changes in Israel's society, the political scene was still dominated by the same figures who had been active in Zionist politics for the past forty years. And outstanding among them was the father-figure of Israel, David Ben Gurion.

Ben Gurion did more to fashion the Israel of today than any other person. He, more than any of his colleagues, thought in terms of statehood and sovereignty long before the State of Israel was established. The party was secondary to him. When he became Israel's first Prime Minister, he left party matters in the hands of his colleagues, while he himself remained engrossed in affairs of the state. He had no great interest in economics, leaving this subject entirely to his Finance Minister. But he was intensely taken up with building up a modern, efficient, non-political army, in establishing a non-sectarian national compulsory system of education, in moulding the people into one united nation, and in laying the foundations of a dynamic foreign policy. His authority and stature were such that both the Government and his party willingly let him decide on all matters with which he wished to deal. He was the man of vision, and he used the party apparatus in order to transform these visions into hard facts. But he himself had little to do with that apparatus. He left the direction of party affairs to his loyal aides, to Mrs Gold Meir, and, increasingly, to Levi Eshkol. They were in command of the party machinery; they directed the party organization; they led the election campaigns. The party was at their beck and call, and they used it to back up the policies laid down by Ben Gurion. Of all the Mapai leadership, Mr Eshkol was Ben Gurion's most loyal and unquestioning lieutenant. Ben Gurion trusted him completely, and, because he always agreed with the Premier's dictates, Ben Gurion assumed that his approach to all subjects was similar to his own.

The Premier was not, however, an easy person to work with. He understood how to deal with issues but not with people. He could evaluate their performance, but rarely their characters. He often rode rough-shod over the feelings of his colleagues, ignoring their demands or belittling their capabilities. He was a leader in his own right, and brooked no opponents and little criticism. His colleagues in the Government and in his party lived in his shadow, governing not with him but under him. He alone made the decisions, took the responsibility. The others complied automatically.

But when in 1960 his ministers and party colleagues saw that this great force was weakening, they rose up against him. The ill-famed "Lavon Affair" supplied the cause.

The origin of this unhappy "affair" went back to 1954 when an Israeli network was apprehended by the Egyptian police after an Egyptian Jew was caught in the act of trying to place a bomb in a Cairo cinema. The Egyptians claimed that one of the assignments of the group had been to place a bomb in the library of the United States Information Service in order to create bad blood between the Americans and the Egyptians. Two of the group were subsequently hanged, one, an Israeli, committed suicide and the others received severe prison penalties. The affair created an outcry in Israel and the question arose: who had given the order for this operation? The "Lavon Affair" revolved around this question. Ben Gurion had, at the time, been in temporary retirement in his Negev home at Sde Boker, and Pinhas Lavon had been serving as Defence Minister in a government headed by Moshe Sharett. Lavon was dismissed, though he denied all knowledge of the operation. In 1960 he produced evidence which purported to show that certain documents had been forged by senior army officers in order to place the blame on him. A committee of seven Ministers, guided by Levi Eshkol, exonerated him. Ben Gurion, however, was dissatisfied with the findings of this committee and demanded a judicial enquiry.*

But the real reason for the crisis of leadership which burst on Israel that year and transformed the political scene was that special relationship which had existed throughout the years between Ben Gurion, the lone leader, and his colleagues, each one of whom had, at one time or another, felt frustrated, insulted or degraded. The "Lavon Affair" provided the excuse to assert themselves, to prove their independence from the stultifying influence of Ben Gurion, and one after the other of the "old guard"—Moshe Sharett, Golda Meir, Zalman Aranne, Mordechai Namir, Pinhas Sapir—deserted him. But Eshkol remained faithful to the leader he had served so well over the years, and when Ben Gurion, sickened and furious over what he considered the moral lapses displayed by the "Lavon Affair" and over the attitude of his erstwhile colleagues, decided to step

* This short summary of the "Lavon Affair" is based on the *Jewish Observer and Middle East Review*, 18 December 1964.

down from the premiership in 1963, he chose Eshkol as his successor.

Ben Gurion did not, however, understand the power incumbent in the position of premiership he had voluntarily relinquished. He knew the meaning of a national leader, he knew his own power, but he never attributed the two to the role of Premier, which he considered of secondary importance. He was convinced that, either in power or not, if he fought for something he would get it. He was certain that Mr Eshkol would continue to do his bidding, as he had done in the past, and that, if he refused, he would not be able to remain in power. But Ben Gurion was wrong, and this mistake was to lead to the most bitter and intense political fight the country had yet seen, and which continued unabated until the outbreak of the June war. For the primary aim of Ben Gurion, when he retired to the wilderness, was to pursue the attainment of justice over the Lavon Affair. In much the same way as the Biblical prophets of old, he lashed out against what he considered was the lowering of the moral standards of the country's leadership and their unwillingness to pursue the search for justice to its bitter end. But Eshkol had no intention of continuing with the "affair" which he considered harmful to the state and to his party; he was now his own master and was not going to take instructions any more from the "Old Man" in Sde Boker. Bitterly disappointed, Ben Gurion took up the cudgels against the Eshkol government.

The new Premier, however, was now in a powerful position. He had for years been in virtual command of the party apparatus; as former Minister of Finance he controlled the country's economic affairs. And now he also wore the mantle of premiership, which, because of the personality of his predecessor, bore a power far beyond the normal precepts of a democratic country. The people had over the years become accustomed to the fact that the Premier decided on all matters of importance. Now this privilege was automatically conferred on Ben Gurion's successor.

He was lucky at the beginning. Ben Gurion's attacks made

him popular. For a time he received the sympathy usually given to the underdog. Internationally, he established diplomatic relations with Germany. His meeting with Johnson proved a success and had a bearing on the arms purchase policy, with a heavier emphasis on a purchase programme from the United States, including Hawk anti-aircraft missiles and heavier armour.

Eshkol believed he could improve relations with Russia and made a few direct approaches to the Russians. He later encouraged Abba Eban, who was appointed Foreign Minister in the new government, in his attempts to promote a "Tashkent"* mood over the Middle East. But the Russians were not interested. Eshkol and Eban (the Foreign Minister) were more successful in their new United States orientation. It had been the policy of Ben Gurion and that of his deputy, Shimon Peres, to maintain close relations with Europe. Shimon Peres, especially, emphasized the need to maintain links with the French Government and improve those with the Germans. These links had developed along mutual defence interests from which Abba Eban was quite remote, and in which he could play only a minor role. Eban preferred a rapprochement with the Americans, who never quite trusted Ben Gurion's flair for independent leadership, and who were willing to back Eshkol to a far larger extent than they had backed Ben Gurion's government. Significantly, in the summer of 1966, General Dayan spent a few weeks in Vietnam, observing the Americans fighting the Viet Cong and the North Vietnamese. He returned convinced that the United States was the one great power in the world. He was impressed by the overwhelming power and economic forces operated by the Americans and it led to his reappraisal of the part that these powers might play in the future of the Middle East.

Thus only a short time before the completely unexpected Six-

* In January 1966 Kosygin sponsored a meeting at Tashkent between Lal Bahadur Shastri and Ayub Khan; in a week of talks, the two Prime Ministers reached an agreement which averted the imminent crisis over Pakistan.

Day War, the three leading Israeli political figures in this war had become convinced that the future of Israel lay with improved relations with the United States.

But it was not only in foreign policy that the Eshkol régime parted from its predecessors. Levi Eshkol himself was a very different person from David Ben Gurion. He was the man of compromise who whenever possible procrastinated in taking decisions on his own. He lacked the visionary force of Ben Gurion's leadership, but made up for it by his ability to rule by committee and by the dexterity with which he manipulated the party apparatus. And the old-timers of the party who had for so long smarted under the authoritarian rule of Ben Gurion, rallied round their new leader. They were not willing to fall once more under Ben Gurion's uncompromising rule, nor were they anxious to draw blood in the party for the sake of his demand for justice over the "Lavon Affair". The more Ben Gurion attacked Eshkol, the more strongly they voiced their support for him. Eshkol became the symbol of their anti-Ben Gurionism. Each had his own grievance, which now blossomed forth in this tenacious support.

Mrs Meir was a typical example. She had for years been one of the most fanatical supporters of all that Ben Gurion had done, but had fallen foul of him during her tenure as Foreign Minister. For Ben Gurion had taken her too much for granted. He had often conducted a foreign policy of his own without consulting her, and, worse still, had encouraged his Deputy Minister of Defence, Shimon Peres, in his pursuit of close relations with France and, to a lesser extent, with Germany. The Franco-Israeli friendship, the pride of Israel's foreign policy in the 'fifties and early 'sixties, had been achieved through Peres's efforts, and Mrs Meir's objections that foreign policy should be conducted by the Foreign Ministry alone were ignored by Ben Gurion. Frustrated and bitter, Mrs Meir veered into the anti-Ben Gurion camp, and became one of his most implacable enemies. Her enmity was directed not only against Ben Gurion himself, but even more against the younger elements in Mapai who had identified themselves with their former Premier, and above all, against Shimon Peres. Her bitterness and anger found expression at the Mapai Convention in 1965 when, taking the rostrum, she launched into an all-out attack on her former mentor and colleague. The majority of the party supported her and Eshkol; 40% voted against them in favour of the Ben Gurionists. The convention marked the turning point. Shortly afterwards, Ben Gurion, together with Peres, Dayan, Almogi and a number of other militants, left Mapai and established a new party, Reshimat Poalei Israel, or, as it was better known, "Rafi".

The emergence of Rafi marked the first open revolt against the old, East European élite. The vast majority of its supporters were young Sabras. Its platform was forward-looking, pragmatic, stressing the need to modernize, to come to terms with the second half of the twentieth century. It was a language the youth could understand. Yet Rafi failed to become the mass party its leaders had hoped for. The revolt misfired, and in the general elections in autumn 1965, Rafi succeeded in gaining only ten seats to the Knesset while Mr Eshkol's Mapai, now aligned with the slightly more left-oriented Ahdut Ha'avoda, increased their majority by gaining a respectable forty-two places in the 120-seat Parliament.

For the Rafi revolt came at a most inopportune moment for the rebels. Israel had, in 1965, reached a stage of economic affluence and political security unsurpassed in previous years. The people had never had it so good and as standards of living soared at an unprecedented rate, materialism was rapidly becoming the dominant characteristic of Israeli society. The new generation, though largely disenchanted with the existing political leadership, were more taken up with their own pursuits than in joining a political crusade. Although much of this economic prosperity had been artificially maintained until after the elections, few people were willing to note the darkening clouds of depression on the horizon. Wages of civil servants were raised by between 15% and 25% in the six months preceding the elections, causing a general wage increase through-out the country and adding to the false feeling of affluence. Economic stability was promised to all. The industrialists and shopkeepers, traditionally right-wing, were persuaded that under Eshkol and Sapir, the Minister of Finance, their lot was a pleasant one, and any change would only be to their detri-ment. Never had Israel witnessed such an intense and antagonis-tic election campaign, in which patronage and economic power were so cynically used. Rafi, without a party apparatus and with a shoestring budget, never had a chance.

Yet, despite their victory, it took Mapai nearly two months to form a coalition, during which time Mr Eshkol had a heart attack which the Mapai leadership tried unsuccessfully to hide from the people. He remained incapacitated for nearly three months, and his power to carry on was increasingly questioned. But the old-timers would not consider replacing him. He was carrying the torch of their independence from Ben Gurion, who, for more than a year, had been ceaselessly repeating that Eshkol was not fit to lead the country. If Eshkol were removed, this would be a tacit admittance that the "Old Man" had yet once more been proved right, over and above his old associates. For Rafi was being largely used by Ben Gurion to continue his personal feud with the elders of Mapai. Neither his followers, nor the second echelon of Mapai were prepared to admit that they were all being used as pawns by Ben Gurion, by Golda Meir and by Levi Eshkol in their conflict as to who was to rule the country.

At the beginning of 1966 the storm clouds finally broke over Israel. The Government had been staving off the beginnings of the economic depression until after the elections. Now the elections were over, and there was no more holding back the cold winds which swept through Israel. Their force was all the greater because of the steps, economically false, which the Government had taken to inject new life in Israel's economy before the elections. There were a number of deep, underlying causes for the depression which now hit the country. Repara-

C

tions from Germany had come to an end. The standard of living had been rising much faster than the corresponding increase in production. The balance-of-trade gap was still proving unbridgeable. Imports per head amounted to more than $500 per annum, one of the highest rates in the world. This figure included, however, imports of arms and of fuel, on neither of which the Government could cut down. In order to pay for these imports the Government was forced to increase the rate of exports. But prices were too high, industries were being managed inefficiently, and the workers, accustomed to the pre-election wage increases, were constantly going on strike to demand yet higher pay. Thus Israel's entire economy needed a through overhaul, and by 1966 this unpleasant task could be delayed no longer.

The first signs of the depression to come were a series of anti-speculation laws and a tougher credit policy, both of which directly affected the building industry and the real estate business—both of which are as important for the economy of Israel as the car industry is to the United States. As the pace of building slowed down, and trading in real estate stopped almost completely, the rate of economic growth churned to a stop and disinflation set in. This tendency was exacerbated by the almost complete stoppage of immigration in 1966, which was another brake on the pace of growth. It was now the turn of the companies closely connected with the Government to feel the pinch of the more stringent monetary controls. Many of them went through a severe crisis, and some went into liquidation, adding to the general decline of the economy. Somerfin, a shipping company with assets of £13 million, was liquidated under a cloud of suspicion of financial incompetence; Zim, the national navigation company, suffered losses of more than £6 million; Rassco, a publicly owned building group, admitted losses totalling more than £7 million. The spiral of depression claimed an ever-increasing number of victims, among them two banks, which went bankrupt after losing £8 million between them.

As the extent of the depression spread, the Government

came under increasingly severe fire for not having initiated in due time sufficiently rigid controls that could have prevented, or at least reduced the size of, the crisis. The pre-election promises of economic stability and prosperity for all were now recalled with growing bitterness. Much of the blame fell directly on Mr Eshkol's shoulders. He had been Finance Minister for a decade, and most of the companies suffering most from the crisis had been developed through his aid. For patronage in Israel is not only political and does not always fall directly within strict party lines. Economic enterprises are developed through large-scale financial aid from the government, and only partly objective criteria are used to decide who is to receive such aid. Very few new successful economic enterprises took root in Israel without such help, which could take a number of forms: financial loans, price fixing, import or export licenses, protection against competition, subsidies, grants, etc. One element was usually lacking in most large enterprises in Israel: very few showed real profits. The government's policy of encouraging competition and boosting exports discouraged real profits, and as a result even successful enterprises were usually satisfied in passing the break-even point and showing a profit of 1 or 2% on turnover. Many did not even reach this target. Thus these enterprises speedily fell by the wayside once depression set in.

Inevitably, the growing crisis led to soaring unemployment. And worst hit were the new development centres in the south and in the Galilee area, where the large textile and other plants had to shut down or reduce production. These were the centres of the new immigrants, especially of those from the Oriental countries. It was they who suffered most from the depression. For the first time since its establishment Israel witnessed hunger marches and demonstrations for bread and work. Yet the crisis was hardly felt in the pavement cafés of Tel Aviv. Private consumption, including entertainment, remained almost as high as ever among large sections of the population. One of the results of the depression in fact, was to increase the polarization between the immigrants of the development towns and the more well-to-do veterans of the towns, villages and kibbutzim.

Thus the crisis was not only economic. It had deep social connotations. And, at the same time, it led to an intensive ideological heart-searching regarding the most fundamental values and faiths on which Israel's very existence rested. The lack of communication between the old "heroic" generation of Zionists and the bulk of the population, the political feuds and personal strife, the lack of faith in the leadership caused by weakness and by broken promises, all these played their part in this wave of pessimism and defeatism which swept over Israel in 1966. One result was a sudden upsurge of emigration, mainly of Sabra youth. They complained of a lack of incentive, of an absence of challenge in the Israel of 1966. They grumbled at the inordinately high taxes which stultified economic advance. These had, indeed, reached a world record, with taxes, including compulsory loans, of 77% on each additional dollar above a yearly income of $10,000 per annum, and 50% on an income of $5,000. Some of the critics went so far as to say that Israel had become a small provincial ghetto in the Middle East and had not lived up to the expectations of her Zionist forefathers.

In such conditions the Israelis were desperately in need of a strong leadership. But the Eshkol government failed to provide it; and it made the cardinal mistake of trying to cover up its mistakes by interfering with the freedom of the press. The leading independent Hebrew daily, *Haaretz*, was viciously attacked by the Minister of Justice, Yaakov Shapira, one of the new Ministers whom Eshkol had brought into his cabinet in 1966. The Minister of Justice went even further when he demanded the secret trial of two editors of a sex-trading weekly called *Bul* who were found guilty of publishing material endangering the security of the state and were locked up without a word of the trial and imprisonment being allowed to reach the public. When this entire unsavoury episode was made public in the *New York Times* a public outcry arose against these high-handed methods.

THE POST-BEN GURION ISRAEL

The symptoms of weakness exacerbated the feelings of disillusionment and loss of faith which had taken root in Israel
during 1966 and which reached their climacteric in early 1967.
Rumours, said to have been deliberately spread by Rafi, of the
imminent downfall of the Eshkol government were persistently
spreading, despite denials. Yet the more the Government was
attacked and the stronger Ben Gurion's Rafi appeared to
become, the closer the ranks of the veterans of Mapai closed
around Eshkol in his defence. One of the reasons for the
phenomenon was the lack of an obvious successor from within
the ranks of Mapai. For Mapai lacked an heir-apparent. Its
second and third generation had been weakened considerably,
first by Ahdut Ha'avoda's secession in 1944, when a substantial
part of Mapai's youth seceded, and later when the loyalists to
Ben Gurion broke away to form Rafi in 1965. Largely in order
to fight Ben Gurion and his associates, Mapai had entered into
alignment with Ahdut Ha'avoda on the eve of the 1965 elections;
and here was to be found a candidate for succession who could
be a match for Shimon Peres or Moshe Dayan. This was Yigal
Alon, ex-commander of the Palmach, the shock forces of the
Haganah who had fought so brilliantly in the 1948 war, who
now served as Minister of Labour in Eshkol's government. Yet
Eshkol and the "old guard" were in no hurry to relinquish power.
Yigal Alon, who might have done much to repair the tarnished
image of the Government, was kept in his place, while inside
Mapai itself deep fissures appeared over the close relations
which the party had developed with Ahdut Ha'avoda.

Thus, in the spring of 1967 Israel was divided among herself
as never before. Only one thing could wash away the differences
and restore her inner cohesion—an outside threat. Arab efforts
to weaken Israel by terror attacks had, in this respect, the
opposite effect; the attacks, in fact, strengthened the position of
the Government. This was particularly the case after the spate of
incidents on the Syrian border in the spring of 1967 which was
followed by the shooting down of six Syrian MiGs by the Israeli
Air Force. Eshkol's popularity soared after that event.

But basically the Israel of early 1967 presented an unhappy picture. Unemployment, bankruptcies, emigration, a weak government—these were her hallmarks. This change in Israel's image was not lost upon the Arabs. The Arab press gave copious space to describing the misfortunes of their enemy. And when the crisis burst upon the Middle East in mid-May it was this picture of a weakened Israel that the Arab leaders bore in mind as they laid their plans and made their threats with such bravado. They failed to comprehend the inner founts of strength in Israeli society. It was a mistake that was to cost them dear.

CHAPTER 4

Terror and its Repercussions

On a chill Wednesday morning in February 1966, Syrian tanks took up positions in the main squares of Damascus. Troops broke into the broadcasting station, others surrounded the houses of General Amin al-Hafiz, Salah ed-din el-Bitar and other leaders. Syrians woke up to the rattle of machine-gun fire. By evening it was all over. A new régime had taken over in Damascus, the most fanatic and extreme left-wing régime the Syrians and the Arab world had yet experienced.

The group of young men, with General Salah Jadid at their head, who took over the reins of power in Syria differed from their predecessors in that they were, far more than any previous Syrian régime, dedicated and imbued with a sense of mission. Jadid and his colleagues were not Communists. But they were left-wing socialists, and some of them at least, such as the new Foreign Minister, Ibrahim Makhous, accepted the tenets of Marxism. They deeply believed in the need to eradicate all vestiges of capitalism from Syria; they also believed that theirs was a crusading mission to plant revolutionary socialism in the other countries of the Arab world so that the basic slogan of the Ba'th party—"unity, liberty, socialism"—could be achieved. They set about achieving their purpose with a determination which brooked neither opposition nor compromise. Nor were they willing to consider the consequences which their actions might have on the economy of their country or on their own popularity. Factories, banks, insurance companies and trading firms were nationalized,* land and property were expropriated,

* These were not new acts. The previous Ba'th regimes had gone a long

and "enemies" of the régime—capitalists and pro-Hafiz Ba'thists—were hunted down, intimidated or arrested.

The result of this policy was catastrophic both for Syria's economy and for the morale of her people. Unemployment figures spiralled, bureaucratic log-jams mounted as inexperienced youngsters took over the key jobs of hundreds of veteran officials who had been discharged because of their loyalty to the previous régime. For the hard core of the Ba'th remained loyal to the ousted leaders.* They resented the heavy-handed methods of the new régime and were bitterly opposed to the alliance it made with the Syrian Communist Party.

Moreover, the Jadid régime relied overwhelmingly on the support of members of the minority groups in Syria, who, over the years, had attained important positions in the army and the defence establishment.† General Jadid himself was an Alawi,‡ so were some of his leading colleagues, such as the commander of the Air Force, General Asad, and the commander of the élite 90th Armoured Brigade. One of Jadid's closest comrades, General al-Jundi, who was head of the all-important Intelligence and Security Services, was an Ismaili. Another leading member of the ruling junta, Colonel Hatoum,§ was a Druze.

The unpopularity of the new Syrian régime, and the minority derivation of its leaders, had a deep significance in the events

way towards nationalizing the major economic assets of the country.

* More than 200 Ba'th party branches were closed down after their members demonstratively boycotted the Party Convention organized by the new leaders on 10 March 1966.

† A Beirut political commentator noted two weeks before the coup that Alawi and Druze officers controlled at least 60% of the military units (*al-Hayat*, Beirut, 5 February 1966).

‡ The 400,000-strong Alawi sect live mainly in the Latakia region of Syria. The vast majority of them are peasants, many of whom have been eager supporters of extreme left-wing ideas. The Alawis are on the extreme fringe of Islam, who believe that Ali was an incarnation of God himself—and that Muhammad was merely his forerunner.

§ Colonel Hatoum attempted to overthrow the Jadid régime on 4 September 1966. His attempted coup failed and he fled to Jordan. During the Six-Day War he returned to Syria to serve his country in the belief that he would be pardoned. He was given a summary trial and executed.

that were to follow in the Middle East. With Jadid's accession to power, the have-nots and petty bureaucrats of Syria succeeded, more than in any other preceding régime in Syria, in gaining a position of paramount influence. They were imbued with a missionary zeal to obtain social equality in their country. But their leaders were not representative of Arab nationalism, because they were not of the majority Arab Sunni sect, and precisely for that reason they felt that they had to be more nationalist than the extreme nationalists in order not to give their opponents the opportunity to whip up orthodox Arab feeling against them.

Thus, to counter its unpopularity among the population, the Syrian Government took to the time-honoured solution of calling for national unity in the face of "outside aggression". The Israelis were deliberately provoked, and the public brought to a state of near hysteria, by nationalist harangues accusing the imperialists—the US with Jordanian and Israeli help—of plotting the overthrow of the régime. Workers were armed, reservists mobilized. And the call went out that Palestine must be liberated by means of armed struggle and popular warfare. To give teeth to this show of nationalism the Syrian Government decided, in July 1966, to assume full control over the Fatah terrorist organization.

The crisis atmosphere which the Syrians generated was not directed against Israel alone. It was aimed equally at the "reactionary" Arab countries, and in particular at Jordan. This was partly due to real fear that the Jordanians, with the help of the Syrian émigrés in Amman, were plotting the everthrow of the Damascus régime. It was also due to socialist fervour. The Syrians, in fact, wanted nothing to do with the Arab "reactionaries", and they made it increasingly plain that they considered the Arab summit conferences to be but a tool in the hands of such men. This view was sharply expressed by Nur ed-din al-Atassi, the Syrian President, at the Ba'th convention in March 1966. He represented it in even stronger terms on 23 May during a tour of army units along the Syrian–Israeli border.

The Syrian President made it plain that Syria would not participate in the fourth summit, which was due to take place in
Algiers in September 1966.

The summits, as we have seen, were the fruit of President
Nasser's initiative and planning. It was he who had pushed the
idea, he who had brought the Arab heads of state together
(although some had come reluctantly) in Cairo in January 1964.
His primary aim, at that time, had been to place a curb on the
Syrian militancy in connection with Israel's water development.
And at the same time these gatherings of the Arab heads of state
enabled Nasser to reassert his authority and leadership over the
Arab world. The Syrians would have none of this.

But Nasser too was becoming disillusioned. The cracks in
Arab solidarity were already evident at the Casablanca conference in September 1965, when Tunisia's seat at the conference
table remained conspicuously empty. And by the end of 1965
the much larger cloud cast by the quarrel between President
Nasser and King Faisal of Saudi Arabia hung menacingly over
the prospects of Arab solidarity.

By the beginning of 1966 this quarrel reached crisis dimen-
sions. The Yemeni confrontation between the two loomed as
large as ever. The Heraj conference, convened in December
1965, to find a solution to the Yemeni problem, had ended in
failure. Then came the British announcement, in February 1966,
that Britain intended to pull out of the South Arabian Federation by 1968. It was soon followed by another declaration, this
time by Marshal abd al-Hakim Amer: the Egyptians, he
asserted, were prepared to stay in the Yemen "even twenty years
if necessary". The writing on the wall was plain. The Egyptians
were preparing for a showdown in the Arabian Peninsula, and
were waiting only for the British to get out before moving in on
Southern Arabia and the Persian Gulf principalities and their oil.

For Faisal the Egyptian presence in the Yemen now took on
new and sinister connotations, and he reacted swiftly. He
ordered modern arms from the US and Britain worth $400
million. He increased his aid to the Yemeni royalists and his

political contacts in southern Arabia and the Persian Gulf principalities (the latter clearly with British connivance). But above all he took the political initiative out of Nasser's hands by calling for a new type of summit conference—not only of the Arabs but of all Muslim countries: a Muslim solidarity conference representing 500 million Muslims to be convened in Mecca in the spring of 1967. To propagate his call, Faisal set out on a series of swift tours of Muslim countries, including Pakistan, Guinea, Mali, Iran and Turkey as well as Tunisia shortly after President Bourguiba had been condemned by the Arab League for his peace-with-Israel statements.

The Egyptians were furious. They denounced the proposed Islamic Pact as a tool of imperialism. They accused King Faisal of undermining the spirit of the Arab summit. The Egyptians had good cause for their anger: Faisal's new initiative was a demonstrative challenge to Nasser's leadership of the Arab world; it undermined Nasser's international image as the recognized spokesman of the Arab World; it impeded his drive to plant revolutionary socialism in the Arab countries, and it threatened to arouse the conservative and religious elements within Egypt itself in renewed activity against the Nasser régime.*

Nasser fought back, and the first casualty was the atmosphere of summit solidarity which had characterized the Arab world for the previous two years. There were, moreover, strong ideological undertones to Nasser's disillusionment with Arab summitry. For he had been steadily moving to the Left. The only political movement allowed in Egypt—the Arab Socialist Union—was being reorganized on Communist lines, and to that end a number of its leaders visited Prague to learn from the Czechs how it should be done. On the economic plane, the most recent nationalization bids were aimed at wiping out the middle class, while collectivization of the land by means of state farms was being accelerated. But most significant was Nasser's return

---

* The activities of the Muslim Brotherhood had in 1966 already reached alarming proportions for the Egyptian régime.

to the definition of Arab unity which he had first expounded in March 1963 after the secession of Syria from the UAR. Arab unity, he said, could only consist of unity of the revolutionary forces of true Arab socialism, for there could be no unity with feudalistic and reactionary régimes. This theme recurred time and again in Egyptian writing during 1966. But there was a corollary: inasmuch as Arab unity was, to Nasser's thinking, an essential prerequisite to a successful war against Israeli, it followed that Palestine could only be liberated after the reactionary Arab régimes had been overthrown and replaced with progressive ones. Israel, according to the Egyptian theorists, could be challenged only after two conditions had been fulfilled: the Arabs must, first and foremost, build up their armies so that they obtained overwhelming superiority over the Israeli army; and they must first wipe out the vestiges of reaction and feudalism in the Arab world and achieve full Arab socialist unity.

The Syrians differed with the Egyptians regarding the means and the time-table for the overthrow of Israel. Israel must be weakened and harassed by constant terror attacks in the form of a popular war, which would prepare the ground for the final onslaught. As for Arab unity, "revolutionary Arabs will unite on the field of battle and not at Summit conferences", in the words of the Syrian *al-Jamahir al Arabiya*.* This difference of attitude was to be one of the prime causes for the June war.

On 23 July 1966, the fourteenth anniversary of the Egyptian Revolution, President Nasser announced that Egypt would not take part in the forthcoming summit. That same month the Syrians took over the Fatah. These two events were closely interconnected.

The termination of the summits meant that there was now no more collective Arab action against Israel. Syria was free to act according to her will and there was no one to curb her in implementing her theories of popular warfare. And to spur her on there were the internal needs mentioned earlier in this

* 24 June 1966.

chapter, and that old aim of all Syrian governments since Syria had left the United Arab Republic, the attainment of recognition for the Ba'th régime by Egypt. For despite the summits, Egypt had still not granted diplomatic recognition to the Syrian régime; no Egyptian Ambassador had been stationed in Damascus since 1958.

Throughout the spring of 1966 the Syrians had tried to coax the Egyptians into a meeting of Arab revolutionaries to which Iraq, Algeria and the Yemen would also be invited.* But the Egyptians were obdurate. They refused to listen to any overtures from Damascus. The Syrians thus once more tried to force the pace of violence on the Israeli frontier as a means to coerce the Egyptians into an alliance.

Throughout the summer and autumn of 1966 the campaign of violence increased in intensity. The Fatah was under the full control of the Syrian Deuxième Bureau, whose officers planned the terror missions, organized special commando units to implement them, and supplied the intelligence, the arms and the explosives needed for their successful fulfilment. Most of these raids were made from Jordanian territory—the Syrian frontier with Israel was much shorter and therefore more difficult to cross undetected—and the Syrians were moreover only too pleased to stir up trouble between the Jordanians and the Israelis. They succeeded only too well. During the month of October 1966 a group of Fatah terrorists encamped in the Judean hills to the south of Jerusalem. They were more daring than most of their comrades. In a series of sorties they dynamited a house in the outskirts of Jerusalem, derailed a goods train on the main Jerusalem–Tel-Aviv line, mined roads and shot up isolated settlements. This wave of terror was accompanied by almost daily shooting incidents between the Syrian and Israeli armies as the Syrians sought to prevent Israeli farmers in the

* The first call for a "revolutionary summit" of these five countries was made by the former Syrian Premier, Amin al-Hafiz, in January 1966 (see *al-Hayat*, 27 January 1966). It was repeated a number of times by members of the new régime.

demilitarized zones of Galilee from cultivating their fields. Israeli public opinion was aroused. It was particularly incensed by the attack in Jerusalem, which was considered a dangerous precedent, and by the dynamiting of the goods train. It mattered little that there were no casualties. If a passenger train had hit the mine—and indeed one had been scheduled less than half an hour after the derailment—there might have been many killed or wounded. But above all the attacks were held to be a challenge to Israel's sovereignty and security, and the Government was urged to act.

The Government was in a dilemma. The attacks came from Jordan, but it knew only too well that the Syrians, and not the Jordanians, were responsible for them. But a conventional retaliatory raid against the Syrian heights was out of question. The Syrians, with Russian help, had spent years in fortifying those heights. An attack on them would entail a high rate of casualties, unless it was carried out with all the supporting devices modern warfare could offer—air strikes, artillery barrages, the use of armour and paratroops or airborne commandos who would be landed by helicopter on the heights behind the wall of steel facing Israel. But such action was tantamount to war. At the very best Israel would be placed in the dock of international opinion as aggressor, with the Soviet Union, Syria's friend and protector, acting as chief prosecutor.

Yet in those early days of November precisely such an attack appeared to have become inevitable. The Fatah theory that terror attacks would lead to war was about to be vindicated. The Israelis were demanding blood—Syrian blood. Foreign observers fully expected Israel to make a paratroop raid on the Syrian garrison town of Quneitra or even on Damascus itself. The Syrians too had become jittery. They hurriedly despatched a high-level mission to Cairo to seek Egyptian help should Israel attack. The Syrians hoped, moreover, that this time they would also gain the political recognition that they had sought so long. And indeed this time the Egyptians had no choice. The Syrians were already too close to the brink, and now there was no summit apparatus to prevent them from teetering over the edge. The Egyptians had to act quickly, or face the consequence of a possible war between Israel and Syria into which they would be drawn. On November 4 Cairo and Damascus announced that a Defence Pact had been signed between the two countries: Egypt would come to Syria's aid if she demanded it; she would also shortly send an ambassador, and a military mission, to Damascus. For the Syrians this was, in fact, a political victory over Egypt, snatched in the hour of the greatest tension. Under the threat of Israeli guns the Syrian régime had obtained the *de jure* recognition from Nasser for which it had been striving so hard. Terror had paid off; the Defence Pact was the price Egypt paid to restrain the Syrians.

But in Jerusalem, where the debate raged behind locked doors, the pact made no impression. For Israel to remain passive was unthinkable; the rising temper of Israeli public opinion on the one hand, and the continued strikes of the Fatah on the other, were forcing the Government's hand. The Security Council was ruled out as a solution, for that body's impotence in dealing with the terror on Israel's borders had only recently been demonstrated by the Soviet Union's power of veto and by the reluctance of other countries to condemn the Arabs. But Mr Eshkol did not want to go to war. And in particular he did not want to cross swords with the Russians. He therefore chose the easier way out—a retaliatory raid on Jordan. After all, the Israeli Government argued, the terror incursions had nearly all come from Jordanian territory, and retaliation would make the Arab villagers on the border more reluctant to provide shelter for Fatah raiders; they would pressure the Jordanian Government to take energetic measures to halt Fatah operations; but, above all, it was comparatively easy, for the Israeli army could cross into Jordan at will. And it would quieten Israeli public opinion.

At dawn on 13 November 1966 an Israeli force supported by tanks advanced across the invisible border line separating Jordan from Israel. Their target was the village of Samu, four miles from the border. Two days previously three Israeli border policemen had been killed on the Israeli side of the border opposite Samu when their command car hit a mine. Now the debt was being repaid. The attacking force had strict instructions to avoid taking human lives. Their objective was to destroy property, as a warning to all the villages and towns along the border that it did not pay to house terrorists. In the first light of day startled villagers were bundled out of their homes by grim-faced, silent Israeli soldiers. Then the explosions began. Forty houses were dynamited in the largest action the Israeli army had taken since Suez. All was proceeding according to plan when suddenly a long convoy of Jordanian army trucks appeared on the Hebron road, heading straight for Samu, which was now in Israeli hands. In the trucks was a Jordanian battalion, thirsting for battle. They were heading straight for the Israeli tanks ringing Samu's perimeter. A suicidal attack of this nature was something the Israelis had not bargained for. In the circumstances, orders had to be changed, and the commander of the task force quickly gave the order to open fire. In the first salvos fifteen trucks were hit. In them were seventy Legionnaires; fifteen of them were killed. The rest of the battalion was allowed to extricate itself and head back for Hebron. The Israelis could have destroyed it to a man. Only later did it transpire that the Jordanian assault in such a peculiar manner was due neither to suicidal heroism nor to madness, but to a fault in communications. The battalion commander had been told that the Israelis were attacking nearby Yata, and he drove into Samu, confident that the nearest Israeli was four miles away.

The Samu raid demonstrated once more that there is no such thing as planned and controlled violence. The unforeseen and the unplanned take over as soon as the safety catch is disengaged and the first shot is fired. And the same is true for the aftermath of violence. The Israeli Government had been prepared for an outcry after the attack. It had expected the Powers to wag reproving fingers and the Arabs to make warlike noises. But they were convinced that the overall effect would be salutary: the Jordanians would increase their vigilance to prevent further raids on Israel. But they were totally unprepared for the wave of revolt which swept through the towns of the West Bank of Jordan immediately after the Samu raid and which posed one of the greatest threats to the rule of King Hussein since he ascended the throne in August 1952.

We have gone to some lengths, in discussions with Arabs of the West Bank, to understand exactly what happened in those days immediately after the raid. The Arabs there were shocked by the ease with which the Israelis entered one of their towns. And the call went out: Hussein has left us defenceless to face the Israelis; give us arms. The people of Hebron, Jerusalem, Ramallah, Nablus and the other towns went on a rampage. Demonstrators stoned Government offices, soldiers and policemen were spat upon and molested, pictures of King Hussein were torn to shreds or burned in the streets. For Samu had released a pent-up feeling of discontent which had been steadily mounting in the West Bank over the years. For the politically conscious among Palestinians were becoming increasingly disillusioned with Jordanian rule. Their share in running the affairs of the Kingdom of Jordan was steadily dwindling. The favoured clique of East Bank Bedouin who formed the Establishment was successfully keeping them out of all positions of influence. There had been a short period when Palestinians, under the leadership of Suleiman Nabulsi, had formed a government, but they had been much too radical for the conservative élite of east Jordan. Since that interlude, the Palestinians had been increasingly suppressed. The leading Palestinian officers in the army, Ahmad Za'rour, Ja'far Shami, Shamkat Sboul, Mahmud Mu'aitar and others, were cashiered or jailed on charges of sedition. Arabs from the East Bank took over leading positions in the administration, the police and in the judiciary in the West Bank towns. The Palestinians, who are probably the most politically precocious Arabs in the entire Middle East, had to make do with junior positions. In the judiciary, for instance, only some 25% of the judges of Jordan were Palestinians, despite the fact that the great majority of lawyers in Jordan were Palestinian. There were, it is true, Palestinians who did reach high positions in the Establishment, but they were looked upon by the vast majority of Palestinians as being "court" Palestinians, unrepresentative of true national opinion on the West Bank. Some were well-known smugglers of hashish or arms, others were nonentities who had attached themselves to one or another member of the Establishment and risen to positions of influence in this manner.

These were not the only grievances of the Palestinians. Development projects were nearly all based on the East Bank. So was the industrialization programme. A Palestinian who wished to invest could get easy credit terms from the Arab National Bank provided his investment was meant for an East Bank project. Moreover, the Palestinians felt that the new, heavy taxation laws which had been promulgated in 1966 were designed to enrich the East Bank at their expense. But the bitterest blow of all was struck in March 1965, when the Jordanian Government decided to disband the Palestinian National Guard whose duty it had been to defend the border villages against exactly such incursions as had occurred at Samu. The official reason for the abrogation of the National Guard was that the Government wished to merge the Guard into the ranks of the Jordanian army, but the Palestinians were convinced that the real motive for the break-up of the National Guard was the Government fear of a self-contained Palestinian military formation on the West Bank. The disbanding of the National Guard was a major error which contributed as we shall see to the swift defeat of the Jordanian Army in the Six-Day War.

All these grievances came to the fore after Samu in the frenzy of violence which took hold of the West Bank. The growing stability, the rising standard of living, the relative prosperity brought about by King Hussein's rule were all forgotten. And in the meantime, in Washington and in London, Israel was accused of having endangered the existence of the régime most friendly to the West in the Arab world. Even in Tel-Aviv there were angry mutterings. The Samu raid, it transpired, had not appeased the popular mood in Israel, after all. The Israelis regarded the Hussein régime with a great deal of sympathy, and construed the attack on Jordan, instead of on Syria, as a sign of weakness.

In the midst of this furore, King Hussein and his advisers were making their own assessment of the lessons to be learned from the Samu raid. One was that the Palestinians were not to be trusted and that surveillance of the nationalist and left-wing elements on the West Bank must be increased. But of far greater importance were the conclusions the King drew regarding Israel. The raid had come as a great shock to Hussein. For it bore out the suspicion that had slowly been forming in his mind, namely, that in any tension between Israel and one of her neighbours, Israel would strike at Jordan, not only because Jordan represented an easier target than either Syria or Egypt, but even more so because the Israelis had not relinquished the dream of occupying the entire area of Palestine up to the Jordan River. After Samu, Hussein became convinced that Israel was determined sooner or later to conquer the West Bank.

Another lesson of Samu for the Jordanians was that in case of Israeli attack no help could be expected from the Arab High Command. The Command had proved to be a paper tiger. No Arab country had lifted a finger during the Samu attack. The impotence of the Arab countries, and in particular of Egypt, in the face of Israel attack was fully exploited by Jordanian propaganda. Radio Amman poured scorn on the Egyptians "hiding behind the skirts of UNEF" while Arab soldiers of Jordan were being killed in the line of battle.

Both the Syrians and the Egyptians construed the Samu lessons differently. The Syrians had goaded the Israelis beyond the limits of their endurance, and had got away with it scot-free. This fact was not lost on them. After Samu there was a lull in terror raids due to Syrian promises to Egypt made before the signing of the Defence Pact. But the lull lasted only six weeks. On 28 December a Syrian army-type mine was discovered in the dust of "patrol alley"—a path taken by Israeli patrols in the north-eastern fringe of Galilee. The next day Syrian army posts opened fire with machine guns in the same sector, and in the ensuing skirmish, tank and artillery fire was exchanged. The Syrians were once more using trouble on the border to cover up internal problems. And this time they had the Samu precedent that no ill would befall them.

The Egyptians, on their part, interpreted the Samu raid in their own manner. They had, over the years, developed their own concept of the strategic play of forces in the Middle East. The Egyptian army, they believed, acted as a strong deterrent force which prevented the Israelis from taking large-scale action against any of her neighbours who were allies of Egypt. Hence Israel had refrained from attacking Syria, and had gone against Samu instead. As the Egyptians read the situation, any aggressive intentions on the part of Israel against Syria would lead to large concentrations of Israeli troops on her northern border. This would leave her southern borders relatively exposed, which would enable the Egyptians to deploy their forces in their forward positions in Sinai, and threaten Israel. The Egyptians were convinced that this strategy had been successful in 1960 when the Israelis had conducted a reprisal raid on the Syrian fortified village of Tawafiq.* At that time the Syrian southern command falsely claimed that the Israeli attacking force had been repulsed with heavy losses. Both the Egyptians and the Syrians estimated that the Israelis would mount a second, larger prestige-saving attack. Nasser, therefore, gave the order to rush troops into Sinai. Four divisions hastily took up positions facing Israel. They stayed for a month. But when all remained quiet on the Syrian frontier Nasser recalled his troops, convinced that their deterrent force had prevented the outbreak of a dangerous conflagration in the north. Now, after Samu the deterrent quality of the Egyptian army, which had been bound by treaty with Syria but not with Jordan, had evidently been demonstrated once more.

The lessons of Samu were repeated in much stronger form,

* Syria then still formed part of the United Arab Republic.

as we have seen, five months later, when on Friday, 7 April, Israeli Mirages silenced Syrian guns which had begun shelling Israeli border settlements and when the Syrians sent up their new MiG-21s, shot six of them down without loss.

The short, sharp battle was a resounding rebuff for the Syrians. But hardly less was it a blow for the Egyptians, who once more had remained idle in the face of Israeli aggressive action. And this time Egypt was bound to Syria by a defence pact. Where, then, was the deterrent quality of an alliance with Egypt? Radio Amman again provided the answer, to the great discomfiture of the Egyptians. Yet the Egyptians did not change their theories. The April raid only strengthened them. They become convinced that the Israelis were acting with such impunity against their Arab neighbours precisely because the bulk of the Egyptian army was occupied in far-away Yemen, because the Sinai was only thinly occupied by Egyptian troops, and because a UN buffer existed between Israel and Egypt. For the deterrent theory to become operative, these basic factors must first be altered.

But for the Syrians there was no turning back from the path of violence. The Syrian régime had gone too far. They had preached war with Israel for too long to be able to halt now. Terror had taken on a rhythm of its own. Frankenstein's monster had been built up slowly, carefully, and now it had a will of its own and there was no stopping it. The nationalist harangues, based on hatred for the Zionists and the imperialists, continued heedless of the warning that had been delivered on that Friday, 7 April. Perhaps the Syrians still believed that their fortifications, perched high above Israel on the jutting cliffs of the Hauran plateau, were well-nigh impregnable. Perhaps the harangues were made necessary by the deteriorating internal situation in Syria. An article attacking Islam in the Syrian army journal, *Yaish ash-Sha'b*, had sparked off the worst bout of riots and demonstrations against the Government which had occurred since the Jadid group assumed power. Hundreds were arrested, including the influential heads of the Ulema, the

Muslim religious dignitaries. The wave of civil disobedience following this move forced the Government to denounce the article and arrest its author. But the tension remained. Violence on the borders, as usual, provided the ideal outlet.

The feeling of impending crisis in the north grew as the Syrians themselves daily became more jittery. On 13 April the Syrians sent a note to the Security Council warning that imminent Israeli aggression was to be perpetrated against Syria. On 18 April, two days after the first Syrian Ambassador since 1956 had presented his credentials in Cairo, the Egyptian Premier, accompanied by the Commander of the Egyptian Air Force, arrived in Damascus. To the accompaniment of air-raid practice alerts in the Syrian capital, the Egyptians began a lengthy discussion with their Syrian counterparts. The Egyptians were trying desperately to obtain Syrian acquiescence to a curbing of violence. But the Syrians were adamant. They insisted that they could not stop the Fatah raiders. The Syrians apparently believed that the Egyptians would be forced into coming to their aid, and that this would either deter the Israelis from attacking or would bring about a general war and the final victory over Israel. From Syrian documents captured by the Israelis it is evident that the Syrians planned* that if war broke out between Egypt and Israel, they themselves would mount an offensive aimed at conquering the entire north of Israel, including Haifa. Thus, once assured of Egyptian intervention, they had every interest in creating further tension.

And the Egyptians, for their part, had to give these assurances. Failure to do so would have lost them their leading position in the Arab world. And only by giving such assurances could they hope to curb the Syrian border activities. The Egyptians believed in their deterrent strength. They were convinced that Israel would not dare to attack Syria if it was made plain to them that Egypt would not stand idly by. Hence, in his traditional May Day speech, Nasser took the opportunity to warn Israel. Egypt,

---

* Syrian army maps captured by the Israelis show in detail the path the Syrian offensive was supposed to take.

he declared, had offered to send planes and pilots to Syria to be ready for any further Israeli attack.

The Russians, too, were becoming increasingly alarmed. On 26 April they sent a strongly worded note to the Israeli Government. It contained a warning to Israel not to provoke the Arabs. Such a policy, it stated, was fraught with danger. On the same day, Gideon Raphael, Israel's new representative at the UN, met the Soviet Deputy Foreign Minister, Semionov, in Moscow, and was given a similar warning. At the same time, the Soviet Ambassador in Damascus warned the Syrian Foreign Minister of the grave consequences which might befall Syria if the Fatah was allowed to continue its attacks.

But the Soviet warning, and the Egyptian pleas, went unheeded. Hardly a day passed without a new incident. On 29 April a water pipeline of Kibbutz Hagoshrim was damaged by explosives laid by Fatah raiders; on 2 May an attempt was made to blow up a culvert on the Dvir–Lahav road; on 4 May a trailer hit a mine on the road near Baram; on the following day Fatah raiders set up a mortar in a field just within the Lebanese border and lobbed mortar bombs on Kibbutz Manara, and an irrigation pump was destroyed near Kfar Nahum; two days later an army truck was damaged by an electrically detonated mine on the main Tiberias–Rosh Pina highway. In the first ten days of May eleven incidents were recorded, more than during the whole of the preceding month. The list was impressive. By 7 May the Egyptians were virtually certain that there would be some sort of Israeli retaliation, and urgent talks were held at army headquarters. They decided to await developments, and be ready for instant action.

The Israelis, for their part, were in no hurry to take action. The reasons which had caused Israel to stay her hand against Syria in November, and attack Samu instead, were all as operative as ever. Now, as then, Israel did not want to contribute to an escalation of tension. Indeed, there had been some criticism inside Israel after the 7 April incident on those very grounds. The Israeli leaders preferred, therefore, to make do with a verbal assault, hoping that this would have the desired effect of bringing the Syrians to their senses. And now the Independence Day celebrations began to play their part in the spiralling tension. Israeli ministers are wont to make speeches with strong patriotic overtones on these occasions. It was only natural for them to choose as their central theme the deteriorating situation along the northern border. The Premier, Levi Eshkol, solemnly warned Syria on 11 May that unless they ceased their acts of aggression the Israeli army would strike back hard, in a manner, place and time of their choosing.* And there was hardly a minister in his Government who did not have something similar to say along these lines, as they appeared in pre-Independence Day gatherings in the various towns of Israel. This concentration of statements was construed in the international press as the forerunner of a massive Israeli attack designed to overthrow the Damascus Government. And, indeed, to the outsider reading the stern warnings of the Premier and his Ministers there appeared little doubt that Israel meant business. The Syrians panicked.

For the Israeli warnings had come hot on the heels of an urgent Soviet message which had been delivered to the Syrian leaders in Damascus, and to Nasser in Cario. The Russians reported that the Israeli were massing large troop concentrations near the Syrian border. An attack appeared imminent. A second Soviet warning was much more specific; it pinpointed the Israeli attack to the hour of 0400 on 17 May.

The Soviet Embassy personnel in Tel-Aviv had every opportunity to see—and to know—that Israel was not at that time preparing an attack on Syria. The reason they made their

* Mr Eshkol's speech *in toto* was much less aggressive than might appear from the excerpts published in the press the following morning. Following the speech, one of the Premier's aides handed out extracts to the press. He chose the most aggressive parts of the speech. Later that night he realized that his choice might have an untoward effect, and phoned the various night editors to soften the tone. All complied, except one, who for technical reasons, did not get the message. It was this paper's report which the news agencies took up and dispatched to the world.

alarmist reports must therefore be sought either in the inter-Arab, Soviet–Arab or internal Syrian arena. In all probability, all three played their part. The Russians had been becoming increasingly concerned at the reckless way in which the Syrians were courting disaster. Their report of Israeli concentrations was in all probability designed to curb the Syrian terror attacks. And they hoped that the Egyptians would also labour the point.*

Their plot succeeded only too well. Alarm and fear gripped Damascus, while in Cairo a tight-lipped Nasser decided that the time had come to put his theory of the deterrent strength of the Egyptian army to the test. On the evening of 14 May, as fireworks burst over the milling crowds of Independence Day celebrants in Jerusalem, Tel-Aviv, and other towns of Israel, the mobilization of the Egyptian army was under way. Nasser had decided.

---

* But there was much more to their deliberate falsehood than mere preventive action. There can be no doubt that the Russians hoped to gain considerable political capital from their ruse. They either envisaged, or planned beforehand during Mr Gromyko's visit to Cairo, that Egypt would have no choice other than to send her troops into Sinai after the Soviet warning. Egypt would in this manner regain her prestige and her position of leadership in the Arab world, from which the Russians would also benefit.

CHAPTER 5
The Arabs on the Move

Some time between the morning of 13 May and noon on 14 May, Nasser and the Egyptian High Command took the decision to move two divisions of the Egyptian army into Sinai, in addition to the one division permanently stationed there. The command issued by Field Marshal abd al-Hakim Amer stressed that the move must be executed as rapidly as possible, and with no regard to secrecy. At 1200 hours on Sunday 14 May, the battalion commanders of the first units to be moved received their orders. They were short and to the point: the battalions must be ready to move out of their Cairo base within three hours. No mention was made of their destination. Shortly afterwards Marshal Amer issued "Battle Order No. 1". The army, it stated, would go over to the highest degree of alert as of 1430 hours on 15 May. The armed forces would prepare for battle on the Israeli front in accordance with developments.

The order to move rapidly was something the army had often exercised. Telephone calls were made, dispatch riders were sent out, officers on leave were quickly and efficiently rounded up. By 1900 hours the battalions, though far from being complete, were ready to leave. No effort was made to hide these preparations. And when the first units of the 16th Brigade left their base at 2030 that evening, they drove through the streets of Cairo in an impressive display of strength.

Why was the order given? What had made Nasser decide to embark on a deliberate course of escalation? In his speech on the anniversary of the Egyptian Revolution on 23 July, Nasser declared that the Middle East crisis began with the Israeli intention "to invade Syria". And he added that he had received information to this effect from different sources. "Our Syrian brothers informed us that the Israelis had a concentration of eighteen brigades on their borders. We attempted to verify this information and found that the Israelis were concentrating not less than thirteen brigades on Syria's doorstep." The Russians, Nasser continued, informed an Egyptian parliamentary delegation visiting Moscow that "the invasion of Syria is near at hand".

By 14 May President Nasser was, apparently, convinced that an Israeli attack on Syria was imminent. The Soviet warning very probably left him in no doubt on that score. This being so, he simply had to move. He could not afford a recurrence of the shame of 7 April, when the Egyptians had stood by idly while six MiGs were shot out of the Syrian sky. But Nasser was not, at that stage, thinking in terms of a full-scale contest with the Israeli Army. The size of the force he ordered into Sinai—two divisions to back up the reinforced division permanently stationed there—was not sufficient to allow for a large-scale assault on Israel, and the elaborate publicity which accompanied the move did not point to offensive intentions. Nasser's motives in giving that order to move on 14 May were twofold: the deployment of forces in Sinai was to act as a deterrent to any Israeli plans of attack in the north; it was also to be exploited politically by Nasser to regain his initiative and his prestige in the Arab world, which he had all but lost by his inactivity after Samu and after the April air battle over Syria. The move into Sinai must, moreover, be viewed against the background of the increasing radicalization of Egyptian foreign policy since the autumn of 1966, when Arab summitry was discarded. Since then the Egyptians had been increasingly drawn in the wake of the extremist line of the Syrians and even began to encourage Fatah activity which hitherto they had strongly opposed. A growing recklessness had been apparent in Egyptian policy for some time. During his visit to the Yemeni capital of San'a in April 1967, Marshal Amer told the assembled Egyptian officers that "the time has arrived for us to prepare for offensive in all directions". Similarly President Nasser declared that he intended to launch a concentrated attack on "the colonialist alliance", by employing "all economic, psychological and military means of combat". Nasser's tactics in South Arabia and elsewhere in the spring of 1967 showed that he was in no mood for compromise. The hot winds of extremist militancy were blowing ever stronger from Cairo.

Yet Nasser did not then think there would be war. In his 23 July speech he claimed that he believed that there was a 20% chance of war breaking out. He was, therefore, not running a great risk. But it was clear to him that apart from preventing an Israeli attack on Syria, he would not be gaining much else unless he neutralized the presence of the United Nations Emergency Force. For his adversaries in the Arab world, and in particular the Jordanians, did not take his moves seriously. "Nasser is making war-like noises behind the protective screen of UNEF," Radio Amman jeered. It was, therefore, imperative that Nasser take steps to fulfil the promise he had made at the third Arab summit conference at Casablanca, that the UN force would not be allowed to stand in the way of offensive operations against Israel.

At 2200 hours on 16 May, the Egyptian liaison officer to the UN force in Gaza, Brigadier Ibrahim Sharqawi,* called on General Rikhye, the Indian Commander of UNEF. He handed him a letter from the Egyptian chief of staff, which had just been brought specially to him by Brigadier Izz ed-din Rif'at. The letter stated that Israel was concentrating troops on the Syrian frontier. If she attacked Syria, Egypt would go to the aid of the Syrians. If war started the UN troops would be in danger, and they were therefore asked to withdraw immediately. General Rikhye read the message through carefully, turned to Brigadier Sharqawi and said: "This is a shock to me. As commander here I can't do anything. I will send it to U Thant to decide."

* He was later taken prisoner by the Israeli forces.

In subsequent clarifications between the UN representatives and the Egyptians, it became clear that the Egyptians were not asking for a total evacuation of UNEF. They demanded a withdrawal from the border only along Sinai and the Gaza Strip into the UN camps at Khan Yunis and Rafa. No mention was made of the UN contingent at Sharm el-Sheikh, at the mouth of the Straits of Tiran. The following day the Cairo news bulletin announcing the request was accompanied on local televison by a map showing the UN posts along the border from which the UN had been asked to leave. The map took in Elath in the south and Gaza in the north. The all-important Sharm el-Sheikh was not shown on the map, and no mention of it was made in the news broadcast. Thus, again, the evidence points very clearly to a face-saving manœuvre, designed to still the guns of hostile propaganda. Nasser was still not thinking in terms of a possible war.

But the UN Secretary-General was not willing to play the Egyptian game. The United Nations, U Thant informed the Egyptian representative at the United Nations, could not be asked "to stand aside in order to enable the two sides to resume fighting". In subsequent talks U Thant took a tough line. The UN, he declared, could not be played with. He would not agree either to a partial or to a temporary evacuation. It was either all—or nothing. The Egyptians could choose between two alternatives: maintain the UN force as it was, or demand its complete and final evacuation. U Thant was evidently gambling on his conviction that Nasser did not want war, and would not want to see the complete disappearance of the UN force. His gamble might have succeeded if he had not made one cardinal mistake: by making public his answer that it was Nasser's privilege to demand the evacuation of the Emergency Force and that no one could oppose such a demand, U Thant forced Nasser's hand. Once this reply had been published in the international press Nasser could not climb down without tremendous loss of face. Characteristically, once Nasser realized that he had no choice left, he decided to make the best

of the new situation, and immediately gave orders to the army
to take over the UN posts, even before obtaining U Thant's
agreement to full evacuation. On the morning of 17 May,
Egyptian troops began occupying the Yugoslav observation
posts on the eastern borders of Sinai, and later that day General
Rikhye received an order from U Thant to withdraw his troops
from the frontiers to rear camps and to prepare a plan for
general withdrawal. On 18 May the Egyptians ordered the
32-man contingent at Sharm el-Sheikh to evacuate the post
within fifteen minutes, and on the same day sent an official
request to U Thant demanding total UN evacuation. A day
later, on 19 May, the UN flag was lowered from UNEF HQ in
Gaza and the force, to all intents and purposes, ceased to
exist. Neither Nasser nor U Thant had foreseen this abrupt end.
U Thant was severely criticized both in the United States and in
Europe for his mishandling of the affair. At the very least, it was
claimed, he should have brought the Egyptian request to the
General Assembly in accordance with the agreement reached
between the former Secretary-General, Dag Hammarskjöld,
and Nasser in November 1956, shortly after the UN forces had
been decided upon in the General Assembly. According to this
agreement, an Egyptian request for the evacuation of UNEF
"would at once be brought before the General Assembly. If
the General Assembly found that its (UNEF's) task was not
completed, and Egypt, all the same, maintained its stand and
enforced the withdrawal, Egypt would break the agreement
with the United Nations."*

U Thant, on his part, later claimed that there was little he

* One of the criticisms levelled against U Thant was that he was being
pro-Egyptian, out of sympathy for a fellow nation of the Afro-Asian
world. The facts, however, do not substantiate such an accusation. On
the contrary, U Thant has gone on record in the past in his sympathy for
Israel. On 17 May 1958, U Thant, then Burmese Ambassador to the
United States, said in a speech to the American Jewish Congress ". . . The
return of the Jewish people to their homeland—the Orient—is looked upon
by many race-conscious Asians as the return of their long-lost relatives to
their own hearths and homes."

could have done to prevent the demise of UNEF. The force had been effectively destroyed by the Egyptians even before their formal request had been made for its withdrawal. Moreover, two of the countries which had sent the largest contingents to the UN Emergency Force—India and Yugoslavia—insisted that Egypt had every right to demand their evacuation and declared that they would immediately pull out their troops even if U Thant bowed to the pressure of two other contributor-nations— Canada and Denmark—to withold evacuation until the Security Council and the General Assembly approved such a step. But U Thant does not explain the extraordinary speed with which he acceded to President Nasser's request.

For Nasser, however, a totally new situation was now unfolding. On 19 May Sharm el-Sheikh stood empty; there was no longer a UN screen between Egyptian soil and the channel, not more than 200 yards away, through which Israeli ships had been sailing to and from the Israeli port of Elath. Nasser knew that all his gains in prestige in the past few days would be wiped out if he continued to allow free passage for Israeli ships and cargoes now that the UN had left. The "reactionaries" in the Arab world would exploit his weakness mercilessly, while even his allies in Damascus and Algiers would probably delight in his discomfiture.

Yet Nasser hesitated. He still did not want war. The Israelis had time and again declared that they would consider the closing of the Straits tantamount to a declaration of war. Nasser had had no intention of closing the Straits before the total evacuation of the UN forced his hand. As late as 20 May Marshal Amer said that there was no intention of closing the Straits of Tiran. "Don't ask me why we cannot do it," he said. "Accept my word that the time is not yet ripe for such a move."* Nasser wanted to gauge Israeli reaction before he took his step. He also wanted to strengthen his forces in Sinai before he declared the Straits closed. From 19 May

---

* This was revealed by Egyptian officers taken prisoner by the Israelis.

onwards, the pace of Egyptian troop movements into Sinai was accelerated. The accent now was put on armoured units. The aim was now more than deterrence. Egyptian paratroops were dropped over Sharm el-Sheikh in order to forestall any possible Israeli move to occupy the vital point; ships of the Egyptian fleet were dispatched through the Suez Canal to the Red Sea and the mouth of the Gulf of Aqaba; units already on the move were reinforced and fresh units were rushed in. But still Nasser waited for the Israeli reaction. For a full four days after the UN departure from Sharm el-Sheikh, he kept quiet on this controversial and explosive question. The Straits were *de facto* closed, for there was now no UN presence to prevent Israeli ships from being fired upon. But he wanted to see what the Israelis would say and do before closing them *de jure* with a public declaration on their closure. The Israelis, however, were in no hurry to oblige. Only on 21 May was it announced that the Prime Minister, Levi Eshkol, would make an important policy statement about the tense situation on the border. This was to be in the Knesset (Parliament) the following evening at 1800 hours; it was to be his first statement since the withdrawal of UNEF. The Israelis were now going to reveal their hand. For Nasser this speech was crucial. He would trim his sails according to it. In the words of one of the senior officers who was later taken prisoner, Nasser did not have a master plan or a pre-determined policy. He took a step forward, looked to the left, looked to the right, saw if there was any danger, and took another step forward.

Mr Eshkol's six o'clock speech was a model of moderation. He called once more for peace between Israel and her neighbours; he demanded that Nasser withdraw his forces from Sinai; he did not mention the Straits with so much as a word.

This was the green light for Nasser. He had looked to the left and the right and there was no danger. The speech confirmed what he had already suspected, that Eshkol's government had no stomach for fighting. This being so, the limited objectives that Nasser had set a week earlier could now be scrapped.

Nasser could now go on the warpath without having too much to fear. He was greatly encouraged in taking this decision by the overwhelming confidence displayed by the Egyptian pilots at the Bir Gifgafa air base when Nasser visited them that day. They were absolutely convinced that they could completely destroy the Israeli Air Force within a matter of hours. Tel Aviv and other Israeli cities cities would then be at their mercy. Their complete self-confidence strongly affected Nasser. He came away from Bir Gifgafa convinced that this time the Egyptians would be more than a match for the Israelis. That same evening Nasser informed his ministers and advisers that he had decided to declare the Straits closed to Israeli ships and cargoes. Shortly after midnight Cairo Radio broadcast Nasser's decision to the world: "The Israeli flag will no longer pass the Gulf of Aqaba; our sovereignty over the Gulf is indisputable. . . . We now stand before war with Israel. But Israel does not have Britain and France on its side as it did in 1956. We are face to face with Israel. The Jews threaten us with war, and we say to them, 'ahlan wasahlan'—go ahead!" The die was now cast.

This was a very different Nasser from the cautious President of a few days earlier. He was now in an ebullient mood. Again according to his 23 July speech, Nasser thought, after closing the Straits, that there was now a 50% chance of war. But he was no longer afraid of war. He had, in fact, very shrewdly assessed possible Israeli reaction, and he elaborated his views to a group of senior officers—some of whom were later taken prisoner—shortly after closing the Straits. Eshkol, he said, was made of very different stuff from Ben Gurion. There was a very good chance that he would not go to war over the Straits, but limit himself to diplomatic and political moves only. But even if the Israelis did take hostile action, it would in all probability be a limited operation only, aimed at occupying the Gaza Strip or possibly the el-Arish region. On no account did he believe that the Israelis would begin a general war along the entire front. Moreover, he felt that his army was sufficiently strong to be able to prevent any decisive Israeli victory. At the very worst, the

D

Israelis might be able to achieve limited and local gains in the Gaza Strip or the el-Arish area before being brought to a halt by the Egyptian defensive deployment combined with Russian moves at the UN designed to bring a hasty cease-fire if the course of the war went adversely for the Egyptians. But in such an event the Straits would still remain closed. The Israelis, and the Americans, would still have to come begging. The trump cards would still be in his hands.

For these reasons Nasser did not at this moment fear the advent of war. But he still did not believe that the Israelis would attack. In his talks with his officers he compared Israel's situation to that of 1956, on the eve of the Suez War. Nasser made the following points:

1. Despite the fact that the fedayeen attacks preceding the Suez War gave Israel a good case with which to justify internationally her attack on Egypt, it did not enter into the minds of the Israeli leaders to go to war on their own. Only after they had been assured that they would be part of a general Western attack on Egypt, and only after they had been promised an air "umbrella" over their cities, did they dare venture to the attack.

2. Israel then fought against a weak Egyptian deployment in Sinai, when the bulk of the Egyptian forces were concentrated near the Canal to stave off any attack from the West; and even then the Israelis did not succeed in capturing the fortified positions of Abu Ageila and Rafiah (which, according to Nasser, the Israelis succeeded in taking only after the Egyptian garrisons had received the order to retreat). Now the whole line was fortified to a much greater extent than in 1956.

3. At that time the decisions had been taken by the aggressive Ben Gurion, with Dayan as Chief of Staff to encourage him. The team in Israel now was very different. Moreover, this time, the weaker Eshkol was facing an Arab world which was from day to day becoming more united in its resolve to stand together in the face of possible Israeli aggression. And this time Israel stood alone, with no guaranteed air umbrella over her cities and no Western Power to open a second front against Egypt.

As if to underline Nasser's evaluation of the situation, the reaction in Israel to his moves was weak, unsure of itself, temporizing. This, more than anything else, strengthened Nasser's conviction that he was gambling on a safe bet.

By now his deployment in Sinai was nearing completion. On the morning after his declaration on the closure of the Tiran Straits, the Egyptians had more than 80,000 troops in Sinai, and more were on the way. Nasser felt confident that he was master of the situation. And by now the irrational streak which had always been evident in Nasser's character began to show through. Flushed with victory—after having suffered one defeat after another for years—he threw caution to the winds and went from one extreme to the other, taunting Israel to attack. His public appearances in the week following the closure of the Straits, his threats and challenges, bore all the hallmarks of a man who had allowed events to take control of him. Nasser, in a sense, was no longer master of the situation; the situation had become master of him.

His victory, in that last week in May, appeared tangible enough. The hostile propaganda in Amman, Riadh and elsewhere in the Arab world had been silenced. In its stead, in every Arab capital delirious crowds were once more cheering the deeds of the great "Gamal". His predominant position in the Arab countries had been restored and there were no challengers. As for the Israelis, they appeared to be in disarray. It seemed almost incredible to the Egyptians that the Israelis could allow their deeds and their taunts to go unanswered. Writing in *al-Ahram* on 26 May, Nasser's close friend and confidant, Muhammad Hassanein Haikal, declared that he saw no alternative to an armed conflict between Egypt and Israel. War was inevitable. The Arabs, he wrote, had now for the first time succeeded in imposing their will on Israel by the use of force. This fact undermined the most basic concepts of security of the Israelis. Therefore, in Haikal's view, Israel had no choice other than to strike, hard. But Egypt was expecting and awaiting such a move on the part of Israel, and would strike back with all its might.

On 28 May Nasser appeared before hundreds of journalists
at a press conference in Cairo. He was supremely sure of himself.
He demanded the Israeli evacuation of the Red Sea port of
Elath and of the Sinai border post of Nitsana, both of which,
he claimed, had been occupied by Israel after the cease-fire had
come into effect after the 1948 war. The stakes were being raised.
And he repeated his challenge: "If the Jews want war, they are
welcome. We are awaiting them."

On the following day he declared to members of the National
Assembly that Egypt had restored the pre-1956 position; now,
with the help of Allah, they would restore the situation to its
pre-1948 state. "I have said in the past that we would decide the
time and the place, and that we must prepare ourselves in order
to win . . . those preparations have been completed and we are
now ready for the conflict with Israel." The problem now was
much larger than that of the Straits of Tiran and the right of
passage through it, Nasser continued. The problem dealt with
the rights of the entire Palestinian people. On the same day
forces of the Palestine Liberation Army stationed in the Gaza
Strip laid a heavy artillery barrage on Kibbutz Nahal Oz and its
fields, setting alight the ripening corn which was already heavy
with grain. War was moving perceptibly nearer.

By the end of May war hysteria had engulfed the entire Arab
world. The talk of war had begun after the expulsion of UNEF:
"As of today, there no longer exists an international emergency
force to protect Israel. We shall exercise patience no more. We
shall not complain any more to the United Nations about Israel.
The sole method we shall apply against Israel is a total war which
will result in the final extermination of Zionist existence,"
declared the "Voice of the Arabs" radio commentator in Cairo
on 18 May. "The irrevocable determination of the Arab people
is to wipe Israel off the face of the earth," commented Radio
Cairo on 25 May. These and similar statements poured from
the radio stations in an ever-growing pæan of hate. Religious
dignitaries called for a "Jihad"—a holy war against the infidel
Israelis. Everywhere the mounting fervour could be felt.

Even the moderates were taken up in the surge of excitement which gripped the Arabs. "The day of reckoning is near; be ready," was a call repeated time and time again during those latter days of May. The excitement reached fever pitch after the closing of the Straits of Tiran, and Nasser's challenge to Israel: "If you want war, 'ahlan wasahlan', we are ready for you." Nasser was now the idol of the people. Demonstrators surged through the streets, chanting slogans of war and death. Radio Cairo daily produced new hit songs, calling on the Arabs to march forward, to smite, to kill, to burn and destroy. "Itbah, itbah, itbah," "massacre, massacre, massacre," chimed one of the favourite "shlagers". In Gaza the enthusiasm was especially great, as rifles and ammunition were distributed to the men in the refugee camps. The general attitude is well reflected in the call made by the Egyptian Chief of Police in the Gaza Strip, Colonel Mahmud Shibli, to his men on 25 May.* "The time has come for the vanguard to move forward," he declared, "and here are the forces of victory breaking through towards the enemy, in order to wipe out the existence of Israel."

The call for war was not limited to Egypt alone. The other Arab states stepped into line, one after the other. "The elimination of Israel is the essential step towards the establishment of a life of freedom and honour for the Arab people," declared a commentator on Damascus Radio on 28 May, while President Aref of Iraq, speaking over Radio Baghdad three days later, echoed these sentiments when he said: "The existence of Israel is an error which must be rectified. This is our opportunity to wipe out the ignonimy which has been with us since 1948. Our goal is clear—to wipe Israel off the face of the map." The Syrians ostentatiously moved up troops through Damascus to the southern front. The Iraqis announced that they had put their army on a war footing, and that it was ready to move "to liberate Palestine". The Lebanese cancelled all leave and took "necessary steps to defend the homeland". Algeria declared

* This was one of the thousands of documents captured by the Israeli forces when they entered Gaza.

general mobilization and Tunisia, Libya, the Sudan, Kuwait and the other Arab countries reported on measures taken to put their armies on a war footing. On 24 May the advance units of a Kuwaiti armoured brigade were flown to Cairo airport and on the same day token forces arrived from Algeria and the Sudan. Even Saudi Arabia and Tunisia, two traditional enemies of Egypt, voiced their support for the Egyptian President. But the greatest *volte-face* of all was made by Jordan. For no other country in the Arab world was confronted with the need of such a great switch in policy during those three weeks before the war as was Jordan.

When Nasser decided to move his divisions into Sinai, the quarrel between Egypt and Syria on the one hand and Jordan and Saudi Arabia on the other had reached extremes seldom seen in the Arab world. The two kings were anathema to the revolutionaries of Cairo and Damascus, whose radio commentators spent almost as much time in vilifying them as they did in attacking Israel. King Hussein was variously described as "a lackey of imperialiam", "an ally of Zionism", "a prostitute", "a pimp", to mention only some of the printable epithets. His downfall was considered to be an essential prerequisite to the elimination of Israel, and the people of Jordan were repeatedly called upon to rise against their "puppet king". King Hussein's most deadly enemy, Ahmad Shuqairi, was allowed by the Egyptians to run a daily radio programme from Cairo directed at the Palestinians of the West Bank of the Jordan, which daily poured slander and insults on the head of the king and called on the people to kill him. The Syrians had taken their propaganda war against Jordan one step further and had sent groups of saboteurs, trained by the Deuxième Bureau, to create havoc and increase unrest. On 21 May, a bomb exploded in a bus at Ramtha, on the border of Syria, killing fourteen persons and injuring twenty-four. This was the last straw for the Jordanians, and on 23 May, shortly after Nasser announced the closing of the Straits of Tiran, Jordan broke off diplomatic relations with Syria, and immediately began expelling Syrian nationals.

Thus when the crisis broke on 15 May, the Jordanians were patently out of step. But during those first days of tension, the Jordanians, like the Israelis, refused to take the Egyptian measures seriously. At first they kept quiet; then they gave details of the Egyptian and Syrian moves, to the accompaniment of derisive commentaries. As proof of the lack of real war-like intentions on the part of the Egyptians, they pointed to the limelight and the publicity given to the troop movements. "If the Egyptians really mean what they say, let them demonstrate their real intentions by expelling the UN force," challenged Radio Amman on 16 May. The following day the Egyptians did just that. Still the Jordanians were not put out. They withdrew to a new line of propaganda, and counter-attacked. "The Egyptians talk big, but Israeli ships still pass through the Straits of Tiran," was their new challenge. By this time Egypt's moves had already led to a steep rise in Nasser's prestige, especially among the Palestinians of the West Bank, a fact of increasing concern for the Government in Amman. There can be little doubt that at this stage there must have been many among the ruling circles of Jordan who hoped for and expected an Israeli attack on Egypt, in order to cut Nasser down to size.

When Nasser took up their second challenge, and closed the Straits of Tiran, the Jordanians were thrown into a state of confusion. Nasser's prestige was now soaring, and internal tension was rising to dangerous heights. Jordanian propaganda was now in full retreat. On 24 May Jordan announced its agreement to the stationing of Iraqi and Saudi Arabian troops on its soil after having previously rejected an Iraqi request to this effect. But the troops did not come. The Iraqis were still furious at Jordan's first refusal; the Iraqi Defence Minister castigated the King for his "treachery" to the Arab cause. During those days immediately after the closing of the Tiran Straits, the Jordanians became more convinced than ever that an Israeli attack on Egypt was imminent. But the internal situation was explosive. They had to step into line, quickly. They now did what they had so contemptuously rejected only a week previously: they sent troops to the front to the accompaniment of all the trappings of publicity that they could muster. Units of the 40th Armoured Brigade and a battalion of heavy artillery were sent through the main streets of Amman in broad daylight on their way to the West Bank. This was the first time that reinforcements for the front had been sent in that manner. They usually took the detour to the north of Amman, at night. A Palestinian from the West Bank, who watched the procession of tanks and guns in the streets of Amman that day (24 May), commented later, sadly: "Little did the people of Amman, who cheered and clapped so enthusiastically, dream that they were bidding farewell to all that heavy and expensive equipment." Equal publicity was given to the mobilization of reserves, and to civil defence decrees which were repeatedly broadcast over the radio.

On 25 May Radio Amman finally stopped all its attacks on Egypt, and voiced its approval of the closing of the Straits. And for the first time, an anti-American approach was adopted. The American Ambassador was summoned to the Prime Minister, who warned him that Jordan would react strongly if the US continued to identify itself with Israel. The following day Radio Ramallah began co-ordinating with Egyptian propaganda.

And still the expected Israeli attack on Egypt did not come. Instead of a show of strength, the Israelis put up a front of weakness, of placatory statements, halting speeches, and defensive actions. Israel was hesitating to attack Egypt, and to King Hussein and his advisers the only plausible reason for his hesitation must be that Israel feared the strong troop concentrations in Sinai. And now the King recalled the situation in November 1966, when Israel, out of fear of attacking Syria, had attacked the Jordanian village of Samu instead. His latent suspicion that Israel had set its eyes on the West Bank was now once more aroused. To attack the Egyptian concentration in Sinai would be a costly affair. But what prevented the Israelis from marching into the West Bank, a much easier and more remunerative affair? Would the Syrians and the Egyptians, who for so long had been preaching his downfall, come to his aid, or would they sit on the sidelines, happy that Israel was doing their work for them, and that one more enemy of the "Arab revolution" was being eliminated? As Hussein saw it, the Syrian–Egyptian Defence Treaty had saved Syria from an Israeli invasion; therefore, a similar treaty could do the same for Jordan.

And there was the mounting tension at home to combat. The situation was daily becoming more dangerous for the King. The people, especially on the West Bank, were hypnotized by Nasser's propaganda machine. Even the most moderate of the Arabs there were now wildly in favour of war. They were convinced that the hour for liberating Palestine was at hand. Nasser, it was argued, must have a master plan ready, for he had always said that when he was ready he would choose the time to attack, and that it would not be dictated to him by Israel. Now that time had come. An unprecedented wave of enthusiasm engulfed the kingdom, not least within the ranks of the army. The King's most trustworthy officers were pressing him to cast in his lot with Nasser. They warned him that they would not be able to control their troops much longer if he did not act quickly.

By 28 May, King Hussein had become convinced that Israel would not attack Egypt. Nasser, he realized, was going to get away with the biggest victory he had yet gained. In such circumstances, he could not afford to sit quietly by. He had to become part of victorious Arab nationalism, or risk the fate that had befallen his grandfather, King Abdullah. Hussein decided to act.

On the morning of 28 May the Egyptian Ambassador in Amman was summoned to the house of the Prime Minister, Said Jum'a. When he arrived he found King Hussein awaiting him. He told the Ambassador that he wished to meet President Nasser, and proposed a meeting in Cairo on 30 May. The Ambassador was asked to transmit this message urgently and secretly to Cairo. The Prime Minister was also sworn to secrecy by the King. Not a word was said to the other Ministers.

Nasser's reply was not long in coming. The King would be welcome in Cairo, but only if he agreed beforehand to certain conditions, so that there should not be any basic differences of opinion between them when they met. These conditions included the dispersal of the strong deployment of Jordanian troops opposite the Syrian frontier, the acceptance of Ahmad Shuqairi and his Palestine Liberation Organization as the legitimate representative of the Palestinian people, agreement to the immediate entry of Iraqi troops into Jordan, and the annulment of the Jordanian intentions to re-establish diplomatic relations with West Germany, after they had been broken off when Germany recognized Israel. Nasser also strongly advised Hussein, for his own good, not to reveal his intention of coming to Cairo. Western agents, Nasser added, might try to prevent his trip, might even endanger his life.

For Hussein those conditions spelt unconditional surrender to Nasser. Hitherto their acceptance would have been unthinkable. But now he felt that he had no choice. He would, at best, be gaining time to enable him to extricate himself from the three-fold danger which threatened him: danger of an imminent Israeli attack, danger from an explosive internal situation inside Jordan, and danger from a renewed propaganda offensive by Nasser.

So Hussein flew to Cairo on 30 May, guided by circumstances over which he had had no control. He had expected Israel to attack after 23 May. The attack did not come. Now he was flying to Canossa in what he believed was a mission to save his country and his neck. In the event, had he waited another week the mission would have been unnecessary and his country would have been saved.

It must have been a bitter moment indeed for the young King when he drove through the streets of Amman at the side of his arch-enemy, Ahmad Shuquairi, who had triumphantly returned with him from Cairo. But the effect of his trip was instantaneous. The internal pressure vanished; demonstrations were held in his favour. Once more the pictures of Gamal abd al-Nasser and King Hussein were paraded side by side through the streets of West Bank towns; not since the brief rule of Suleiman Nabulsi in 1956 had such a spectacle been witnessed.

For the King the die was now cast. On 1 June the Egyptian chief of staff of the Joint Arab Command, General abd al-Munim Riad, arrived in Amman, and took command over the Jordanian armed forces. He scrapped all existing military plans and prepared new ones based on the immediate entry into Jordan of a division of Iraqi troops. For one of the main points that Hussein had accepted in his Cairo talks with Nasser was that the Iraqis would take up offensive positions along the Jordanian–Israeli frontier in order to draw Israeli troops away from the southern front facing Egypt. The plan was to concentrate four Iraqi brigades, including one armoured one, opposite Natanya and in the Jenin hills. Such a concentration of troops and armour would represent a very real danger for Israel. The distance between the Jordanian border and the Mediterranean Sea at Natanya is only eleven miles. Israel has always been susceptible to any possible threat to cut the country into two at this narrow waistline. By agreeing to this plan in Cairo, King Hussein agreed to his country becoming a possible battlefield. And, indeed, once hostilities were opened, this threat without doubt played a major role in the Israeli decision to drive on to the Jordan River. Their major preoccupation was to forestall the Iraqi division at the Jordan crossings.

The Saudi Arabians were none too pleased by Hussein's dramatic switch of sides. Saudi Arabian troops, who were to have entered Jordan, were retained at the last moment, and they also witheld equipment they had previously promised to the Jordanians. Even less pleased were the Syrians, who persisted in considering Hussein as a reactionary whose overthrow was an essential objective for revolutionary Arabs. The Ba'thists, in particular, were furious. One of the more revealing documents captured by the Israelis in Quneitra* is a report written by

* Doc. No. 29/34, dated 3 June 1967. marked "Top Secret—Personal—

Muhammad Ibn abd al-Hadi Aat, head of Intelligence of the south-western sector of the Syrian front, on 3 June, two days before the war broke out. The report assessed the reaction in the army and among the people to the Nasser–Hussein pact. "A decisive blow to the revolutionary forces in the Arab world; the pact is part of a plot against Syria, and abd al-Nasser personally, together with Israel, is keeping Hussein on his throne", are some of the reactions given in the report, which concludes with the following words: "The army was enthusiastic to enter into battle. They expected the downfall of the Jordanian King in those circumstances, but Nasser's step in signing the defence pact with Jordan has saved the King from the anger of his people and has left the army with a bitter feeling. They don't want to have anything to do with Nasser and feel ever closer to the [Ba'th] party and the Syrian revolution." The Syrians, even at this late hour, were still more engrossed in their inter-Arab quarrels than in the war against Israel.

The Syrians were also angry that Nasser had signed the pact without first consulting with his Syrian allies or even informing them beforehand. They continued attacking Hussein after the pact was signed, and the Egyptians, fearing a rupture with Syria at this crucial stage, hastily sent Zakaria Muhi ed-Din to Damascus to calm frayed tempers. But this incident undoubtedly played a part in the Syrian refusal to come to the help of the Egyptians once war broke out.

Apart from this one discordant note all was now harmony in the Arab world, and all were now engaged in last-minute preparations for the war which Hassanein Haikal, as early as 26 May, had said was inevitable. The enthusiasm which engulfed the Arab world also gripped the Arab students in Europe and, first and foremost among them, the members of the Fatah who had acted as the spark which eventually ignited the Middle East. As tension rose, a fever of excitement took hold of the Palestinian students. Fatah members toured the

Urgent", addressed to General Intelligence, Branch 255.

universities and demanded that all Palestinian students immediately stop their studies and report for military training in Algeria. Several hundred students were dispatched forthwith to the training camps in North Africa. The day the Fatah had worked for was fast approaching. They wanted to be in at the kill. The Algerians joined in the general enthusiasm. Radio Algiers announced that all Palestinian able-bodied men in Algeria must report for training immediately, adding that their families would continue to receive their salaries. But the Algerians proved to be inefficient. They were incapable of handling the sudden influx of well over a thousand volunteers. The training camps were poorly organized and the military instruction of low standard. Many of the students returned to Europe in disgust after a few days. Of those training only approximately one hundred made their way to Syria and were infiltrated after the war into the Israeli-occupied West Bank to organize acts of terror and sabotage.

Meanwhile, on 2 June, Marshal Amer issued his top secret "Battle Order No. 2".* It makes interesting reading, in the light of future events:

Officers and soldiers of the armed forces, Israel has tried, and is still trying, to obtain direct support from the US for her planned operations against Egypt. But because of the firm stand taken by the Soviet Union and her readiness to intervene if any Great Power enters into war with Egypt, it is now clear that the American Government will not on any account enter into any military adventure on the side of Israel.

Israel will not be able to maintain the burden of mobilization for any length of time. It has already completely paralysed Israel's economy. And in the meantime there have been two developments in the inter-Arab arena: Jordan signed a defence pact with Egypt; Iraq decided to participate in the conflict, with large forces, operating from Jordanian territory.

* This document, together with Battle Order No. 1, was captured by the Israelis.

After the establishment of a national government in Israel, extremist elements have joined the government who call for war against Egypt. I estimate that Israel reckons that the entry of Iraqi forces into Jordan and their deployment along the border with Israel will take approximately two weeks. Israel, therefore, plans to attack Egypt before this deployment is completed.

In accordance with this I have completed my plans and issued my orders for the execution of operations. I call on every one of you to fight with maximum aggression, to follow faithfully after the instructions within the framework of the general plan—until the fulfilment of the objectives of the Egyptian command. Our aim is to defeat the major part of the Israeli Army. Our armed forces, the numbers and the equipment that are at their disposal, are capable of attaining this objective.

I am certain that each one of you will fulfil his duty and will think of nothing else except his contribution to the general plan. The contest awaiting us will be fateful for Egypt and fateful for the entire Arab nation.

The honour of the Arab armed forces depends upon you. I have full confidence in our victory. Allah guard you and may you be successful.—*signed:* Field-Marshal abd al-Hakim Amer, Deputy Commander in Chief of the Armed Forces.

From this document it is clear that the Egyptians were expecting an attack within two weeks. On the following day, forty-eight hours before the outbreak of the war, Nasser once more convened his Ministers and his military advisers and told them that in view of the changes within the Israeli Government, he considered war to be now inevitable. But he was not worried. He thought there might be losses and that the Israelis might reach the outskirts of el-Arish. But this would be more than offset by the capture by the Egyptians of Elath. General Shazli* had two hundred tanks and five crack battalions of

* General Shazli first came to the notice of the British public when, as

paratroops and commandos for this special mission, Nasser told his audience. Later that day, Nasser declared that all the steps he had taken so far had been guided by logic, and that logic prescribed that further measures would be taken against Israel. Nasser's confidence was not shared by all his officers. On that day some of them, led by Marshal Amer, urged on him to put into operation forthwith the special plan they had prepared for a pre-emptive air strike against Israel's airfields. But Nasser dallied. Despite his statement to the officers that war was inevitable, he was still not sure. The Russians had assured him that Israel would not attack. The Americans had warned him not to fire the opening shots. So had de Gaulle. Nasser stayed his hand. Moreover, one of the most basic tenets of Egyptian strategic thought over the years had been that the Arabs should not fire the opening shots of their war with Israel, in order not to estrange world opinion. The Egyptians had long ago reached the conclusion that, once their army was ready to overcome the Israelis, they should goad the Israelis into beginning the war, and they would then smash the Israeli army in a massive counter-offensive. At the beginning of June, Marshal Amer urged Nasser to scrap this strategy,* but the Egyptian President would hear none of it. This was to become the principal source of the quarrel which burst out between the two friends after the war.

On 3 June the first units of the Iraqi division reached Jordan, and two Egyptian commando battalions were flown into

---

Egyptian military attaché in London, he became involved in a deal with Colin Jordan, the British fascist leader. See *Sunday Telegraph*, at the beginning of October, 1962.

* The existence of this strategy was later borne out by the evidence of the former Minister for War, Shams ed-din Badran, during his trial. Badran, who was accused of plotting the overthrow of President Nasser, told the court in Cairo on 26 February 1968 that they preferred Israel to open hostilities so that, when Egypt replied, she would have to fight against Israel alone. If Egypt was the first to strike, she would have to fight not only against Israel but against the American Sixth Fleet, Badran told the court.

Amman. Forces of the Kuwaiti army took up positions in the Sinai alongside the Egyptians. On 4 June the Iraqis signed a defence agreement with Egypt, and a squadron of Iraqi MiGs was flown into the Jordanian air base Mafraq and the Egyptians took over the command of the Jordanian Air Force. On the Syrian Heights, high above Israel, 24,000 Syrian troops and 380 tanks were in position. In Jordan, the bulk of the army was deployed along the long border with Israel. It included 32,000 men and 170 tanks. And within forty-eight hours the four Iraqi brigades were scheduled to join them. In Sinai the Egyptian deployment had been completed; seven divisions, composed of 100,000 men and a thousand tanks, stood arrayed against Israel. It was Sunday, 4 June. The Arab deployment had been virtually completed. In Tel Aviv that morning the decision had been taken to go to war if the Arabs made any further aggressive moves. For a few brief hours history stood still as the armies, poised in readiness, stood facing each other.

CHAPTER 6

The Powers Back Down

Neither the Soviet Union nor the United States wished to become involved in a Middle East conflict. Both Powers sought to disengage as the crisis unfolded in the latter days of May. But neither succeeded, for neither was willing to abdicate its influence in the region to the other. The Russians feared that an Israeli victory could jeopardize the hard-won positions which the Soviet Union had gained in the "progressive" Arab countries, in particular in Egypt and in Syria. The Americans feared that a victory of the Egyptians and Syrians over Israel—whether political or military—would bring in its wake the downfall of all the Western bastions in the Middle East, which would be transformed into a Soviet-influenced region. From the Russian point of view, the political gains made by President Nasser after 15 May were advantageous in the extreme, provided they did not involve Egypt in a war with Israel. They removed a direct Israeli threat against the pro-Soviet régime in Syria. They restored the leadership of the Arab world to President Nasser and the "progressive" forces. They silenced the pro-Western Arab régimes which, the Russians believed, had been plotting the downfall of the Syrian Government. The New Middle Eastern situation at the beginning of June would enable the Soviet Union to consolidate its position in the region and spread its influence in the wake of a victorious President Nasser. Arabia, the Persian Gulf principalities, Kuwait, Jordan and Iraq would, in all likelihood, fall within the orbit of President Nasser's influence. Reactionary régimes would be overthrown and the

Arab world would join the ranks of the progressive forces of the world. This was the rosy picture which must have presented itself to Soviet eyes in those last days of May. The fly in the ointment was Israel. Israel must be prevented at all costs from going to war with Egypt. It was to this endeavour that all the Soviet efforts were directed.

For the same reasons, President Nasser's gains spelt disaster for the United States' policies in the Middle East. A victory of the Russian-backed Egyptians and Syrians would have a direct bearing on American prestige in the entire Third World. Therefore, the efforts of the United States in those crucial weeks before the war were directed first and foremost at negating the gains President Nasser had made.

But, as we have already said, neither the Soviet Union nor the United States wished to be directly involved. Both feared an escalation which could lead them, at best, to a new confrontation; at worst, to a thermonuclear world war. But direct disengagement was possible only if the other side was not directly engaged. To ensure this was the first and highest priority of both Powers in those crucial three weeks before the war. The Russians made guarantees to the Egyptians that they would prevent the Americans from actively helping the Israelis;* the Americans assured the Israelis that they need have nothing to fear from direct Soviet intervention. This mutual cancelling out of the Great Powers paved the way for the direct confrontation between the local forces—Israeli and Arab—on the battlefield.

We thus have the frames of reference for the Great Power activity between 15 May and June 5. It was neither in the Soviet nor in the American interest to intervene. But each had its own interests. The Egyptians expected the Russians to neutralize the West, and the Israelis expected the Americans to neutralize the Soviet Union. There was thus from the very outset a certain symmetrical pattern created by the relations between Egypt and

* This was admitted by Marshal Amer in his "Battle Order No. 2". See p. 109.

the Soviet Union on the one hand, and between Israel and the United States on the other. But the Egyptians did not take into account the overall inferiority of the Soviet position in global affairs, vis-à-vis the United States. They overestimated the Soviet ability to influence the march of events. It was a mistake that was to prove costly. For in the event, the Soviet moves, far from being adroit and machiavellian as they have since frequently been described, were based rather on a series of miscalculations, and were thus unable to obtain their major objectives.

During the first week of the crisis the Russians were still almost totally preoccupied with the situation along the Syrian frontier. They paid only scant attention to the gathering storm clouds in the south. They were convinced there would have to be an explosion along the Israeli-Syrian frontier if the Fatah terror attacks continued. In order, therefore, to safeguard the pro-Soviet Ba'th régime, they wished to stop the terror strikes, but their influence on the leaders in Damascus was not sufficient to persuade them to change their policy. They therefore scared the Syrians by their reports of an imminent Israeli attack, and, as Egyptian influence in Damascus had increased since the Defence Pact was signed, they passed the story on to the Egyptians as well, hoping that they might have better luck than the Russians in dissuading the Syrians from persisting in terror tactics. Security experts in Israel, who know a great deal about this sort of thing, are absolutely convinced that the Russians must have known that their story of a concentration of thirteen Israeli brigades along the border and of an impending Israeli attack on 17 May was completely untrue. The Soviet Embassy in Tel Aviv had a number of means of checking this story, and thus could easily have discovered that there was no truth in it. Yet the Russians persisted in their lie, and both the Syrians and the Egyptians believed them. But the Russians were not content with crying "Wolf" over Israel. They were far more interested in directing Arab sentiments against the West. They therefore persisted in their "Western plot" story, according to which a joint conspiracy of the Western powers, together with Jordan and Israel, existed, aimed at overthrowing the socialist régime in Damascus. As late as 23 May, the day Nasser declared the closing of the Tiran Straits to Israeli shipping, a Soviet Government statement on the situation in the Middle East dwelt more on this so-called conspiracy than on the situation in Sinai. This was the first major statement the Soviet Government had issued since the crisis broke on 15 May. Yet the closing of the Tiran Straits was not mentioned by so much as a word, and the expulsion of UNEF was only briefly referred to. At the same time a Note was presented to the Israeli Ambassador in Moscow which warned Israel in the strongest language not to attack Syria. The accent, at this late hour, was still on Damascus.

All these points are not conclusive evidence that there was no active Soviet–Egyptian collusion. That the Russians informed the Egyptians of an impending—and imaginary—Israeli attack on Syria is certain. That they advised Nasser to send in his troops to the Sinai to act as a deterrent force is possible, but there is no evidence that such advice was in fact given. That they encouraged him to demand the evacuation of UNEF and to close the Straits of Tiran is highly unlikely. There was, in fact, no Soviet–Egyptian collusion in the accepted sense of that word. But, if the number of times that the Soviet Ambassador was called to the Egyptian Foreign Ministry during that first week of the crisis is anything to go by, the Russians were very probably kept in the picture, and their Ambassador was informed of the Egyptian move regarding the Gulf of Aqaba shortly *before* the Straits were closed, as the Egyptians have themselves admitted.

Indeed, the Soviet leaders in Moscow only realized the full implications—and the dangers—of the Middle East situation on 25 May when the Egyptian Minister of War, Shams ed-din Badran, arrived in Moscow. Significantly, one of the first conclusions they reached after hearing the Egyptian Minister was to change their Ambassador in Cairo for a much more veteran and seasoned diplomat, someone who would be able to conduct a dialogue with Nasser personally, and not through the Foreign Ministry. The decision to appoint Vinogradov as Ambassador was, in all likelihood, taken then, though he took up his post some time later. The Russians would hardly have taken that decision if their ambassador had been party to the developments in Cairo of the past week. Badran had come to Moscow to ask for urgent delivery of new military equipment, and to obtain Soviet political support specifically in neutralizing any possible American intervention in the crisis. He received affirmative replies to both requests; in Nasser's speech to members of the National Assembly on 29 May he said that "after hearing Badran's report on his talks in Moscow, I can tell you today that the Soviet Union is a friendly country, standing at our side in the honourable manner of a friend". But the Egyptian Minister did not ask for direct Soviet aid, and the Russians made it clear that they would not intervene directly unless the Americans did.

Within twenty-four hours of the departure of the Egyptian War Minister, a Syrian delegation arrived in the Soviet capital headed by the Syrian Head of State, Dr Nur ed-din al-Atassi, also to ask for Soviet aid. Moscow was now moving into high gear. Their gains in the Middle East were greater than they had dreamt possible. Nasser's moves had been dangerous, both for him and for his Soviet allies. But they transformed the entire Middle Eastern situation to the greatest benefit for himself and his Soviet friends. The Russians now went into action to ensure that these gains would not be lost in war. To their mind, there were four possibilities:

1. A US–Israeli collusion, leading to war. This could lead to an extremely dangerous situation.

2. The US would not give the green light to Israel to go to war. Israel would be left without American backing, and the political gains of Egypt could thus be preserved and consolidated.

3. The US would act unilaterally, or in conjunction with other maritime powers, to force open the Straits of Aqaba for Israeli shipping. Such a move would throw all the Arabs into the

pro-Soviet camp and strengthen the Soviet Union's position in the Middle East.

4. Despite lack of US backing, Israel might decide to go it alone.

Soviet contacts with the US were primarily designed to prevent the first possibility. Their main approach was made to the US on 26 May, when the Soviet Premier, Alexei Kosygin, proposed that the two Powers should both act to lessen tension in the Middle East. Kosygin proposed that President Johnson act to restrain the Israelis; he, on his part, would do his utmost to prevent aggressive action on the part of the Egyptians. President Johnson concurred, and on the night of 27 May a Note was drafted to Mr Eshkol, calling on him to desist from using force. A copy was sent to the Soviet Premier. The Israeli Foreign Minister had just left Washington. His visit, as we shall see later, had had a demoralizing effect on the Americans. In the circumstances they were only too willing to accept the Soviet proposal. But they were not going to limit their restraining influence to the Israelis only. In his talk with Dean Rusk, Eban had said that Israel possessed information according to which Egypt intended to attack. The Americans were sceptical. But they did not want to take any chances. Late that night they woke up the Egyptian Ambassador in Washington, Mustafa Kemal, informed him of Mr Eban's fears and urged the Egyptian Government not to take hasty action.* They also informed the Soviet Government of Eban's assertion. The Russians, too, were doubtful. But they could not be sure of their Egyptian allies. The American report lent urgency to their promise to act in Cairo to prevent hostilities. At 0300 hours the following morning the Soviet Ambassador in Cairo contacted the President's office and asked for an immediate interview with the President. He wished to deliver a Note from the Soviet Government, and he could not brook delay. Reluctantly the order was given to wake Nasser, and a sleepy President listened as the Ambassador read out the contents of the Note. It was

---

* Hassanein Haikal writes of this episode in *al-Ahram* of 16 June 1967. Nasser also mentions it in his speech of 23 July.

from Kosygin. But the contents were almost identical with the
Note that had been delivered through Mustafa Kamal from
Washington earlier that night. Both urged restraint. Aggressive
action, Kosygin added, could have dire consequences for the
entire world.

But Kosygin's main efforts were directed against Israel to
prevent the fourth possibility (of Israel going to war alone).
The Russians did not believe that the Israelis would go to war.
This belief was strengthened after they received the copy of
President Johnson's Note. They estimated that Mr Eshkol was
too weak to take such a fateful decision. They understood—
perhaps better than the Americans—the limitations and the
internal brakes of Israel's political system which made such a
move so difficult during the rule of a weak Prime Minister.
They knew of the activists in opposition but did not believe
they would be able to influence the Government's decision. And
they set out to calm the Government, to remove its fears, and
thus make a decision to take the extreme step of war more
difficult. This explains the sudden change of attitude of the
Russians towards Israel during the last few days of May. They
were suddenly full of smiles, accommodating, and certain that
everything could be worked out without Israel needing to worry.
On 27 May the Soviet Ambassador in Tel Aviv, Mr Zubachin,
twice asked to see Mr Eshkol in order to deliver Notes from the
Soviet Premier. On the first occasion the Soviet Ambassador
called at 0230 in the morning. The impeccably dressed Ambassador and the pyjama-clad Premier settled down to a two-hour
conversation in Russian in Mr Eshkol's study, during which,
in Mr Eshkol's words, the Ambassador, poker-faced, successfully parried awkward questions. But the Note itself was
couched in surprisingly polite and even cordial terms. In it
Kosygin asked his Israeli counterpart not to follow the
imperialists, and urged him to exercise restraint. The Soviet
Union, he declared, was doing its utmost to restrain the Arabs.
The Second Note was similar in content. During the days that
followed there were several more contacts between Soviet

representatives and Israeli officials. The theme was always the same. Israel need have nothing to fear. A satisfactory solution would be worked out. During this period the Russians carefully avoided voicing their support for the closing of the Aqaba Straits. They wished the door to remain ajar for a settlement.

The Russian mistake stemmed from their wrong reading of the internal situation inside Israel. They failed to realize that the point of no return had been reached; they failed to remember the effect that a threat of extermination can have on a people's determination to fight. Stalingrad, and all it stood for, had long been forgotten. Russian Intelligence also underestimated the overwhelming superiority of the Israeli army to that of the Soviet-equipped Egyptian armed forces. Russian experts had told Egyptian officers that, in any war between Israel and Egypt, the Israelis would not be able to achieve total victory. They believed in the strength of the Egyptian defence, which was based on Soviet doctrines. How much these basic mis-calculations on the part of the Russians affected Nasser's actions in that crucial crisis period we may never know. But at the very least, they prevented the Russians from exerting greater influence on the Arabs to avoid the disaster into which they had manœuvred themselves.

Compared to these Soviet moves, the American actions were much more complex. This was, to a large extent, natural: the Russians wished to preserve and safeguard a situation which had been created by the Egyptians; the Americans wished to change it. The problem that confronted the Americans was how to restore the former position in the Middle East without taking direct action themselves. During the first days of the crisis, they shared the opinion held in Israel, that the Egyptian President was rattling his sabre, but did not seriously intend to go to war. Nasser was putting on a show, a dangerous one, but none the less a show. But this attitude changed abruptly after the evacuation of UNEF. The Americans were shocked by the alacrity with which U Thant agreed to Nasser's demand. ". . . We are dismayed at the hurried withdrawal of the UN Emergency Force

from Gaza and Sinai after more than ten years of steadfast and
effective service in keeping the peace, without action by either
the General Assembly or the Security Council . . .", declared
President Johnson on 23 May. The Americans did not hide their
scepticism that U Thant's talks in Cairo on 24 May could
appreciably alter the situation.

That situation had, in their view, been fundamentally altered
after Nasser's act of closing the Straits of Aqaba. Up to that
time there had been no act on the part of the Egyptians which
officially changed the status quo or which exceeded the legitimate rights of Egypt as a sovereign country. The massing of
Egyptian troops and armour in Sinai, and the expulsion of the
UN Emergency Force were not, in themselves, acts of war
which justified a military reply. The Egyptians had gained
political advantages, had endangered American interests, but
there was not much that could be done about it. Indeed, during
that first week American officials in Washington repeatedly
warned the Israelis not to take rash action. But Nasser's act in
closing the Straits changed the situation entirely. For it provided
Israel with what the Americans considered to be a legitimate
casus belli. But the Americans did not want a general war in
the Middle East. They feared the dangers of possible escalation.
The problem, as they saw it, was essentially one of free passage
of shipping through the Straits. This was the *casus belli*, and
on this question the Americans were directly involved by
guarantees given by previous American governments, which
they could not ignore.

When the President and his advisers heard the news that the
Straits of Aqaba had been closed to Israeli shipping and
cargoes, they were convinced that the Israeli armed forces would
almost immediately swing into action. This conviction grew
when they read Nasser's aggressive speech announcing the
blockade. Nasser had thrown down a challenge and it seemed
almost inconceivable that the Israelis would not hasten to pick
it up. But the Americans, as we have said, did not want a general
war in the Middle East. They feared complications which might

hinder their efforts in Vietnam. They therefore felt it incumbent upon them to try to stamp the crisis out, by political means, before it got out of hand. There was not a moment to lose.

That same day, 23 May, the Israeli Ambassador in Washington, Avraham Harman, was summoned to Mr Eugene Rostow, Assistant Secretary of State, who was now assigned by Dean Rusk to co-ordinate activities on the Middle East crisis. The Ambassador was asked to pass an urgent request from the President to the Israeli Prime Minister. It was to withhold all action for forty-eight hours to allow the US to use her good offices to reopen the Straits. The Israelis were given to understand that they had nothing to fear, that Washington was taking it upon itself to solve the problem.* At the same time President Johnson issued a statement saying, *inter alia*, that the US Government regarded the Gulf of Aqaba as an international waterway, and that the blockade of Israeli shipping in the Gulf was "illegal and potentially dangerous to peace". And he added: "The right of free, innocent passage of the international waterway is a vital interest of the international community. . . . We have urged Secretary-General Thant to recognize the sensitivity of the Aqaba question and to give it the highest priority in his discussions in Cairo. To the leaders of all the nations of the Near East, I wish to say what three Presidents have said before— that the United States is firmly committed to the support of the political independence and territorial integrity of all nations of the area."

On the same day, the US Ambassador-designate to Cairo (he had not yet presented his credentials) called on the Egyptian Foreign Minister, Mahmud Riadh, and delivered a letter that had arrived that morning from President Johnson to President Nasser, and a Note from the American to the Egyptian Government. Both were later published in full by Hassanein Haikal, the editor of *al-Ahram*.† The President, in warm and mild tones, urged President Nasser to do his utmost to avoid an armed

* See Mr Eshkol's interview in *Maariv*, 4 October 1967.
† *al-Ahram*, 23 June 1967.

conflict. The Note was more formally worded. It supported the efforts being made by U Thant in seeking a solution and noted three aspects of the crisis giving rise to particular concern: the terror attacks against Israel, the evacuation of the UN Emergency Force, and the large concentration of troops along the borders. The Note reiterated the American Government's support for the freedom of all shipping in the Gulf of Aqaba and called on the Egyptian Government to co-operate "within the framework of the UN and outside it" in lessening the tension in the region.

The Israelis agreed to the forty-eight hour delay. The Egyptians did not reply then to Mr Johnson's letter, but there was an indirect response. On 24 May they announced that as of noon on the previous day the entrance to the Gulf of Aqaba had been effectively closed by mining, land batteries, and armoured sea and air patrols. That evening U Thant announced that he was cutting short his stay in Cairo and was returning forthwith to New York. His mission had, only too evidently, ended in failure.

The Americans were left with one last glimmer of hope before the forty-eight hour period expired. In New York that day the Security Council met to take up a request by Canada and Denmark for "an urgent meeting . . . to consider the extremely grave situation in the Middle East which is threatening international peace and security". But the debate proved to be a dismal demonstration of UN impotence. Mr Goldberg's attempt to transfer the discussion into a programme of action failed to gain support. "I have been authorized", he declared, "to announce that the United States, both within and outside the United Nations, is prepared to join with all the other great Powers—the Soviet Union, the United Kingdom and France—in a common effort to restore and maintain peace in the Near East."

But after the Soviet, Bulgarian, Indian and Malian representatives had stated that they would not participate in any consultations on the draft resolution "until further notice", the

Council was adjourned with no date being set for the next meeting. Once more the Security Council had demonstrated its inability to deal effectively with crises of this nature.

The forty-eight hours had by now nearly passed. The Egyptians were more obdurate than ever. Reports were flowing into Washington of mobilization of reserves, of troop movements and of mounting tension. More direct means would be needed to tackle the situation. The Americans realized that nothing would be achieved by normal political and diplomatic pressure. In a renewed evaluation of the situation, they saw two possible ways in which the crisis could be resolved:

1. Israel would act on her own, without involving the US, in a limited military action designed to break the blockade of the Gulf of Aqaba. This, in their view, would be the ideal solution. It would not entail a general conflagration, to which they were strongly opposed, but would wipe out Nasser's gains and cut him down to size.

2. If Israel did not act the US would have to find a solution on its own. For the Americans could not possibly enter into any joint action with Israel. There must, on no account, be any collusion. That accusation must be prevented at all costs. On the other hand, to remain inactive and allow Nasser's victories to go unchallenged would be just as damaging for US foreign policy. This was to become the major dilemma of the Americans before the war.

They now hoped for, and expected, a solution along the lines of the first alternative. After the forty-eight-hour period lapsed they fully expected Israel to unleash her armies. But they could not encourage the Israelis to act for fear of being accused of collusion. To their amazement, the Israelis not only remained inactive, but they also demanded that the United States come to their aid. This was the one solution which the Americans refused to envisage because of the stigma of collusion which it entailed. The Americans were all the more surprised at the Israeli attitude because they estimated that militarily the Egyptians were weak and Israel had nothing to fear. Their chagrin, therefore, was great when the Israelis informed them that their Foreign Minister, Abba Eban, was on his way to Washington. This was a visit they definitely did not welcome. For it meant that Israel was postponing action. And far worse, any action Israel might take after the visit would be immediately construed as having been taken as an outcome of the Minister's talks with the American President. Collusion again.

The Americans hardly bothered to hide their disapproval when Mr Eban arrived in Washington on 25 May. He was kept waiting for nearly a whole day before the President received him. Mr Rusk was more than curt with him. And when the Israeli Minister in Washington, Mr Evron, was called to the President two hours before the Israeli Foreign Minister was due to arrive at the White House, Johnson told him pointedly that he had nothing to say to Mr Eban which had not already been said to him by Dean Rusk. The President warned "Eppie" Evron that Israel would be completely on her own if she decided to fight. He reminded him that any US action would require Congress approval, which might be a protracted affair. This was a particularly sensitive point in view of Senator Fulbright's attacks at the time on various acts of the Administration which had been taken without agreement or even knowledge of Congress. US involvement in the Middle East crisis without Congressional approval was unthinkable.

But when the Foreign Minister was at last admitted to Mr Johnson's office, he presented a strong case. He reminded the President of a firm American commitment to uphold the principle of free and innocent passage through the Gulf of Aqaba. Now was the time to fulfil this commitment. Mr Eban declared that Israel would not be able to live with the Straits closed, and would be forced to take every action needed to reopen them. But the President would give no firm undertaking. He was not shirking the responsibility which had been put on his shoulders by the commitments of previous Presidents. He would make the utmost endeavours to fulfil those commitments. But there were difficulties. Congress would have to ratify US involvement.

They would not be keen on unilateral action. Other maritime powers would have to be consulted. All this would take time. He would need another two weeks at least during which he needed to be assured that Israel "would not jump the gun".

Before meeting the President, Mr Eban had talks with the Secretary of State, Dean Rusk, and the Defence Secretary, Robert McNamara. The meeting had been an unhappy affair. Mr Eban had found a lengthy dispatch waiting for him at the Israeli Embassy when he arrived in Washington. It had been cabled to him by Dr Yaakov Herzog, Director-General of the Prime Minister's Office, and contained an evaluation of the military developments around Israel's borders since Eban's departure from Israel early the previous morning. The cable stressed that the most burning issue was no longer the blockade, but the threatening concentration of troops and armour in Sinai. Mr Eban gained the impression from the contents of the cable, which arrived in a somewhat garbled form, that an Egyptian attack on Israel was imminent.

But it became apparent that the Americans did not share these alarmist views. General Wheeler was called in to join the meeting and he gave the official evaluation. He had no information of any Egyptian intention to attack, he declared; if anything, it was the Israeli army that was pressing to begin hostilities. And he repeated that in the Pentagon's view Israel had nothing to fear. Her army was, in their estimation, far superior to that of Egypt.

Eban's visit forced the Americans to revise their evaluation of Israel and thus of the entire Middle East crisis. They had expected the Israeli Foreign Minister to take a tough line; instead he spoke of the dangers threatening the very existence of Israel. They were now suddenly faced with a new situation. Israel was not so strong and firm as they had estimated previously, not from the military, but from the political point of view. They were, therefore, forced to consider the second alternative in their assessment of ways of solving the crisis:

action by the US without Israel. The ball was now passed to Dean Rusk and his assistant, Eugene Rostow.

There now began a new phase in American thinking during the crisis period. Rusk's first concern was to assure that he would not be hindered by a hesitant Israel taking it upon itself to act after the Americans had decided to move. A swift Israeli action to force open the blockade, as the Americans had first contemplated, was one thing; but an action mounted together with the Americans must be avoided at all costs. Mr Rusk made this point clear in an addendum to the Note President Johnson sent to Mr Eshkol on 28 May, after the Russians had proposed that the two Powers exert pressure on Egypt and Israel to refrain from war. The tone of Johnson's message had been mild. But Rusk's addition to the Note was worded much more sharply. An attack by Israel could have catastrophic consequences, he warned. He wanted the deck cleared for his own action, and he did not mince words.

For Mr Rusk and the State Department officials knew they could not remain inactive. As the crisis deepened they began to fear that the United States might be completely ousted from the Middle East. This fear was greatly strengthened when King Hussein made his dramatic flight to Cairo. They thus began to view the situation from the point of view of long-term policy. The officials of the State Department, some of whom had all along felt that the President was too Israeli-oriented, now urged that matters be discussed with the Egyptians. A *modus vivendi* could be reached with Nasser without necessarily sacrificing Israel. They could fulfil previous commitments, but not necessarily in the manner Israel would like them to be fulfilled. In this new thinking varying possibilities of compromise solutions were considered; their implementation would have transformed Israel into a virtual American Protectorate.*

* One such solution was that the world would accept the closure of the Aqaba Straits by Egypt, and that the US would compensate Israel financially and also be responsible for importing oil to Israel in place of the oil which had previously been brought through the Aqaba Straits to Elath.

The Egyptian Ambassador was once more contacted, and informed that a special emissary of President Johnson would be leaving forthwith for Cairo where he wished to meet the President. The way out by appeasement and compromise was already being prepared.

But first other possibilities suggested by the President had to be explored. Johnson had told Eban that the US envisaged a four-phase plan of action: Congress would be asked to endorse a resolution upholding freedom of navigation in the Gulf of Aqaba; the resolution would then be brought before the Security Council; the sea-going nations would be asked to endorse the resolution; the Americans would then propose the formation of a multi-national flotilla, including an oil tanker, which would sail through the Straits of Aqaba to the Israeli port of Elath. If the flotilla were fired on from Sharm el-Sheikh, they would force their way through.

This was, at least, what the Israelis had understood from the Johnson–Eban talks. This they now believed to be the master-plan according to which the crisis would be resolved without war. And, apparently, the British were willing to go along with the plan. George Brown called for consultations among maritime nations in a speech to the House of Commons on 30 May. But the Foreign Secretary had his own views on how to solve the problem. He wished, in the words of one of his colleagues, to "do a Dulles" on Israel. Action could be postponed for several months by talk of maritime consultations. By that time the Israeli army would have been deterred from taking action, its reserves would have been demobilized, and tension would subside. But the following day the scope of action which the Americans had in mind was revealed in the following statement issued by the State Department spokesman, Mr McCloskey:

"The focus of our effort to solve the Middle East crisis without hostilities is in the United Nations. We regard its responsibilities as essential and fundamental, and we are

1. Prime Minister Levi Eshkol with the Minister of Defence, General Dayan, conversing during visit on West Bank

2. Chief of Staff, General Yitzhak Rabin, with General David Elazar, Commander of Northern Front

3. A member of the Israeli Tank
   Corps

4. An El Fatah member in an Israeli
   court

doing everything in our power to seek a fair and just outcome of the crisis in that forum. As part of that effort, and in support of that policy, we are supporting the British initiative which was announced by Foreign Minister Brown yesterday. We are consulting other maritime powers as to their views on the international character of the Straits of Tiran and the Gulf of Aqaba in the light of the President's statement of May 23rd."

The emphasis was still on consultations, nothing more. The forum was still the United Nations, with all its limitations.

There now began a phase of intensive activity on the part of the US and Great Britain, aimed at obtaining the support of the maritime powers to an Anglo-American declaration affirming the right of free and innocent passage through the Gulf of Aqaba. Some twenty maritime nations were contacted. According to the Washington correspondent of *The Times*, the declaration contained three major principles: the Gulf of Aqaba was an international waterway open to all shipping; the signatories were prepared to exercise their right of free and innocent passage; and that this right applied to all nations.

But by now the sands were fast running out. In Israel a new National Government had been sworn in. Even the British, who had been thinking in terms of months, now realized that, in the words of Mr Wilson, "time is not on our side". Wilson flew to Ottawa on 2 June for talks with Lester Pearson, and from there continued to Washington. At a Washington press conference later in the day, Wilson stressed that freedom of shipping in the Gulf of Aqaba was the key to the Middle East crisis. "We must use every minute," he declared. Failure to end the blockade peacefully could lead not only to a Middle East war but to a "much larger conflict" within hours.

But the other nations procrastinated. Only Australia, New Zealand, the Netherlands and Iceland gave their unqualified support to the declaration. The French refused to endorse the principles. In the words of M. Gorse, Minister of Information,

E

the declaration would "not fit into the framework of the Four-Power contacts we wish for, and would not help matters forward". The French attitude in particular was disappointing for the Israelis. France had, since 1956, been considered Israel's special friend. Israel's planes and a great part of her military equipment were purchased there. Special agreements covered a large variety of subjects on which the two countries co-operated. A special friendship had been struck up between General de Gaulle and Israel's former Premier, David Ben Gurion. The Israelis assumed almost as a matter of course that they would enjoy the full support of the French. And, indeed, French public opinion went out of its way to voice that support.* But President de Gaulle felt differently. He felt that Israel had fallen too far under American influence. And he had his own designs in the Middle East. He demonstrated his disapproval in his talk with Mr Eban, the Israeli Foreign Minister, who had stopped in Paris on 24 May while on his way to Washington. Mr Eban had intended to explain Israel's stand in the Middle East crisis. But he was not given much chance to do any talking. President de Gaulle lectured to him in lofty and general terms, beginning many of his sentences with the neutral "Il faut que . . ." But abruptly he came down to earth and sharply told Mr Eban: "You must on no account start a war. The country that fires the first shot will lose the friendship of France." Mr Eban stated that Israel would never start a war, but that, in this particular case, the war had in effect already been started by the closing of the Straits. President de Gaulle demurred, whereupon Mr Eban read out the text of the French statement

---

* This support was strong, particularly in the French Ministry of Defence and in the armed forces. The French Minister of Defence, M. Messmer, backed by M. Schumann and M. Debré, urged the French Government to continue its pro-Israel policy. Shortly before the war broke out the French"loaned" the Israel Government 20 *Mystère* planes on the understanding that they would be used for defence if hostilities broke out. The planes were flown out to Israel by French pilots and were subsequently returned after the war. This was revealed by a Gaullist deputy, M. Clostermann, in an interview on German television.

supporting the right of free passage in the Gulf of Aqaba, which had been issued in 1957. The French President made a derogatory gesture with his hand. "Times have changed since then," he declared, "And, besides, I wasn't President then." The French called for a four-power meeting to settle the crisis, but, as was to be expected, the Soviet Union rejected the proposal.

General Dayan has since commented that President de Gaulle could have prevented the Middle East war if he had come out unequivocally against any aggressive acts in the forty-eight hours after Nasser had closed the Aqaba Straits. For at that time President de Gaulle's prestige among both the Arabs and the Israelis was such that he could have brought about a lessening of the tension by energetic action. But instead, the half-hearted reactions of the French to the closing of the Straits encouraged Nasser to increase his threats.

At the end of his visit to the US, Mr Wilson stated that he had reached complete agreement with President Johnson that Britain and America should work for a "multilateral solution" of the crisis through the UN. But, as his own Foreign Secretary had said only three days before in the House of Commons, ". . . the United Nations is at the end of the day only the sum of its members, and there are clear limitations on it at this moment". Nobody seriously believed that the United Nations would have it in its power to find "the multilateral solution" which Mr Wilson talked about. On 3 June, the day Wilson issued his statement, the Security Council held another of its indecisive meetings. Nothing came of it. Indeed, nothing could come of it, with the Soviet power of veto lurking in the background.

At the same time, a State Department spokesman denied that the US was contemplating the formation of a naval flotilla to force its way through the Straits. He repeated the statement that the US considered the United Nations to be the proper forum to deal with the problem. In this respect, he declared, the US was consulting maritime nations with a view to issuing a joint declaration concerning the rights of free and innocent passage through the Gulf of Aqaba. The multilateral maritime action, which the Israelis had believed was being organized, was thus reduced to a joint declaration!

But by now a significant change had once more occurred in the American approach. It was a change that was not imparted to their British allies. The Israelis had become aware of the false interpretation they had given to American intentions. They decided to send a leading personality post-haste to Washington to discover whether the Americans were in fact preparing a naval flotilla or not. And this time there were no misunderstandings. The chances of such a solution were, he cabled his Government, virtually nil. But, while in Washington, the Israeli visitor succeeded in imparting to some top American officials a feeling of quiet confidence that the Israeli army would settle the whole crisis quickly and efficiently. Once more, opinion swung round in official circles to the view that perhaps it would not be such a bad idea after all if the Israelis took matters into their own hands. This change of attitude was not lost upon the Israelis, and had a profound effect on their deliberations, as we shall see.

But in the meantime, the special emissary from President Johnson had arrived secretly in Cairo on 1 June. He was taken immediately to President Nasser, where, if the version of Hassanein Haikal in *al-Ahram* is to be believed, he made two observations: President Johnson was still waiting for a reply to his urgent letter of 23 May; the President proposed sending the Vice-President, Hubert Humphrey, to Cairo so that direct contact could be made on the highest level between Egypt and the United States.

This time President Nasser answered forthwith. He replied at length to the points raised in the Note sent by the American Government on 23 May.* He agreed to Mr Humphrey's visit and proposed that the Egyptian Vice-President, Zakaria Muhi ed-Din, should go to Washington at the same time.

* The full text of President Nasser's Note is given by Haikal in *al-Ahram*, 23 June 1967.

The visits were confirmed. Zakaria Muhi ed-Din was to arrive in Washington on Wednesday, 7 June,* and on the same day the American Vice-President was to arrive in Cairo.

But these moves came too late. The warriors did not wait for the politicians. On Monday, 5 June, war broke out in the Middle East.

---

* According to Haikal (see note, p. 132). According to Nasser, in his speech on 23 July, the Americans proposed that he arrive a day earlier.

CHAPTER 7

Israel's Hour of Indecision

The first report of the Egyptian troop movements into Sinai reached Israel's Chief of Staff, General Yitzhak Rabin, on the evening of 14 May, as he was visiting a friend's home in Jerusalem. It was the eve of Independence Day. Nineteen years earlier the State of Israel had been proclaimed in a quiet but impressive ceremony in Tel Aviv. Now the people of Israel were celebrating that event. Crowds milled in the streets as fireworks cascaded in the skies above. Loudspeakers blared out local hit tunes as couples danced jostling in the public squares. At the Hebrew University Stadium the army was performing a night tattoo, and the crowds cheered appreciatively at the display. There was a feeling of relaxation and also of permanency. The novelty and the excitement of the first years of the state's existence had long since worn off. Israelis no longer celebrated their Independence Day with fervour and wonder. A generation had passed since those days in 1948 when the state had been established in the heat of war. The memory of that war, when Israel's new-found existence was threatened with extermination, was now a distant dream. Everyone in Israel, from the Prime Minister and the Chief of Staff downwards, would have scoffed at the idea that war would soon be knocking once more on Israel's doors, and that Israel would once more, as in 1948, be engaged in a life-or-death struggle with the combined armies of her neighbours.

General Rabin was not unduly concerned by the information that was passed to him. Nor was the Prime Minister. In Mr

Eshkol's words, "In the last two years there have been a number of reports of one brigade or another entering Sinai, of one division going in, another coming out. . . ."* Nor were they particularly alarmed the following day, when Radio Cairo informed the world that Egypt was moving troops up into Sinai "in view of Israel's threats to invade Syria". "We were told on the same day," Mr Eshkol said later,* "by the Great Powers that we had nothing to worry about, that the troop movements were meant only for show."†

But the Premier and other Cabinet Ministers did not need the soothing words of the Great Powers. Their confidence was based on the evaluation of the Army, that Nasser would not be ready to start another war before 1970 or 1971 at the very earliest. They based this conclusion on the pace of development of the Egyptian army. Since its defeat in Sinai in 1956 that army had been steadily growing in size and in fire power. By 1970, they estimated, it would become formidable enough to allow Nasser to risk with impunity another test of arms with Israel. But not before. This evaluation was supported by the words of Nasser himself, who had repeated time and time again that Egypt was not yet ready for the decisive battle against Israel. Any attempt by Nasser to attack Israel before 1970 would in the opinion of Israeli army commanders be suicidal for him, and this particularly so as long as he maintained a large expeditionary force in the Yemen.

So the Israeli leaders were not worried. The Premier and the cream of the army command attended an Independence Day party given that evening at one of the Air Force bases. The following day, the Premier gave the order for a limited and

---

* In an interview in the Tel Aviv afternoon paper *Maariv*, 4 October 1967.

† Yet, according to Mr Charles W. Yoss, the Israeli Government instructed on 15 May "its representative at the UN, Ambassador Rafael, to request the Secretary-General to assure Cairo on its behalf that it had no intention of initiating any military action. The Secretary-General immediately complied with the request"—see Charles W. Yoss, "How It Began", *Foreign Affairs*, New York, January 1968, p. 309.

partial mobilization of the reserves, but at the Cabinet session he dismissed the flow of troops into Sinai as a show of strength designed more to impress the Arabs than to frighten the Israelis. Thus assured, the Ministers settled down to discuss the plans for the World Jewish Congress and to hear a report from the Minister for Social Welfare on his visit to the Auschwitz death camp.

Throughout that first week of the crisis, as the flow of Egyptian troops eastwards continued uninterrupted, the Israelis maintained their attitude of unconcern. The army commanders continued to stick to their original assessment: the Egyptian army was not strong enough to be a match for Israel; Nasser himself knew this to be the case; therefore, his threats need not be taken seriously. When, however, the UN force was expelled, the first doubts took root. The irrational factor was taken increasingly into account. Yet, despite growing concern, they refused to believe that Nasser would dare close the Straits of Tiran, or seriously contemplate an attack on Israel.

Logically, as the results of the war were to show, their evaluation was correct. The Egyptians were not a match for the Israeli army. In this the estimates were precise to an amazing degree. If anything Intelligence over-estimated the strength of the Egyptians as compared to the Israeli army.* But their mistake was in not taking the irrational factor sufficiently into consideration. For Nasser, who should have known better, was persuaded by his own Intelligence that the Egyptian army was already sufficiently powerful to defeat the Israelis. He reached this conclusion by means of mechanical, and not qualitative, intelligence. He compared the manpower figures, the number of tanks, the firing power of artillery, the size of the two air forces, and saw that—on paper—his forces enjoyed considerable superiority. And he allowed himself to be carried away by this comparison.

The Israelis knew better. But because they could not know of

* This is the view of General Rabin. See his interview in *Yediot Aharanot*, 4 October 1967.

Nasser's terrible miscalculation, they refused to believe right up to the very last moment that he would be reckless enough to risk a war which could only end in disaster for him by closing the Straits of Tiran to Israeli shipping.

This understandable attitude on their part was to play a cardinal role in the events that were to follow. For when, despite previous predictions of the army, Nasser did close the Straits, the Israeli Government found itself totally unprepared for this new situation. It began to feel uncertain of itself, and some of the Ministers even began to doubt the confidence they had previously felt concerning Israel's military superiority over the Arabs. They were particularly concerned over the possibility that Tel Aviv and the other cities might be bombed; conversely, they were not fully prepared to believe in the danger of an imminent Egyptian attack despite the ominous signs in the south. Significantly enough, the only Minister who from the very beginning favoured going to war and who refused to budge from this stand was the Minister of Transport, Moshe Carmel, who was a brigade commander in the 1948 Palestine War, and had served as commander of Israel's northern front. The Minister of Labour, Yigal Alon, who had been commander of the Palmach in 1948, also took a pro-war line, though somewhat less consistently.

The civilian leadership hesitated and procrastinated, to the chagrin of the army commanders. Only on 19 May, when it became evident that the UN force was leaving, did the mobilzation of reserves take on a greater momentum. Diplomatic activity was accelerated. The Prime Minister sent Notes to the Heads of the Western Powers. The Foreign Minister summoned the Soviet Ambassador, M. Zubachin, and pointed out the dangers involved in the concentration of troops in Sinai. But the President, Zalman Shazar, did not cancel his visit to the World Exposition in Canada, and the Government failed to work out any plan of action. By now, however, the attitude that it was all only a show put up for the Arabs was fast disappearing. As Mr Eshkol put it later, "When we saw that they

they were putting [in Sinai] 200 tanks, 250 tanks, and then 400 and 500 tanks, the whole affair began to be dangerous. . . ."*
On 22 May, the Premier made his first important policy announcement since the crisis began. Speaking in the Knesset (Parliament) before a crowded house, Mr Eshkol was a model of moderation. At the Cabinet's behest, he was careful not to provoke the Egyptian President. There were no specific warnings, no formulation of policy, no reference to the Straits of Tiran. It was a speech of appeasement, and the army and, increasingly, the general public, were bitterly disappointed. They had expected a tougher line in the face of Egyptian threats.

Within hours of Mr Eshkol's speech the news came through that Nasser had done what the Israelis had been certain he would not dare to do. The Straits were closed. The gauntlet had been thrown down. "Now it means war", was the reaction throughout the length and breadth of Israel.

But the Government, as we have seen, had not been prepared for the eventuality. The reaction was one of shock and of bitter realization that Israel might, after all, be heading for war. Speeding to a meeting of GHQ in Tel Aviv early that morning, Mr Eshkol muttered to his Political Secretary, Adi Yaffe: "It looks as if there is no other way out." For the first time the Prime Minister began to feel that they had passed the point of no return. But hope dies slowly. Mr Eshkol did not want war. Nor did the other members of the Cabinet. And when, later that morning of 23 May, the Government received an urgent cable from the Israeli Ambassador in Washington saying that the US would do everything it could to re-open the Straits, the Government grasped at the straw. Later in the day, they agreed with alacrity to the American request for a forty-eight hour postponement of action. Here was a possible way out. It had to be explored thoroughly before returning to the other, unpalatable alternative of war. The Chief of Staff, to the surprise of some of the Ministers, was himself not hostile to the

* *Maariv*, 4 October 1967.

proposal of the US. The mobilization of reserves had not yet been completed. The army could well utilize the extra time, was his comment.

It was generally believed in Israel at that time that, if fighting should break out, the Army would try to gain a bargaining counter for the opening of the Straits of Tiran. The Gaza Strip was an obvious choice.

But the turn of the army was not yet to come. For as the Cabinet met on that day after the Straits had been closed, Mr Eban, the Foreign Minister, came forward with a plan of his own, based on the Washington cable. Israel, he declared, had cast-iron guarantees from the Western Powers regarding freedom of its shipping in the Gulf of Aqaba. It had been on the basis of these guarantees that she had agreed to withdraw from Sinai in 1957 after the Suez war. Now was the time to draw on those guarantees, he urged. He therefore proposed that he leave forthwith for Washington to press on the American President the need to take urgent action to reopen the Straits.

Mr Eban worked on the axiom that there must not, on almost any account, be a war. He tried everything to prevent it. He was convinced that the crisis could be resolved by diplomatic action. As an alternative, he felt it incumbent upon the Great Powers to back up the cast-iron guarantees they had given in 1957 with force, if necessary. Israel, in his view, should on no account take action on her own. Eban pushed his line with all the vigour he could muster. Of all the ministers in the Cabinet, only he and Mr Carmel, the Transport Minister, knew clearly what they wanted, and Eban, at least, had the power of persuasion to back him up.

But the Government needed a great deal of persuasion to agree to Mr Eban's voyage, whose immediate result would entail postponement of further action until his return. Carmel opposed the idea of sounding out the Western Powers. This might tie our hands, he declared. Mr Eshkol temporized, suggested sending Mrs Golda Meir, the former Foreign Minister, who could be expected to take a tougher line than

Mr Eban. But Eban persisted, and to back up his plea he flourished a cable from the Ambassador in Paris saying that if Mr Eban came to Paris there was a good chance of arranging a meeting with President de Gaulle. Finally, towards evening, Eshkol agreed to the journey and Eban left in the early hours of the following morning. Only Mr Carmel had insisted in his opposition.*

Thus with the approval of the American request for a forty-eight hour postponement of action, and with Mr Eban's departure, the period of waiting began; it was to last two weeks.

The shadow and the lessons of the Sinai War hung heavily on the decision-makers. There was a feeling of isolation in the face of growing danger. There was no certainty as to whether the United States would support Israel, especially if she went to war, and there was a great deal of apprehension regarding the role of the Soviet Union in such an event. The possibility of a Russian air umbrella over Egypt, or even of Russian "volunteers" joining the Egyptian forces, was not ruled out by the Ministers, though the army had no such fears. This feeling of uncertainty was heightened by conflicting estimates on the outcome of the war. There was no doubt of an Israeli victory; but the rate of casualties would, it was feared, be very high in view of the strong defence deployment of the Egyptian army, the possibility that the Egyptians might use their navy for offensive operations, and the uncertainty regarding the use of missiles. A retired general sought out Mr Eshkol and warned him that if he went to war he could expect at least 10,000 casualties if he won; if Israel lost, there would be two million as good as dead. The Ministers remembered 1956, and Ben Gurion's insistence that Israel should on no account fight without allies. In such circumstances, even the activists felt it

* Yigal Alon, who was representing his Government at an international conference in Leningrad, voiced his opposition on his return to Israel the following day. But by then Mr Eban had already left. The tardiness of his return was probably one of the greatest mistakes of Alon's political career.

was wise to sound out the American attitude before deciding on action. Mr Ben Gurion himself contributed to this feeling. He felt the country could not go to war unless it enjoyed the support of one of the Great Powers, and unless it could be assured on a steady flow of arms even after the war to replace those that would doubtless be destroyed in the course of the fighting. Ben Gurion had another reservation. A government at war, he declared in the Knesset, must be prepared to take dozens of decisions daily. His implication was clear. The present leadership was not, in his eyes, capable of waging war success-fully. These views, stated in the usual forceful and cogent style of the grand old man of Israel, strengthened the determination of the anti-war party in the Cabinet, and in particular the ministers of the Religious Party and the left-wing Mapam.

They also gave weight to the growing discontent within the political parties, Government and opposition alike, with the country's leadership. Mr Eshkol, for all his political acumen, was not an ideal leader in time of crisis. He lacked the strength, the decisiveness, and the charisma which are the essential qualities of a war leader. By 24 May the first tentative feelers were already being put out in the Knesset towards the establish-ment of a National Unity Government by including members of the opposition and, above all, Ben Gurion himself. The key figures in these moves were Menahem Begin, one-time leader of the Irgun Zvai Leumi* dissidents and leader of the opposition since the establishment of the state, Shimon Peres, former Deputy Minister for Defence and close disciple of Ben Gurion who had become Secretary General of Rafi, Ben Gurion's breakaway party, and Moshe Haim Shapira, the Minister of Interior and leader of the Religious Party, which, unlike Peres' Rafi and Begin's Gahal, was a co-partner in the Government coalition. Begin had been a lifelong adversary of Mapai, the Government Labour Party, and particularly of its former leader, David Ben Gurion. In the past years the two had often been

* The Dissident Group which had split from the Haganah and carried out terrorist acts against the British during the period of the Mandate.

locked in bitter and acrimonious exchanges across the floor of
the Parliament. Now in the shadow of the dangers threatening
Israel, Mr Begin was willing to forget past animosities. With the
full agreement of Ben Gurion himself, and of the Religious
Party, he called on Mr Eshkol and proposed that he step down
in favour of Ben Gurion, and continue serving as Deputy Prime
Minister. It was in the interests of the country, Mr Begin
pleaded. But if Ben Gurion could be likened to an Israeli
Churchill, Mr Eshkol certainly was no Chamberlain. He scoffed
at the idea, as he did on the morrow when the Minister of
Interior, Moshe Shapira, came to him and proposed that Ben
Gurion be incorporated in the Government as Minister of
Defence. "I have the situation completely under control," Mr
Eshkol told him. "You need not worry."

But this was one thing that Shapira and a great many others
were doing. They were becoming increasingly worried by the
lack of control which Mr Eshkol displayed. By now Mr Peres
had also become active. He made good use of the large number
of contacts he maintained with members of Mr Eshkol's party,
Mapai, to urge them to think in terms of national needs, and
not of narrow party interests. "The country needs a National
Unity Government," he urged. "It needs a change of leadership,
one that can lead us out of this crisis."

By now, too, the general public in Israel had become
thoroughly alarmed. It did not share Mr Eban's optimism that
the Great Powers would protect Israel from any harm. The
public heard the threats of annihilation that were being hurled
at them from all sides; they listened to the near-hysteria, the
calls to kill and destroy, that were being broadcast by the hour
from the Arab broadcasting stations; they read of ever-larger
concentrations of Egyptian, Syrian, and Jordanian troops on
their borders, of movement of Iraqis and Saudis towards Israel,
of detachments of Kuwaitis, Sudanis and Algerians being flown
in to bolster up the front against them; they witnessed the
supreme act of aggression against them—the closing of the
Straits of Tiran—and they waited for Israel's reply. And that

reply did not come. There were no directives, no speeches, no explanations from the Government Ministers. Only silence, and Mr Eban's departure for Europe and the United States. As the alarm grew, the rumblings of discontent at the Government's inaction became louder. A quarter of a million young men were now under arms, confident in themselves and in their power to deal with the situation. They could not understand why the Government restrained them.

The rumblings soon broadened into a public outcry for a National Government. On 25 May the Mapai Secretariat met to discuss the situation. But now the *éminence grise* of the party took over the proceedings. The party secretary, Mrs Golda Meir, took the stand. A former Foreign Minister, Mrs Meir was probably the most powerful figure in Mapai. She was now in fighting fettle. She was adamantly opposed to all talk of broadening the Government, she told the meeting. Such a step was unnecessary. It was also harmful. It was tantamount to a vote of no confidence in the Government in its present form. The representatives of the opposition could be called in for consultations, could even be invited to discussions of the Ministerial Defence Committee, but no more than that. All talk of a National Government should be stamped out immediately. As was the case so often in Mapai, Mrs Meir carried the day. But the next day reaction in the press and in the party was immediate and hostile. Pressure mounted. The public demand grew louder. There was talk of demonstrations. Party branches of Mapai, and in particular the powerful Tel Aviv and Haifa branches, threatened revolt. Within the Coalition, the Religious Party and the Independent Liberals pressed strongly for a broadening of the Government. Finally, on the evening of 24 May, Mr Eshkol gave in to popular demand. The Sunday papers the following morning appeared with Mr Eshkol's announcement agreeing to a National Government, side by side with a long diatribe against the idea made public the previous day in a lecture by Mrs Meir. It was a black mark for Mrs Meir. Her popularity was dwindling fast.

The decision had been made. It now had to be implemented. But this proved to be not so simple. For the question immediately arose: what of the Defence portfolio? The demand that Mr Eshkol should relinquish this post had become stronger than ever.

But for the moment this question was pushed into the background. For in the evening of 27 May, shortly after Mr Eshkol had agreed to the National Government, the Foreign Minister returned from his talks with the leaders of the three Western Powers. This was the moment the entire nation was waiting for. What promises of help was Mr Eban bringing back with him? The Government now had to decide what course to take, and it was clear to all that the Cabinet session following the Foreign Minister's return would be a decisive one.

On that Saturday night wagers were being placed in Tel Aviv that by the following morning Israel would be at war. The one logical reason for Israel to stay her hand for so long—her wish to consult first with the Western Powers—had now been removed with Mr Eban's return. A feeling of deep foreboding, mixed with anticipation, had taken hold of the people. The strain of waiting was beginning to tell. All able-bodied men, and many women, had long since disappeared from the towns and villages as mobilization of reserves was completed. Vehicles vanished as they, too, were pressed into the military machine. Buses stopped running, factories closed down, schools shut their doors as children were called out to dig trenches, clean out air-raid shelters, or deliver mail. Nobody thought the war would be a walkover. People expected the cities to be heavily bombed. Many recalled the fact that Nasser had over the years been developing long-range missiles, and that he had been using poison gas in the Yemen war. There was trepidation, anxiety, but no panic, as war slipped perceptibly nearer with each day that passed.

These thoughts must have crossed the minds of the Ministers as they assembled together that Saturday night in Tel Aviv to hear Mr Eban's report. They knew that they were being called upon to make a decision which could be decisive, and fatal, for their people. Not all of them relished this role which history had bestowed on them.

But Mr Eban's report was optimistic. He did not mention the rebuff he had received in Paris from General de Gaulle, but dwelt entirely on his talks in London and Washington. The United States, he reported, would solve the question of the Straits within a matter of weeks. A multi-national flotilla would be organized which would force its way through the Straits if necessary. But the Americans had impressed upon him that Israel must not attack. If she did, the United States would not support her; but if Egypt attacked first, Israel could be sure of swift and effective intervention by the Americans. For President Johnson had decided to take a tough line against Nasser, Mr Eban told the Cabinet.

The message was plain: sit tight; don't do anything; the Americans will pull the chestnuts out of the fire for you. But the Ministers were not convinced by Mr Eban's optimism. Most of them did not like the idea of Israel falling back on American warships for the protection of its vital sea lanes. And not all of them accepted Eban's explanation of America's intentions. Those opposing Mr Eban's point of view based their stand on three fundamental tenets: continued inaction would, under the present circumstances, invite an Arab attack on Israel which could inflict heavy casualties and damage; on the other hand, the present form of deployment of the Egyptian army in Sinai was such as to enable Israel to strike a crushing blow against Egypt and remove the threat from the south for many years to come; the Americans would not be adverse to Israel taking action into its own hands.

They argued their case at the Cabinet meeting cogently and forcefully. They were particularly explicit regarding the attitude of the Americans. They rejected Mr Eban's conclusions out of hand. They were convinced that the US had really wanted Israel to act. There were many signs to back up their belief. they told the Cabinet.They claimed that President Johnson had not really wanted to see the Foreign Minister at all, and had broadly hinted as much to the Israeli Minister in Washington, Mr Evron. They pointed to the conversation between Mr Johnson and Mr Evron, in which the President had as much as said: "You are on your own. Don't expect us to do anything for you." This, they asserted, was in direct contrast to what Mr Eban had reported. But above all, they pointed to the fact that the Americans had not explicitly threatened Israel with reprisals or sanctions if she went to war. There was nothing like the tough line the United States had taken after the Suez War. If the Americans had really been so anxious that Israel refrain from any action, she could have made her point in a much clearer manner than she did, the army leaders concluded.

The deliberations lasted far into the night. By early morning it had become clear that the Cabinet was evenly divided. The Ministers of the Religious Party, of the left-wing Mapam, and the lone representative of the Independent Liberals, ranged themselves solidly behind the plea of the Foreign Minister against war. They were joined by two Ministers of Mapai, the Ministers of Finance and Education. Nine Ministers against war. The other Mapai Ministers, together with the three moderate left-wing Ahdut Ha'avoda representatives, were in favour of immediate action. Among them was the Prime Minister, who after all the Ministers had had their say, joined the side of the "hawks". Nine Ministers in favour of war. Mr Eshkol could have used his authority as Prime Minister to decide the issue. But he did not. He did not try to lead, direct, or even influence the proceedings. The hour was too late, he said, to decide on such a vital matter. The Ministers dispersed without reaching a decision as the first light of dawn spread over the distant hills of Judea.

With Mr Eshkol formally in the camp of the "hawks", there was every likelihood that the final decision to go to war would be taken on that Sunday morning, on 28 May, as the Ministers reassembled. But in those few intervening hours there had been a dramatic development. One after another, the Soviet and

American Ambassadors in Tel Aviv, Dmitri Zubachin and William Barbour, each contacted Adi Yaffe, the Prime Minister's Political Secretary. Each had a Note to deliver. Neither brooked delay. Both urged Israel not to take matters into her own hands. Of the two, the American Note, coming as it did on the heels of the Government debate on American intentions, was infinitely more important. The Note, as we have seen in the previous chapter, was composed of two parts: a declaration on the part of President Johnson that he would do everything in his power to attain freedom of shipping in the Aqaba Straits within two weeks, coupled with a warning that he had reason to believe that the Russians would react strongly to any military action; and a much more strongly worded addendum by Dean Rusk warning Israel not to go to war.

To the Ministers who heard Mr Eban read out the Note it appeared as if Eban's claims were vindicated. The Americans would oppose unilateral Israeli action. They failed to note the different emphasis of the President's message from that of the Secretary of State. The pendulum now swung in favour of Eban's anti-war party. Even the leading "hawks", such as Yigal Alon, now switched sides. Only Mr Carmel obstinately insisted that Israel should attack immediately. He reiterated what the army leaders had been saying for days, that the problem of forcing open the Straits of Tiran had become of secondary importance; the real issue was no longer the right of free shipping in the Gulf of Aqaba, but the large concentrations of hostile troops in Sinai and elsewhere along Israel's borders which were threatening the continued existence of Israel as a sovereign state. But the others decided to give the United States and the maritime powers a chance to resolve the crisis in their own way. After a day-long debate, Mr Eban finally got his own way again: Israel, for the time being, was not going to war.

There now occurred one of those unfortunate episodes which can have a devastating effect on the morale of a people. Now that the chips were down, the Prime Minister insisted on broadcasting that very evening to the nation, to lift them out of their suspense. His haste was to cost him dear. The broadcast, a live one, was disastrous. Mr Eshkol was, by then, exhausted from the long hours of deliberations. He had twice been routed out of bed in order to receive the Soviet and the American Notes.* Mr Eshkol is never an inspiring speaker at the best of times. But in such a condition he was pitiful. He fumbled, stuttered, lost his place in the script; what he did say, and how he said it, appalled the nation. Israel would try to resolve the crisis by diplomacy, and not by war, he said. But, if necessary the army could be relied upon to defend the State. This declaration had a shattering effect, especially on the army. The country had been keyed up for Mr Eshkol's speech. Most people expected him to take up Egypt's challenge. The least they expected was an ultimatum regarding the Straits. People openly wept in the streets after the broadcast. Was this the man chosen to lead the people of Israel out of the Valley of Death? Even those who had been staunch political supporters of the Prime Minister now forsook him.

The impatience of those who felt that rapid action was essential had now reached its climacteric. The military knew that each day that passed would increase their casualty rate. In the eyes of the militants, Israel was being held back by a group of elderly men who did not know how to make up their minds.

But Mr Eshkol's unfortunate radio speech hardened the resolve of those who wished to remove him from his post of Minister of Defence. These were now joined by many who, until that moment, had stood staunchly by him. The Prime Minister himself had no inkling of the storm that was brewing against him. When the parliamentary faction of the alignment of his own party and the Ahdut Ha'avoda party met on Monday evening, 30 May, Mr Eshkol, completely at ease, urged his comrades to speak openly, and hide nothing. They did, and what they had to say had a shattering effect on the Premier. Speaker after speaker demanded that he step down immediately

---

* But, wisely, he had put in six hours sleep on the day before.

from the Defence Ministry post and hand over the portfolio either to Moshe Dayan or Yigal Alon. Among those who were most outspoken were some of Mr Eshkol's closest colleagues—the Speaker of Parliament, Kadish Luz, the bright hope of the younger generation of Mapai, Arieh Eliav, the veteran Shaul Avigur, etc. The meeting was a cruel blow for the Premier, but even at this late stage he did not realize the weight of public feeling which was now aroused against him.

This lack of comprehension of national feeling by the "old guard" of Mapai—Mr Eshkol, Mrs Meir, Mr Aranne, Mr Sapir —was to cost them dear. They were, as we have seen, implacable foes of Ben Gurion, whose breakaway party, Rafi, was anathema to them. But Rafi contained the heroic figures of Israel to whom the public now turned: Ben Gurion himself, Moshe Dayan and Shimon Peres, the victor and the architect of Sinai. The spotlight was in particular turning ever more on Moshe Dayan, as the one man who could lead Israel to victory. But Dayan was the one man (in addition to Ben Gurion) that the "old guard" of Mapai did not want. He was a supporter of Ben Gurion. He was a member of Rafi. And now, at this late hour, with the "enemy"—not the Arabs, but Rafi—knocking at the gates, the Mapai leadership belatedly produced their own candidate for the post, Yigal Alon, former commander of the Palmach and hero of the 1948 Palestine War. Alon was not a member of Mapai; but he was one of the leaders of Ahdut Ha'avoda with which Mapai was aligned. The two parties were on the verge of a merger, and Alon was generally considered in Mapai to be the favourite candidate for eventual successor to Mr Eshkol as Prime Minister.

Alon had been in the Soviet Union when the crisis erupted on 15 May. He returned only on 24 May, immediately donned khaki and set out on a tour of the southern front together with Mr Eshkol. From that moment onwards Alon was constantly at Eshkol's side. He took part in all the meetings with the army generals. He examined the plans, offered suggestions, visited the troops. Though Minister of Labour, he fitted naturally into this new task of unofficial adviser to the Premier on military affairs. Had Eshkol, when the furore over the Defence Ministry post first began, stepped aside and handed the mantle to Alon, the country as a whole would have accepted the change with relief and the demand to install Dayan would never have arisen. Rafi would then have had the choice of entering the National Government, as Mr Begin's Gahal eventually did—with a Minister without portfolio, or of staying in the opposition.

But even at this late hour, after the open rebellion of the Parliamentary Party faction against their leader and Prime Minister, the urgency of the situation was not realized by either Mr Eshkol himself or by Mrs Meir, the power behind the throne. Mr Eshkol could not understand why his colleagues had turned against him. "What have I done to make you think I am a bad Defence Minister?" he asked, plaintively. Far from surrendering to the will of the party, he countered with such remarks as "So what will I do if I give it [the Defence Ministry] up," and even "over my dead body". To calm his opponents, he proposed that both Alon and Dayan be made deputy-premiers to deal with defence under him. When that proposal was turned down by all concerned he proposed a special defence committee composed of all the ex-Chiefs of Staff* to act in an advisory capacity to the Premier. But this, too, was rejected.

By now matters were rapidly coming to a head. On the morning of Wednesday, 31 May, the political committee of the Mapai-Ahdut Ha'avoda alignment met, and decided to call on Mr Alon to be Defence Minister.† Several speakers spoke of offering the command of the southern front to General Dayan in order "to quieten the people". The alignment leaders spoke hopefully of a situation in which Mr Begin's Gahal would agree to join a National Government, while Rafi would refuse to do so.

* The average term of duty of the Chief of Staff of the Israeli army is only three years. Since the establishment of the state there have been seven Chiefs of Staff, including the present one.

† The only one who abstained was Mrs Meir, who declared that she would not press Mr Eshkol to step down, if he himself did not feel it necessary.

They assumed that, if Dayan was not offered the post of Defence Minister, Ben Gurion would prefer to keep his party in opposition.

It was with this in mind that Mrs Meir assembled the Mapai Secretariat that evening, at the same time that Eshkol was putting the proposals regarding Alon and Dayan before the Coalition Ministers. The meeting proved to be one of the stormiest in Mapai's history. The participants denounced the tactics of their leaders. They demanded that the proposals be first studied by the Secretariat before being agreed upon by the Ministers. Hard words were exchanged with Mrs Meir, who refused to go to the Ministers, who were then in session, and inform them of this decision. "I won't fulfil this decision, even if I have to resign as Party Secretary," stormed Mrs Meir.

But the Coalition had already rejected the proposal to give the Defence Ministry to Alon. The leader of the religious party, Mr Shapira, declared that he did not mind personally whether Dayan or Alon received the post. All he wanted was that there should be a National Government. And this was impossible unless Dayan was given the post, for neither Gahal nor Rafi would agree to join the Government under any other terms. Shapira hinted that unless a National Government was formed, the Religious Party would resign from the coalition.

For twenty-four hours the situation remained fluid. During that time the leaders of Israel were engaged in a political free-for-all. Mr Eshkol met Dayan and offered him a number of posts; Dayan rejected them. The Premier then proposed that he take over the southern command. Dayan replied: "If you wish me to take up a military command, call me first to the colours and I will be willing to take any command you decide upon." Thus fortified, Mr Eshkol returned to his coalition colleagues only to find that his partners in the alignment, Ahdut Ha'avoda, had, in the meantime, evolved another plan. They had become increasingly annoyed with Eban, who they believed had allowed his zeal for peace to impede his judgment. Together with the Justice Minister, Yaakov Shimshon Shapira, they now proposed that Dayan replace Eban as Foreign Minister. Eban would be "kicked upstairs" to the powerless post of Deputy Premier. And the key post of Defence Minister would remain open for their own candidate, Yigal Alon. Eban, greatly offended, threatened to resign. The Premier assured him that he would not be sacrificed, and the proposal was dropped as rapidly as it had been raised. The Government had by now been hopelessly splintered into "Dayan" and "Alon" factions, with the Eban–Ahdut Ha'avoda quarrel adding to the general confusion. Over it all, like the sword of Damocles, hung Shapira's threat to pull the Religious Party out of the coalition, and thus bring about its downfall, unless a National Government was immediately set up.

The end came the following day, on Thursday, 1 June. The Mapai Secretariat met once more, this time with Mr Eshkol. Outside, a demonstration, largely composed of women, arranged by Mrs Peres, quietly paraded slogans calling for a National Government and for Dayan as Defence Minister. The morning newspapers carried the same message. Inside the conference hall the atmosphere was tense as Mr Eshkol got up to speak. But Eshkol even now had not given up the fight. Dayan should be given the southern command, Eshkol declared, adding that that was what Dayan himself most wanted. He hinted that Dayan would not be a good Defence Minister, for his inclinations would lead him to spend most of his time with the troops at the front, as had been the case in the Sinai War ten years earlier. This was too much for most of the members of the Secretariat. In the ensuing debate 80% of those present spoke against the Premier and in favour of Dayan. This was now a full-scale party revolt, backed by overwhelming public opinion.

Mr Eshkol made one last try. When the Secretariat adjourned for lunch, he hurried to meet representatives of Gahal, Begin's party, in an effort to persuade them to come into the Government without Dayan. But they would hear none of it. Only then did Eshkol finally admit defeat. That afternoon, he closeted himself with the Minister of Justice, Yaakov Shimshon Shapira, who, together with Mrs Meir and the Education Minister,

Zalman Aranne, had led the opposition to Dayan's appointment,* and together they reached the conclusion that they could not return to the Mapai Secretariat without a concrete proposal for a National Government, and that this was not possible without the appointment of Dayan. At four o'clock Mr Eshkol assembled the Political Committee of the alignment and, in a toneless voice, formally proposed that he relinquish the post of Minister of Defence in favour of Dayan. The proposal was unanimously accepted. At seven o'clock the performance was repeated at the Mapai Secretariat. Rafi and Gahal were notified. Both agreed to join the Coalition. Mrs Meir, who was also asked to take on a Ministerial post in the new broadened Government, refused angrily. Her efforts had failed. But in the country at large a tremendous sigh of relief went up as the news was broadcast later that evening on Kol Yisrael. The news had the effect of an electric current being shot through the life-stream of Israel. Shoulders straightened, faces brightened, toasts were drunk to a victory which now, with the appointment of one man to the helm of leadership, had, it seemed, become certain. Late that night, the new Government held its first session with the participation of Begin and Dayan.

Nearly a week had been spent in these political manœuvres. The Government of Israel had passed through a painful period. Hard words had been said, long-standing friendships had been destroyed, political alliances had been upset. But now that the house had been put in order, the Government could once more turn to the agonizing problems which faced it.

Time was pressing. The Arab build-up was becoming daily more menacing. King Hussein's dramatic flight to Cairo on 30 May, followed by news the next day that Iraqi troops and armoured units were entering Jordan, posed for Israel a threat which was even more grave than the closing of the Tiran Straits.

* Shapira had special reason to feel vindictive against Dayan's Rafi party. It had singled him out for special attack for his ceaseless attempts to besmirch Ben Gurion whom, at one time, he had accused of being a fascist.

For the problem of the Straits had by now become secondary, almost unimportant for Israel. The military leaders were taken up entirely with the ring of Arab armies poised on Israel's borders, far outnumbering the Israeli army in troops, tanks and planes, which might at any moment decide to attack.

This change of emphasis was not fully understood in the West. At a press conference in Ottawa on 2 June, the British Premier, Harold Wilson, described the Gulf of Aqaba as the "flashpoint" in the Middle East situation, and said that both he and Mr Pearson felt strongly that the solution to the problem lay through the United Nations. To the Israelis such a statement was so palpably wide of the mark, so completely inadequate, that the found it almost amusing. The emphasis placed on action through the United Nations, both by Mr Wilson and by a State Department spokesman, underlined for them the lack of seriousness of the Western efforts to find a solution. Israelis have become extremely sceptical over the years of the efficacy of United Nations' action.

If they were left in any doubts regarding the much-vaunted action of the Maritime Powers, in which Eban had placed such faith, they were dispelled during that week in a number of talks held between Israeli and American officials. The Israelis were given to understand that the interpretation which Eban had placed on his talks in the United States had not been correct. Far from promising to resolve the crisis on their own or in conjunction with other maritime powers, the Israelis were told that the United States did not see any possibility of any action being taken by them in the foreseeable future. The Americans, for their part, were shown a different Israel from the picture they had received during the Foreign Minister's visit. Then they had been confronted by a man of peace, begging, with cap in hand, for help against the Arab bully. Now they were told plainly: the problem is not the Straits, but the troop concentrations. These the Israeli army could handle on her own fully and adequately, without any help from outside quarters. This was underlined by Dayan's statement on 2 June that Israel did not want American or British soldiers to get killed for her sake.

On 2 June Dayan met the generals and went over the operational plans with them. He was already familiar with them all. He had made good use of his time while the Ministers had been arguing. He knew now what he wanted. This was something much more than the Gaza Strip and el-Arish, to be used as a bargaining counter for the opening of the Straits. The Egyptians, he feared, were liable to say: "Keep Gaza, with its 400,000 Arabs. Choke on them. We will keep the Straits closed." What was needed was a much wider plan, one that was aimed at destroying the Egyptian army in the heart of Sinai. "Only if we take as large a slice of Sinai as possible, and smash the Egyptian army, can we be sure of opening the Straits and removing the threat against us," he averred. He was enthusiastically supported in this viewpoint by General Haim Barlev, who had been appointed deputy Chief of Staff on 31 May. Both he and the other Staff Generals, and in particular the Chief of Staff, General Rabin, agreed fully with the Defence Minister that the weight of the attack should be directed against Sinai. Orders were issued to the effect that the attack, if and when it came, would be mounted along three axes into Sinai, in the general direction of Bir Gifgafa and the Mitla Pass.

Dayan was convinced that Israel would have no choice other than going to war. The Jordanian–Egyptian Defence Pact and movement of Iraqi troops into Jordan removed his remaining doubts. It was now only a question of choosing the right moment. The Government had first to give approval, but by now there were no more doubters. Eban's anti-war front, based as it was on the assumption that the US would act, collapsed when it became evident that the US would do nothing. And if that was not enough, there was King Hussein's trip to Cairo and the Iraqi troop movements to underline the dangers of added procrastination. On Sunday morning, 4 June, the Government met once more. Before it was a proposal to give the Prime Minister and the Minister of Defence authority to give the Israeli army the order to take action if circumstances necessitated such a step. This time there were no discussions. All the Ministers voted in favour except the two left-wing members of Mapam who asked for time to consult their party caucus. They later sent in their affirmative vote. After three weeks of indecision the die was now cast. Less than twenty-four hours later Israel and the Arab countries were at war.

Part II : The Six-Day War

THE BORDERS OF ISRAEL AT
4 JUNE AND 11 JUNE 1967

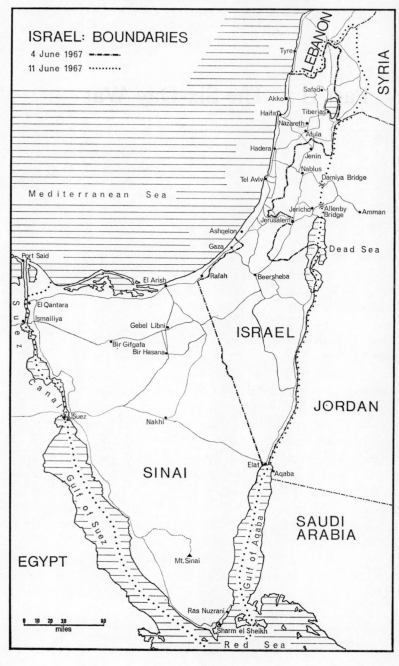

ISRAEL: BOUNDARIES

4 June 1967 ▬·▬·▬·▬

11 June 1967 ·············

CHAPTER 8

Prelude

Dawn breaks early over Sinai in the month of June. The hills and wadis, the sand and the rocks emerge with a startling suddenness from the gloom of night, and for a brief hour are bathed in a chill, pastel-coloured light before the sun rises overhead and transforms the scene into the harsh tones of a film-set desert. This is the glorious hour of Sinai, the hour before the flies plague and the sun burns. On Monday, 5 June, it was the hour in which the soldiers of Egypt snatched their last minutes of peaceful sleep, huddled in their fox-holes or beside their tanks or in the deep underground concrete fortifications which lay, unseen to the casual eye, across the eastern access routes to the peninsula.

There were, on that Monday morning, nearly 100,000 Egyptian troops encamped in that ocean of nothingness. It was by any standards a formidable army of men and machines of war. Seven divisions and a thousand tanks had been deployed in this gigantic show of strength. Conscripts direct from garrison duty in the Yemen, seasoned troops from the Suez War, hastily mobilized reservists from Cairo and Alexandria, fellaheen from the fields of the Delta, village schoolteachers, government clerks and university students, they were all there, in their fox-holes and bunkers, sharing the same experiences and enduring the same discomforts of soldiering in the desert.

The Egyptian High Command had, as captured documents later revealed, deployed its forces both for defensive and offensive purposes. Its planning was, however, guided princi-

pally by topographical factors. The border between Israel and
the Sinai, though 139 miles long, was made largely impassable
by rolling sand-dunes in the north and rocky outcrops, interspersed with tracts of soft sand, in the south. Only three routes
traversed this sea of sand and rock. Of these, the shortest and
best-surfaced was the northern road from the Gaza Strip
through Rafa and el-Arish along the coast to al-Qantara on
the Suez Canal. The central route crossed the Israel frontier at
Nitzana and continued to Abu Ageila, and through the desert
oases of Gebel Libni, Bir Hama and Bir Gifgafa to Ismailia.
A third route, which was nothing more than an earth track,
crossed the Sinai farther to the south, via the oases of Bir
Thamade and Nakhl, and passing through the Mitla Pass, a
narrow gorge cutting through steep hills, before eventually
reaching the Suez Canal to the north of the town of Suez. These
three routes were connected by a number of secondary roads
and tracks, the main points of intersection being at Abu Ageila,
Gebel Libni, Bir Hasane and Bir Thamade.

Any Israeli advance into Sinai could be expected to come
along one or more of these access routes. The Egyptian deployment was therefore placed accordingly. The most dangerous
area, in Egyptian eyes, was the triangle of territory in the north-
eastern corner of Sinai, bounded on one side by the Mediterranean coast from Rafa to el-Arish, by the Israel border on the
second side, and back to the Mediterranean at el-Arish through
Quseima and Abu Ageila on the third side. Through this triangle
passed the two major access routes, and it was there that the
Egyptians constructed their most elaborate fortifications to
prevent any Israeli break-through. By the beginning of June
they had deployed four divisions to defend this triangle: the
7th Division, heavily reinforced with artillery and armoured
units, manned the fortifications in the Rafa-el-Arish area along
the coastal road; the 2nd Division, with additional armour, held
the vital Abu Ageila cross-roads; the 3rd Division was placed
to the west of the triangle, astride the Gebel Libni and Bir
Hasane cross-roads, giving depth to the positions held by the

5. *Right:* Arab refugees from Jordan after crossing the Allenby Bridge

6. *Below:* A Bedouin Sheik from Southern Sinai on visit to Tel-Aviv, overlooking the city from the Shalom Tower

7. A captured Egyptian SAM missile produced in Russia

8. Israeli soldiers during a lull in the fighting in Jerusalem

7th and 2nd Divisions at el-Arish and Abu Ageila. In addition, the 20th Palestinian Division was assigned to the Gaza Strip to guard against a flank attack through the Strip against the Rafa–el-Arish complex.

Farther south, another division, the 6th, was spread out along the southern access route from Kuntilla to Nakhl.

With such a formidable defence of the roads leading into Sinai, the Egyptians felt confident that they could prevent any break-through. But High Command provided for such an eventuality. The 4th Armoured Division, the pride of the Egyptian army, was held back in general reserve, in the Bir Gifgafa–Mileiz area. Its main task was to hold the second line of defence in case of an Israeli break-through and to ensure that the vital passes through the range of hills some forty miles to the east of the Suez Canal remained in Egyptian hands.

The 4th Armoured Division was also, however, assigned offensive tasks. Documents captured by the Israelis during the fighting have revealed that the main offensive action of the Egyptians was to have been undertaken by the special task force under General Shazli, supported by elements of the 4th Armoured Division. This force was to invade Israel to the north of Elath and would head for the Jordanian border, in order to cut the Negev into two and isolate Elath. Elath would be occupied and this would solve once and for all the question of the right of shipping in the Gulf of Aqaba. It would also give Egypt for the first time a common land frontier with Jordan which could be exploited for future purposes. These moves would be preceded by a massive air strike against strategic targets within Israel, above all with the aim of destroying the Israeli Air Force on the ground.

According to these documents, the main task of the divisions in the north in case of an Israeli attack was to engage and hold the Israelis in battle in order to allow the forces in the rear to go over to the offensive in an encircling movement behind the enemy. Local counter-attacks were planned in the northern part of Sinai, on the assumption that the Israelis would fail to break

F

through the Egyptian fortified positions. The main counter-attack in the north was to be launched by the 7th Division. It would be spearheaded by the Egyptian 14th Armoured Brigade and supported by troops of the 11th and 16th Brigades, and their objective was to sweep into Israeli territory south of Rafa and capture the Israeli settlements of Kerem Shalom and Nir Yitzhak.

The Egyptian High Command did not believe that the Egyptian army was strong enough to overrun Israel or even to take Tel Aviv. It considered, however, that even if only a stalemate was achieved, this would be a great victory for the Egyptians. It would force the West to settle with Egypt on Egyptian terms. The Straits of Tiran would remain closed, and the whip would stay in Egyptian hands. If the Israelis decided to fight rather than to submit, this would be turned into Egypt's decisive victory.

To the Egyptian leaders this seemed a valid expectation. They had been building their desert fortifications for the past ten years. Israel's access routes into the Sinai peninsula were barred by a great array of barbed wire, minefields, pillboxes, underground bunkers, hidden gun emplacements and fire trenches. The Egyptians were ready for the war. It seemed to them that they had made it impossible for the Israelis to spring any possible surprise attack on the Egyptian defences. On paper, moreover, the Egyptians had a safe margin of superiority in men, weapons and fire-power.

Pitted against the seven Egyptian divisions, the Israelis mustered a force of slightly more than three divisions. The first, commanded by General Israel Tal, was composed of two brigades, almost completely armoured. The second, headed by General Arik Sharon, was more in the nature of a mixed task force. It was made up of three brigades, which included armour, artillery, infantry and paratroop units. The third division, under General Avraham Yoffe, was actually assembled only at the end of May and was composed of two armoured brigades made up entirely of reserve troops which, when hostilities broke out, operated independently of each other. In addition to these three divisions there were several independent forces including a mixed infantry and armoured brigade facing the Gaza Strip, an armoured column in the Kuntilla area north of Elath, a battalion in Elath and certain reserves of battalion strength of paratroops who were earmarked for the possibility of fighting in the Tiran Straits area and also in the south-west of the Sinai peninsula near the oil-fields.

The force was, both in manpower and in fire-power, far inferior to the Egyptian army in the Sinai. The Egyptian High Command had thus every reason to feel confident on the eve of the war, and their confidence was imparted to President Nasser.

But the situation in the field was vastly different from that depicted on the wall-maps and in the secret files of the Egyptian High Command. The chaos and the confusion in the forward positions of the Sinai army hardly percolated through to General Headquarters.

Hasty deployment on the scale embarked upon by the Egyptian army in the second half of May calls for outstanding proficiency, excellent training and efficient supporting units. The Egyptian army was soon found to be lacking in these qualities. The present authors were able to gauge the measure of inefficiency which characterized the entry of the Egyptian army into Sinai from conversations they had with Egyptian officer prisoners of war. One of the sure signs of lack of co-ordination and of sufficient planning was the constant switching of units from one sector to another throughout the waiting period before 5 June. These interminable troop movements, unintelligible to officers and troops alike, did much to demoralize the army and to reduce its fighting capacity. They led to confusion in supplies and to administrative chaos. A typical case was that of one of the battalions of a reserve brigade which had moved to el-Arish at the end of May. Shortly after arrival, they were given marching orders to Bir Hasane, although the brigade headquarters remained in el-Arish. They bivouacked in the vicinity of Bir Hasane in an open area. They had neither water nor food—apart from their battle rations, which they were forbidden to touch. Communications did not function, and they had no ammunition. But they were told that the brigade headquarters would soon arrive and then all deficiencies would be rectified. For forty-eight hours the men waited impatiently for HQ and supplies to arrive, under the burning sun, with no orders and with nothing to do. By that time many of the troops were already in a state of near-collapse and there was still no word or sign from brigade headquarters. The battalion commander gave the order to open battle rations and dig in. The following day, 5 June, the battalion was attacked from the air. The dug-outs were not ready and many, including the battalion commander, were killed. They had not even known that fighting had broken out.

Typical also was the case of one of the armoured brigades which had moved into Sinai in the latter half of May. The brigade was sent to Gebel Libni where they remained for nearly a fortnight before moving on to Sheikh Zued, near el-Arish. From there they were sent to Bir Hasane where they remained until the outbreak of the war, and on 6 June they returned to Gebel Libni. By that time the large distances the brigade had covered were beginning to tell on the tanks, many of which needed servicing. But this was by no means the end of the brigade's Odyssey. The brigade commander received orders to return once more to Bir Hasane with all the speed he could muster. On arrival he gave an order to establish defence positions to the south of Bir Hasane. But towards the afternoon the brigade received orders to continue to Um Katif. They were told that Israeli tanks were moving southwards from el-Arish and that they must be stopped. The brigade went into action against the Israelis but by this time the troops were exhausted and demoralized by the continuous movement, and the tanks were in poor condition. The battle was lost before they even began it. One of the battalions started retreating after having lost touch with the brigade. Soon afterwards the entire brigade was dispersed by repeated air attacks and most of the tanks were destroyed. This story of lack of planning and wasteful movement could be repeated by unit after unit.

Thus the Egyptian occupation of fortified positions in Sinai, far from being the smooth and well-oiled operation that would have been expected from a modern, well-trained army, was faulty from the very beginning. Entire battalions and even brigades spent days without food or water. Others were isolated because of faulty communications and were thus virtually immobilized. Reserve units in particular were hard hit by the logistical inefficiency: many units were sent to the front with guns but no ammunition. Others arrived at forward positions still dressed in their *galabiyas*, as there had been no time to issue them with uniforms. Entire units were lost in the desert, or arrived at the wrong positions, adding to the general confusion.

Much of this disorganization was caused by the haste with which the army was sent into Sinai. There was no gradual build-up of strength but a headlong rush of troops eastwards. But the army should have been prepared for exactly such an exigency. The Egyptian High Command should have had its plans prepared down to the minutest detail. That it had not is a telling pointer to the real state of the Egyptian army before the war. To understand that army is not easy. One has to understand also the mechanism of Egyptian society in general, and the revolution that it had gone through in the past fifteen years: its successes and its failures, its ambitions and frustrations. The *fellah's* lot had hardly improved over the past fifteen years and he provided the privates and most of the NCOs. The junior officers were drawn mainly from the poor lower-middle classes in the cities and the towns around the Nile delta, and it was only the senior officers who came from the new ruling classes in Egypt. Many of these officers had an academic education and had studied warfare ever since they joined the army. Some had served in the Egyptian army under Farouk and were trained in the officers' school which was still influenced by British military doctrine. More recently, with the Russians becoming the main suppliers of arms to the Egyptians, many of them had gone to Russia to study in the staff colleges and in other military schools. They were trained in the Russian way of military thinking, though an attempt was made to adapt it to the Egyptian way of life and to desert warfare.

The first course in the Soviet Union for senior staff officers took place in 1957, and then a second one for a longer period was held in the winter of 1958–9, and a third course in 1961. There were other courses for junior staff officers of the ranks of captain and major which lasted three years, the first having taken place in 1960. There were courses for brigade officers in 1960, and others in which communications, supplies and engineering problems were studied. Parallel to the training of Egyptian officers in the Soviet Union, the Russians sent military experts to Egypt to help in organizing and reorganizing army units. They first arrived in 1958 and went to work to reorganize the 3rd Division and the 4th Armoured Division which were reshaped according to the Soviet pattern. A group of ten Soviet specialists was attached to each of the divisions, where they operated as direct consultants to the division's commanding officer and his senior staff. Soviet advisers also operated in the training branch of the Egyptian army, teaching Soviet military doctrine and helping in the reorganization of the training in all branches of the armed forces. They brought with them manuals, usually drawn up in English, on which all training in the Egyptian army was patterned. In 1959 a new group of Soviet officers began reorganizing the 2nd Division according to the Soviet doctrine. They were also attached to the various commands for training, but at no time did they take part in complete operational planning or in operational tasks of the combat divisions.

This training transformed the officers into a hard professional corps. Moreover, many had fought in 1948 against Israel and many more had participated in the 1956 war. And most of them had at some time or other served in the Yemen in the gruelling

five-year war which had ravaged that country. Almost all of
them were devoted followers of President Nasser. Politically
they were not interested in any policy which was not approved
of by the Egyptian Government. They were convinced of the
justice of the Arab case over the question of the Palestine
refugees. Most of them believed that the Israelis were usurpers
and that in the long run war was inevitable, for there could be
no peace in the Middle East until Israel was annihilated. But
their knowledge of their enemy was very limited. They regarded
Zionism as an international capitalist movement, controlling
most of the world's capital; they believed that Israel was
corrupt and evil, living off outside help, that the great powers
had saved Israel in 1948 when the Egyptians were only ten
kilometres from Tel Aviv. The lower ranks had very little
information about the Israeli Defence Forces. They were certain
that it was a weak army, substantially weaker than the Egyptian
armed forces. This belief was based simply on the fact that Israel
was a small nation of two and a half million people.

About one-third of the army that was moved into Sinai was
composed of reservists. These reservists included officers up to
company commanders, while battalion commanders were all
regular army officers. The difference in standards of the battalion
commanders as compared to the lower-ranking officers was
most evident. Company and platoon commanders remembered
very little of the theoretical courses they had gone through.
Many of them arrived in Sinai for the first time in their lives,
had no knowledge of the terrain and were uncertain where the
Israeli lines were, what their neighbouring units were, or of
whom they were composed. They hardly knew their fellow
officers and did not know most of their troops. They based their
command on disciplinary measures which were, more often than
not, very harsh. They would be surprised if asked whether they
knew by name their NCOs or any of their privates. "It just
isn't done in the Egyptian Army," they would reply. Their
knowledge of topography was nil, they could not read an aerial
photograph, and they relied instead on the highly detailed and

specific orders they received from their seniors (orders and battle plans are invariably given in writing in the Egyptian army and are usually very precise, detailed and clear). They were not trained to act independently and, as a result, when on occasion communications broke down after the war broke out, there were few cases where junior officers assumed command and acted independently. The lack of initiative and lack of flexibility displayed by the Egyptian officers during the war was probably one of the prime causes for the enormity of their defeat. Unlike the Israelis, most of the officers and men did not feel intensely involved in the crisis on the eve of the war. When they were moved, say from Bir Gifgafa to Gebel Libni, and expected other movement within the next three or four days, they would bivouac but not train. They would not dig in or carry out any army exercises. They just waited for futher orders, passing the time trying to find some shade or playing "sheshbesh". They received very little information on what was going on and were disinterested in politics. Few of the officers or men expected war, and although told that they should prepare defences, they did not work too hard at it. Most of the officers thought that the occupation of the Sinai forward line was no more than a political move on the part of President Nasser, aimed at deterring the Israelis from attacking Syria. For this reason there was very little of the tension and exhilaration of an army on the brink of war. The morale of the men was as usual, with the usual friction and complaints of troops under field conditions. Personal relationships between the officers and the men, and among the officers themselves, were not very good. There was little affinity or trust; there was very little cameraderie, hardly any cases of group loyalty. This lack of *esprit de corps* was one of the dominant characteristics of the Egyptian army which had a profound effect on its fighting qualities. There was no fraternization between officers and other ranks, and not much friendship among the officers themselves. To a large extent it was every man for himself, in sharp contrast to the basic character of the Israeli army.

Again, in contrast to the Israelis, an unbridgeable gap existed between the educated officers and the vast majority of the soldiers, whose standard of living was one of the lowest in the world. Poor, ignorant, often in bad health, the Egyptian soldier lacked intellectual interest, inquisitiveness in his surroundings. He was a passive participant in events which were far too large for him to understand. He put his trust in Nasser but would not trust his colleagues who were living next to him. He performed automatically, passively, accepting the fact that he was there as an inevitability about which he could do very little. There was little hatred in him: in the words of one senior Egyptian officer, "The *fellah* has no idea what Israel is and what the Israeli question is about"; while another officer said, "They cannot think in terms of coming to help the refugees, when their own conditions are so bad."

There were other signs of weakness in the Egyptian army. The standard of maintenance of the equipment was well below the average expected of a modern army. This was particularly noticeable in the air force. The number of sorties the air force could make was based on the assumption that half an hour would pass between the landing of an aircraft and its next sortie, while the Israeli Air Force proved that its planes could refuel, re-arm and take off within ten minutes and sometimes within seven and one-half minutes after landing.

Similarly the tank corps was not up to par and numerous tanks broke down in Sinai long before the fighting broke out because of bad handling and poor maintenance.

Not all the Soviet equipment of the Egyptian army was of good quality and much of it had not been adapted to the exigencies of desert warfare. But the breaking point of the Sinai army as far as equipment was concerned was its electronic and communication instruments. Experts who examined captured Soviet equipment after the war found these to be lagging fifteen years behind comparable equipment in the West. The Soviet-supplied radar was the equivalent to that used by the West in the early 'fifties. It was cumbersome, difficult to operate, and the mobile radar units were still equipped with an oven for heating, but with no cooling system. The latest Soviet radio-telephone supplied to the Egyptians was a copy of an old German model. But the Egyptians preferred field to radio telephones. As a result Sinai was criss-crossed with telephone lines, many of which were cut as soon as the fighting began, which led to the virtual break-down of the entire Egyptian communications network. The Egyptian armour still used a number of "19 sets" which had been purchased by the army in the early 'fifties. These sets are supplied with a hundred crystals which enable a choice to be made of four out of a hundred frequencies. In sets captured by the Israelis during the war it was found that the Egyptians were still using exactly the same four frequencies that they had been using during the Suez War. This was as telling an example of lack of initiative as any found by the Israelis in Sinai. The most effective of all the Soviet equipment, in the opinion of experts, was the artillery, which, in many cases, was superior to its Western counterparts. As for the tanks, they were of good quality, but were much harder on their crews, as far as elementary comforts were concerned, than western armour. Many of the T–55 tanks knocked out in Sinai were very obviously brand new. Some had still not been painted over with camouflage colouring suitable for Sinai.

Yet despite weaknesses, the Egyptian army was extremely powerful, far superior in numerical strength and in fire-power to the Israeli army that was facing it. But this numerical inferiority of the Israeli's was more than made up by the special qualities inherent in the Israeli army, which were derived from the basic differences in the social and economic structure of Israeli as opposed to Egyptian society. The army in Israel was not a profession or a way of life, but an integral part of the country's existence. Israel's regular army was small by comparison with any of the armed forces in the Arab countries. Her strength lay in the reserve units which added more than 200,000 men and women to the army, or something like 10% of the entire population. Every citizen, on completion of his two-and-a-half year service in the standing army, is placed in a reserve unit. Usually reserves are called up for a month's training or guard duty a year, but very often the period of mobilization is much longer. At the age of 45 the Israeli's obligation to serve in a reserve unit ceases and he is transferred to the Civil Defence Force. Women, who are called up for two years' National Service, are liable for reserve duties until they become mothers, or until they reach the age of 29. The average age of the reservists is between 28 and 32. They thus may be slightly slower and less mobile than their younger brothers doing their National Service, but against that they have more experience. They are more knowledgeable and better acquainted with their fellow soldiers and officers. The Israeli Defence Forces are, therefore, a citizens' army in every sense of the word.

The reservists understand the need for their call-up, but they are not militarists. They adapt themselves almost like chameleons to their army service, but they are only too happy to be demobilized as early as possible. They grumble, but they do not complain. They are amateurs, but they act professionally. They realize only too clearly that no war may be lost. The possibility of war is not an abstract, theoretical concept, but something every Israeli soldier lives with. He knows that when hostilities commence it will be a total war; he knows there will be casualties and that he will have to give his all, for defeat means annihilation, the end for him, his family and his people. These are not the vague tenets of patriotism. It is almost as if each soldier realizes that victory is up to him, personally, that he at any point may have to make decisions independently and act independently; although the army acts as a unit and obedience is total, these men are ready at any point to take command and responsibility into their own hands.

It is an intensely democratic army. The officers, from the generals down, are known by their first names, or, equally commonly, by nicknames. General Gavish is called "Shaike" (short for his rather cumbersome first name, Yeshayahu); General Narkiss, "Uzi"; General Elazar is far better known by the name of "Dado" than by his correct name, and so on through the ranks. In many cases a company or platoon commander has his employer in civilian life as one of his subordinates in the army. This is accepted by all and creates strong personal bonds, a greater reliance on each other, and understanding that all are cogs in one big machine.

There is no barrack-square atmosphere, no spit-and-polish attitude (to the horror of foreign military persons who have visited the Israeli Defence Forces and been shocked by the ragamuffin look of its soldiers and the lack of all the outward attributes of militarism). But although there is hardly any parade-ground drill training, battle training is intensive and most soldiers are taught more than one trade. In the armoured corps, every member of the tank crew can drive the tank, act as gunner and usually also act as tank commander. A captain in the infantry may act as intelligence officer, deputy company commander or mortar officer, and is always ready to lead a platoon. He is encouraged to be interested in technical gadgets and handles his equipment with imagination and care, and can, when need be, see to repairs himself. The officers meet frequently when they are not on active duty, and they usually have a common language with their superior officers. The brigade commander as a rule knows all the company commanders of his battalions and many of the other officers. The company commanding officer knows each member of his company by name and is familiar with his personal problems. Even the battalion commander knows many of the privates in his battalion and most probably all his NCOs. Through this absence of distance through rank, trust grows—trust in one another, trust in one's superior officer, trust in the men to be led into battle. The men know that it is their commanding officer who will be going in, leading them into battle. They know that the company commander is the hardest-working man in the company, and that the battalion commander is the toughest, most professional soldier of the battalion. They trust him and they follow him, for the officers maintain their authority by personal example.

It had become a tradition in the Israeli army that the officers always led their troops into battle. They were always the first to storm into an enemy position; they were always at the head of an attacking column; their battle cry was never "forward" but always "follow me". The result was an abnormally high casualty rate among the officers. This was particularly the case in the June War. But to maintain the pace and the drive the officers had to lead, and to lead they had to be seen. And when they were seen by their troops they were also seen by the enemy, with the result that many of them were killed. Of the Israeli casualties in the June War, more than 25% were officers and NCOs, a very high percentage.

In 1948 the Israelis had fought in units of platoons, companies and, very rarely, in battalion strength. There was little artillery and virtually no air force. Most of the attacks took place at night. They were simple in principle and there were rarely any frontal attacks.

The war of 1956 was a prelude to the war of 1967, but far more primitive. Then the infantry still went on foot into battle. There was a lot to improve in co-ordination between artillery, air attacks and the final attack of the infantry. The tank corps was used more as mobile artillery and rarely as an independent fighting unit.

By 1967 the Israeli army had been transformed. In 1956 the infantry made up the great majority of the Israeli land forces; in 1967 its proportion had declined to less than half. The armoured corps in 1956 represented a small fraction of the total; by 1967 this had risen to a significant percentage. More than half of the defence expenditure went into the air force. Armour and air power had become the two decisive factors. With the infantry more mobile it had no mean part to play. For Israeli military thinking was governed by three basic premises: victory is assured to the side that obtains complete superiority in the air; armour should be used as a concentrated mailed fist to smash through the fortified positions of the enemy; once the break-through has been achieved, the accent is on exploitation with maximum speed and flexibility. This doctrine had been fashioned by the prevailing conditions: the terrain, a vast empty desert ideal for armoured warfare, for speed of movement in which air support for the ground forces can be used to maximum effect; the character of the adversary—the Israelis had already discovered in previous wars that the Egyptians are at their best in defending static positions, but quickly lose their heads in a fast, rapidly moving battle; and, most important of all, the limitations of time created by outside intervention which, in Israeli eyes, made speed an essential factor in every plan. Thus, in the period immediately before the war, Israeli thought moved along the following general lines:

1. It seemed unlikely that if a war should break out, it would last much longer than forty-eight hours. By that time the UN would intervene and impose a cease-fire. Possibly the war would be even shorter—not more than twenty-four hours.

2. Over such a short time it would be difficult to make any deep penetration in the Egyptian lines. It would be virtually impossible to reach, take and hold Sharm el-Sheikh and open the Straits of Tiran. Even if Sharm el-Sheikh was captured by an airborne force, it could only be held for a limited time unless the hinterland, i.e. Sinai as a whole, was also captured.

3. The target should therefore be limited to capturing territory which could be used as a bargaining-counter for the opening of the Straits. This was to be a limited offensive at best, whose scope would be dictated by the length of time the fighting lasted.

This, at least, was the concept in the days immediately following Nasser's declaration of the closing of the Gulf of Aqaba. But with the rapid massing of Egyptian troops in Sinai, it became clear that the problem was not merely one of forcing the Tiran Straits, but a confrontation of a threat to Israel's existence. The bargaining counter thus became of doubtful importance. Instead, the destruction of the Egyptian army became the prime objective, and the accent in the plans was put on pushing into the Sinai as deeply as possible. The overriding character of these plans was, however, their flexibility, for they were constantly revised in accordance with the Egyptian deployment and with political developments.

The most important tactical objective for the Israelis was the complex of fortifications which the Egyptians had built up over the years in the Rafa–Abu Ageila–el-Arish triangle, and which, as we have seen, the Egyptian High Command had rightly considered to be the most likely area for an Israeli attack.

Despite the difficulties involved in overcoming these highly fortified defensive positions, the Israelis felt they could not afford to by-pass them and leave them intact in their rear. An imposed cease-fire with Israeli forces in the Sinai, and with el-Arish and Abu Ageila still in Egyptian hands, could place the Israelis in a very dangerous position. The first stage of their plan of action was, therefore, to break through the "triangle". General Tal's division was assigned the task of breaking through on the coastal road, while General Sharon's division was to overcome the Egyptian defences at Abu Ageila. The third division, under General Yoffe, was to advance through the sand-dunes between the Egyptian lines and make its way to the rear of the Egyptian troops, blocking their escape routes across the range of hills to the east of the Suez Canal. The Israelis would then be in a position to execute their prime objective, the destruction of the Egyptian army.

Thus, by the beginning of June, both the Israelis and the Egyptians had their plans and their deployments ready. The final preparations had been made. The battle-lines were drawn.

THE RIVAL DEPLOYMENTS IN SINAI

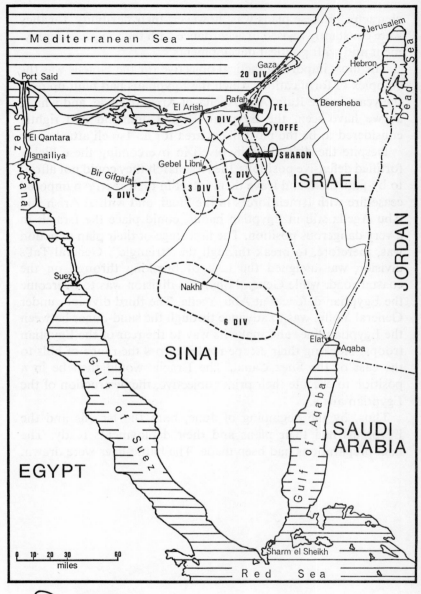

THE ISRAELI LINES OF ADVANCE

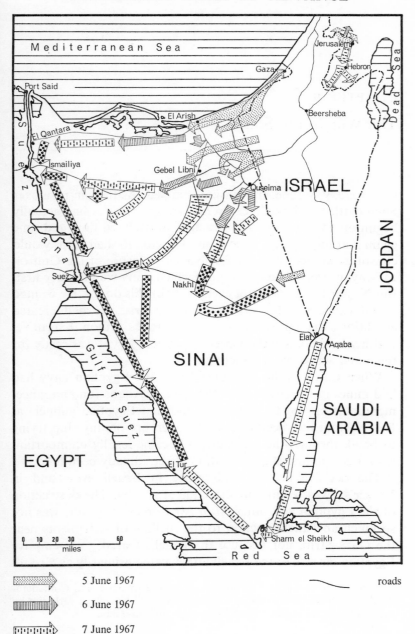

5 June 1967	roads
6 June 1967	
7 June 1967	
8 June 1967	

CHAPTER 9

The War in the South

On Monday, 5 June, the tension snapped. As the sun rose over
Sinai battle was joined. Yet in many ways, the war had actually
begun on 23 May. For the Israelis had declared time and time
again that the closing of the Gulf of Aqaba to their ships would
constitute an act of war. After Nasser's closure of the Gulf on
23 May, it was only a question of which army would move first.
But Nasser for one did not even harbour this doubt. He wanted
—and expected—the Israelis to move first. He had created
conditions, he informed the Arab Trades Union Executive,
which would compel the Israelis to attack. Egypt was ready for
them and set to crush Israel.*

When Cairo Radio announced that the Egyptian navy had
laid mines in the entrance to the Gulf of Aqaba (an announcement later proved to be untrue) and that Egyptian gunners at
Ras Nasrani had been ordered to open fire on any ship trying
to break through the blockade, it became legally unimportant
who fired the first shot. It had, in effect, already been fired.

The decisive act of belligerence in Israeli eyes—and in
Nasser's—was sealing off the Gulf of Aqaba. The destruction
of the Egyptian and other Arab Air Forces on 5 June was not
so much an Israeli reaction to the shelling of settlements near
the Gaza Strip, nor because the Israelis feared a pre-emptive
Egyptian air strike: the Israeli attack came primarily as a result

* Speech made to the Central Council to the International Confedera-
tion of Arab Trade Unions on 26 May 1967, and broadcast verbatim by
the "Voice of the Arabs" from Cairo later the same day.

of the war which was started on 23 May when the Egyptians closed the Gulf and defied the Israelis to do their worst.

They did. They now put their military doctrine to the test.

It proved its worth beyond all expectations. Basic to their entire concept of swift, mobile warfare was the need to gain mastery of the air. This was also necessary to remove the anxiety felt in the country for the safety of its cities. It had been largely this concern that had caused a majority of the Cabinet to oppose the decisive step of going to war until the last possible moment. In the event, the Israeli air force succeeded in destroying in three hours nearly three hundred Egyptian aircraft, and in putting out of action virtually the entire Egyptian air force. The threat to Tel Aviv and the other cities was removed and the Israeli Air Command was free to turn to the air forces of Jordan, Syria and Iraq, and to give air support to their embattled forces in Sinai. We asked General Rabin to what extent this air support was crucial in the desert victory. He was emphatic in his answer: the air strikes against Egyptian columns destroyed Egyptian mobility and prevented the Egyptians from deploying their armour according to their needs. The two massive counter-attacks which the Egyptians planned thus never materialized.

The success of the Air Force's strike was due to near-perfect execution of a plan on which the Israelis had worked for years. Hard training over the years had transformed the air force into an efficient and compact group of professionals. The ground crews had reached an astonishing level of performance in maintenance and in speed. By refuelling and re-equipping aircraft within eight to ten minutes, they proved a new mathematical equation: the strength of an air force depends not only on the number of airworthy aircraft available, but on that number multiplied by total flying time. The ground crews worked at such a pace that at the height of fighting in the first two days of the war aircraft were airborne more than 80% of the day, although most of them had been repeatedly hit by Arab anti-aircraft shrapnel or by small-arms fire. The fast turn-around schedule put the planes back into the air more than three times faster than the Arabs were capable of doing. It was this feat of the ground crews which led the Arabs to believe that the Israelis were operating with the help of foreign air forces and which lent credence to President Nasser's charge that there had been American and British participation in the air strike. He had asserted on 9 June that "the enemy was operating with an air force three times stronger than his normal force". This calculation fitted perfectly with the reckoning of Egyptian turn-around performance, but failed to take into account the greater speed of the Israelis.

But above all, it was the training of the pilots themselves, coupled with the extraordinarily detailed intelligence at their disposal, which enabled the Israeli Air Force to fulfil its mission in such a spectacular manner. The deadly accuracy with which they pinpointed their targets was all the more striking when compared to the haphazard way in which the Arab planes that succeeded in reaching Israel jettisoned their bombs.

The Iraqis attacked Natanya, dropping several bombs in the suburbs where they hit a factory and caused some casualties. Soon after this attack, the lone Tupolev plane, piloted by an Iraqi colonel, was shot down by the Israeli anti-aircraft batteries. The Israelis, on the other hand, always made certain their target was worth while before attacking it. This necessitated coming in low over the target area, often into the thick of anti-aircraft or small-arms fire. But precision was almost perfect, as many discovered later when they visited the battle areas and saw how few cannon shells had been wasted in the attacks. Coming back from assaults the aircraft were very often full of bullet-holes, evidence of the intense fire they flew through as they dived right into the centre of enemy concentrations. Of the thirty-six planes lost by the Israelis during these six days, three were lost in air battles while the remainder were shot down by ground fire. As against the three shot down in air battle, the Israelis claimed to have downed forty-two planes in air-to-air combat.

The plan of the air attack had been to attack concurrently

seventeen airfields in pre-emptive strikes, destroying first the runways to prevent any aircraft from taking off, and then all aircraft in sight. By noon on 5 June this mission had been successfully accomplished. In seventeen air bases in Egypt huge columns of black smoke rising above destroyed planes were the index of that success. One of the Egyptian pilots attending a course on the new Sukhoy-7 planes, who was captured later by the Israelis, gave this account of the attack: at 0845 (Cairo time) on Monday, 5 June, he was sitting in one of the hangars of the Faid air base when suddenly he heard a huge explosion. The windows of the hangar disintegrated and they could see planes swooping in low to the attack. They ran for cover to a nearby building where the air raid shelter had already filled. Due to the suddenness of the attack, the anti-aircraft guns were not ready and did not operate. They did, though, when the next wave of planes came in about ten minutes later. In these attacks most of the planes on the ground were hit and destroyed. When the runway was damaged, after the first attack, the ground crew went out to try to repair it. However, a second wave of Israeli planes came and killed seven of the crew, after which no more attempts were made to go out to work on the runway. By noon all the MiG-21s and the MiG-19s were destroyed and only five remained of all the Sukhoys.

The victory of the air force was the most dramatic in the war. But the breakthrough of the tanks corps under the command of General Tal in the first day of the war, when one of his battalions reached el-Arish, was no less decisive. This battle, together with the night attack of General Sharon over the hills of Um Katif and Abu Ageila, broke the back of the Egyptian defences, in the fortified "triangle" area and made the dash towards Suez possible. The only precise orders that Tal and Sharon had received from General Rabin were to overrun the Egyptian fortifications as rapidly as possible. Further advance depended upon two factors: the speed with which these two positions were taken, and the amount of time left to the Israelis before a cease-fire was imposed.

General Tal's division, almost completely armoured, was the first to attack this Egyptian hedgehog in the northern sector along the road from Rafa to el-Arish. Facing it were units of the Palestinian 20th Division and the Egyptian 7th Division, comprising some six infantry brigades, two artillery brigades and 100 tanks. The attack began at precisely 0815 on Monday 5 June, half an hour after the first waves of Israeli aircraft had taken off to attack Egyptian airfields. One of the Israeli armoured brigades broke through the Egyptian lines to the north of Rafa, headed rapidly for the town of Khan Yunis, and then turned southwards and attacked the Rafa complex from its flank. The speed and power of this assault carried the brigade through the town, and, without pausing to secure its hold on it, the brigade swept on along the road to el-Arish, engaging in battle with Egyptian units all the way. At the same time other units in General Tal's division engaged the main Egyptian forces in the Rafa perimeter, who outnumbered the Israelis by more than two to one, and who had the advantage of defending well-entrenched positions. After five hours of bitter fighting, in which both sides suffered heavy casualties, the Egyptian defence caved in. The Israelis then sent a brigade to back up the armoured force battling its way towards el-Arish, while the remaining force continued to deal with the powerful remnants of the 7th Division in the Rafa region. The battle was by no means the walk-over imagined by so many. The Egyptians fought resolutely and determinedly. During the day they reassembled their forces and reorganized their lines. Rafa and other fortified positions had to be taken and retaken twice or even three times in a day of hard fighting. One of the present authors entered Rafa in the wake of the armoured brigade and found the town a death-trap, as Egyptian snipers shot at Israeli soldiers, and others continued to put up fierce resistance, even though the town had fallen into Israeli hands hours earlier.

But the swift pace and the momentum of the onslaught were too much for the Egyptians. In the first twenty-four hours of the war, the Israeli armoured brigade, commanded by a 35-year old colonel, advanced more than 35 miles to beyond el-Arish, overrunning four fortified positions manned by three Egyptian brigades on the way. The 16th and 11th Brigades of the Egyptian army had been well entrenched on both sides of the highway at Sheikh Zued, approximately half-way between Rafa and el-Arish, and were supported by units of the 49th Field Artillery Brigade. The 57th Artillery Brigade was in position at Giradeh, a strongly fortified point 10 miles to the west of Sheikh Zued. The 16th Brigade held up the Israeli advance, but an Israeli force outflanked the 11th Brigade and succeeded in breaking into Sheikh Zued. According to Egyptian planning, their forces should have fallen back to their second line at Giradeh, but the momentum of the Israeli attack made an orderly retreat impossible. Of thirty-six 122 mm howitzers of the 49th Brigade at Sheikh Zued, only four reached Giradeh. But the Egyptians fought on with everything they had. They succeeded in encircling one of the Israeli armoured battalions which had swept forward to the outskirts of el-Arish, and prepared an ambush for it in case it tried to retreat. But once more the Israelis proved to be masters of the indirect approach. A second battalion came to the aid of the encircled forces by advancing along the sea-shore without the Egyptians noticing it, and, at the same time, the main Israeli force outflanked the Egyptian positions to the south. By midnight on 5 June el-Arish was in Israeli hands, and the remnants of the 7th Division were fleeing westwards.

Meanwhile, farther south, the two other divisional groups of the Israelis, under General Yoffe and General Sharon, were on the move. General Yoffe, a burly 54-year-old reserve officer, ran the Nature Reserve Authority until he was mobilized for the war. He had taught the Israelis not to pick wild flowers and had done a great deal to develop nature reserves in Israel. Now he was commanding two armoured brigades composed entirely of reserve troops. The task of one of these brigades was to make their way through the sea of sand-dunes between the northern road to el-Arish and the central axis of Abu Ageila and reach the roads linking el-Arish with Abu Ageila and, more important,

with Gebel Libni, in order to prevent any counter-attack from
being mounted to save el-Arish, and to ambush the fleeing
remnants of the 7th Division as they made their way southwards.
Throughout the first day of fighting General Yoffe's men moved
forward along a route which had been considered impassable,
often floundering in the deep sands. For them the enemy that
day was the terrain, not the Egyptians. But by evening they were
firmly astride the roads, intercepting every Egyptian vehicle
attempting to pass.

The most formidable of the Egyptian defences was the complex of fortifications in the Abu Ageila area. This was one vast
concrete stronghold of underground tunnels and bunkers,
sunken pill-boxes, communication and fire-trenches stretching
for two miles, and surrounded by innumerable barbed-wire
entanglements interspersed with deep minefields. The fortifications had been built according to Soviet precepts and under the
supervision of Russian engineers. It was now manned by four
battalions of infantry and six regiments of artillery, supported
by ninety tanks ready to mount a counter-offensive in case of
an Israeli attack. Abu Ageila, more than any other spot, was
the key to Sinai. It lay astride the central axis and the road from
the north-east to the centre of the peninsula. Whoever controlled
these vital cross-roads held the Sinai open before him. The
capture of Abu Ageila was entrusted to General Arik Sharon,
who, in his late thirties, was the youngest of the generals on the
southern front. With a handsome, slightly Roman face, his hair
turning grey and slightly too big a paunch, his personality would
be striking among any group of men. In the early 'fifties he had
been given command of the paratroopers and turned them into
the crack commandos who executed the difficult retaliatory
raids that preceded the Sinai Campaign. He combined a first-
class theoretical mind with an adventurous—verging on
dangerous—use of military force, and the plan he now devised
was so complicated and daring that the Chief of Staff objected
to it and had to be persuaded of its feasibility. The plan
envisaged a simultaneous night attack by infantry, armour and

paratroop forces coming from three different directions. Lack of co-ordination could easily have brought disaster, but the entire operation went off with clock-like precision. The paratroops were landed by helicopter behind the Egyptian position and dealt with the artillery regiments. The main body of infantry was, incongruously enough, brought up to the attacking point in mud-smeared civilian buses which had vanished from the roads of Israel during the period of crisis. This infantry force bore the brunt of the fighting which continued throughout the night as trench after trench was cleared, often in hand-to-hand fighting. But by morning Abu Ageila had been taken, and the road to the centre of Sinai lay open.

By this time the Egyptian High Command was already fast losing control of events. General Mortagi, commander of the Egyptian forces in Sinai, sought to save the situation by ordering two massive counter-attacks, one to recapture el-Arish, and the other against General Sharon's forces which were still engaged in bitter fighting for Abu Ageila. The first attack was foiled by the brigade of General Yoffe's division which had taken up positions south of Bir Lahfan on the roads leading southwards from el-Arish to Gebel Libni to the south-west, and Abu Ageila to the south-east. As the Egyptian armoured force moved northwards toward el-Arish they drove straight into General Yoffe's brigade which, with the advantage of surprise on its side, almost completely destroyed the attacking force. The second counter-attack never even got started. The 14th Brigade, which was given the assignment, was pinned down by constant air strikes and got nowhere near Abu Ageila. After these two attempts the Egyptian High Command ceased to play any part in the unfolding battle. It gave the general order to retreat, but from then on it was up to every field commander to extricate his men and equipment as best he could. The rout had begun.

Yet at that time more than half the Egyptian forces in Sinai, including the crack 4th Armoured Division at Bir Gifgafa, the 6th Division in the Nakhl area, the 3rd Division at Bir Hasane and the Shazli task force, were still virtually intact. They had not yet seen battle, and were still fresh at a time when the smaller Israeli attacking force had, with the exception of only a number of small units, been fighting uninterruptedly for twenty-four hours. With determination, initiative and leadership, the Egyptians could still have put up a stiff fight and halted the Israeli advance, or, at the very least, avoided the disorganized rout which cost them the larger part of their army and the loss of all Sinai. But these factors were sorely lacking. By the second day of the fighting the communication system had broken down. The Egyptian High Command had only a hazy notion of what was happening at the front. And it had no means of passing down orders to isolated units locked in battle with the Israelis. There were thus no instructions, and the lack of leadership, of independent judgment and of initiative now began to tell. Very few officers were willing to take matters in their own hands. The retreat was on, and as they moved down the few roads available in Sinai they were pounded again and again by the Israeli Air Force. In the confusion created by large masses of tanks and half-tracks, both Egyptian and Israeli, moving in the same direction, there were numerous clashes. At one time an Israeli armoured unit found itself moving in the midst of a larger Egyptian force. The tanks advanced together for several moments until the Israeli commander gave a curt order to his men: "Wheel off sharply to the right of the road and shoot up every tank that remains on the road."

The Israeli objective was now to destroy the Egyptian forces in Sinai; the Egyptian aim was to achieve an orderly retreat to the second line of defence, hinging on Bir Gifgaga and Bir Thamade. For the Israelis to achieve their purpose, they would have to block the two roads leading through central Sinai to the Suez Canal: one to Ismailia through Bir Hama and Bir Gifgaga, the other to Suez through Bir Thamade and the Mitla Pass. Thus, more than ever, speed became the essential factor as the Israelis strove to cut off the Egyptian retreat along these roads.

All three Israeli divisions took part in this headlong advance eastwards. General Tal's division had, as we have seen, entered el-Arish by midnight on 5 June. His forces thereupon split into two, one continuing to advance along the coastal road, while the other, turning southwards, occupied Bir Lahfan without losing a man, and continued to advance on the road to Gebel Libni and Bir Gifgafa. By nightfall on 6 June General Tal's troops had advanced half-way across Sinai along the coastal road while his second force had passed Gebel Libni and reached the vicinity of Bir Hama, in the area held by the still-intact Egyptian 3rd Division. General Sharon, after capturing Abu Ageila on the morning of 6 June, turned southwards and headed through difficult terrain for the key oasis of Nakhl, in an attempt to cut off the retreat of the troops of the Egyptian 6th Division. By the night of 6 June his troops had covered only a small part of the way. Throughout 7 June they continued their advance southwards, reaching Nakhl on 8 June. The third Israeli division, as we have seen, had made its way through the sand-dunes to the Gebel Libni cross-roads where it was later joined by troops of General Tal's division. Thereupon they split forces, Tal's men advancing along the central route to Bir Gifgafa, and Yoffe's heading for Bir Thamade and the vital Mitla Pass. By nightfall on 6 June Yoffe's advance armoured brigade was pressing steadily forward, but still had a long way to go before reaching the Egyptian second line of defence at Bir Thamade, held by units of the Egyptian 4th Armoured Division.

Thus, by the morning of 7 June, after forty-eight hours of fighting, the situation of the Egyptians was grave but all was not yet lost. They had lost their forward positions; their troops were in retreat, but the Israelis were still a long way off from their second line of defence, and a large part of the Egyptian armoured force was still intact.

But by the end of the third day of fighting, on 7 June, the chances the Egyptians might have had of halting the Israeli advance were fast disappearing. Throughout the day armour clashed with armour as the Israelis continued their rapid advance into the areas held by the Egyptian 3rd, 4th and 6th Divisions.

By nightfall the northern arm of General Tal's armoured division had captured the village of Rumani, and only swampland separated it from the Suez Canal. Tal's second force had captured the air base at Bir Gifgafa after inflicting heavy losses on units of the 4th Armoured Division, which did not, however, prevent the Egyptians from making a surprise counter-attack on an Israeli force of light AMX tanks, a number of which were knocked out. Further south, a series of tank battles was being waged between the Egyptians and General Yoffe's men, in which superior marksmanship, deeper knowledge of getting the maximum out of their tanks, and greater initiative of their commanders gave the Israelis the upper hand despite the fact that they were engaged with forces far larger than their own. By nightfall Bir Thamade had fallen and the Israelis had reached the vicinity of the Mitla Pass. The road to Suez was now barred to the Egyptians, and a scene of terrible destruction unfolded as hundreds of Egyptian tanks, half-tracks and trucks converged on the Pass, only to be pounded to bits by the guns of General Yoffe's tanks and the cannon of the Israeli Air Force. In all these battles hundreds of Egyptian tanks were put out of action or were abandoned intact, and their crews joined the ever-growing stream of soldiers making their way on foot to Suez. The Israelis were by this time almost completely exhausted after having fought non-stop for three days and two nights, but they fought on, not giving the Egyptians any chance to regroup.

Almost unnoticed, a force of Israeli troops were landed unopposed at Sharm el-Sheikh and occupied the vital entrance of the Gulf of Aqaba without firing a shot. The following day, 8 June, saw the final collapse of the Egyptian army in Sinai as Israeli troops reached the Suez Canal and occupied the western coastline of the peninsula. On that day General Sharon's troops reached Nakhl, where an entire Egyptian armoured brigade was wiped out in a pitched battle with one of General Sharon's brigades. Fierce battles continued all day long as the remnants of the 6th Division sought to extricate itself from the trap that General Sharon had sprung by taking Nakhl.

By the end of the day it was virtually all over. Sinai was in Israeli hands. The Egyptians had left behind the debris of their army. The wrecks of their tanks, guns and trucks lay scattered across the sands, a wanton memorial of their defeat.

THE LINES OF DEPLOYMENT IN
JORDAN AND SYRIA

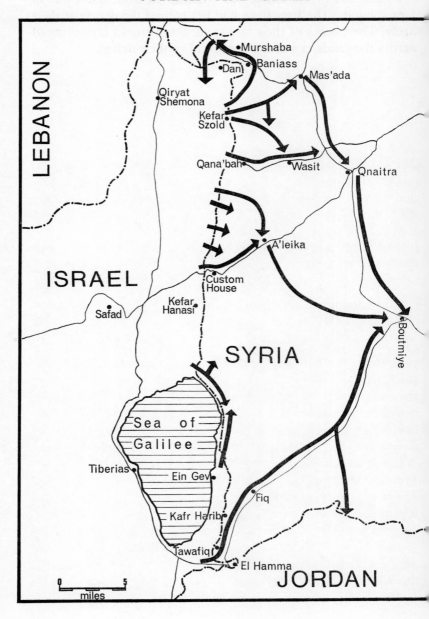

CHAPTER 10

The War in the North

The fighting had ended in Sinai, but Israel was still at war. Her leaders had hoped to limit the fighting to the southern front, and to this purpose had sent a Note via General Odd Bull, the Chief of the UN Truce Supervision Team, informing him that Jordan would not be attacked if the King kept his country out of the war. This message, whose receipt in Jordan was confirmed by General Bull, read:

> "We are engaged in defensive fighting on the Egyptian sector and we shall not engage ourselves in any action against Jordan, unless Jordan attacks us. Should Jordan attack Israel, we shall go against her with all our might."

In the 1956 Suez War Jordan, despite its defence treaty with the Egyptians, had kept quiet. The Israelis were confident that the same would happen this time. General Uzi Narkiss, commander of the central front, was told that Headquarters calculated there would be no war with Jordan. The number of troops assigned to him was, therefore, kept to a bare minimum. When Jordanian artillery began shelling Jewish Jerusalem on Monday morning, 5 June, the Israelis were not unduly alarmed. They were convinced that King Hussein was anxious to prove his loyalty to the Arab cause, and was sending off, in General Narkiss's words, "some salvos to uphold his honour". A second Note was sent off past-haste calling on the King to desist. At this time the Israelis still had no intention of attacking the West Bank. Their deployment was purely defensive. Troops were given strict orders not to take any offensive action (not even patrols) along the border. Each sector had its offensive plans "just in case", but the order was not to use them. But when the Jordanian shelling intensified, not only in Jerusalem but along the entire border, and when troops of the Jordanian army occupied UN headquarters at Government House, the former residence of British High Commissioners, the Israelis realized that the Jordanians were not just putting on a show, and the war began in earnest.

Few wars, however, could be more different from the war in Sinai than the fighting in the hills of Judea and Samaria. Whereas the Sinai war was one of movement of large masses of tanks, the fighting in the West Bank was conducted in heavily populated areas, and in the hills where the movement of armour was hindered, manœuvrability was less extensive, and the forces involved were far smaller. While over ten divisions of Egyptians and Israelis were fighting in the Sinai desert, the war for the West Bank was conducted by smaller units, of battalions and brigades, and the total size of both armies involved was only slightly larger than three divisions. But the fate of Jerusalem was involved, which, for Arab and Jew alike, had an emotion-laden importance out of all proportion to its military significance. It was around Jerusalem that the main battles were fought. The Jordanians had eight brigades deployed on the West Bank. Of these the 3rd ,or King Talal Brigade, was stationed in Jerusalem, a second was situated in the hills to the west of Jerusalem, a third, the 29th, was to the south of the city and a fourth, the 27th Brigade, was in reserve half-way between Jerusalem and Jericho. Against this force the Israelis mustered three brigades, all three of which were composed of reserve troops. The main strength on the Jordanian front was, however, to have been the Iraqi forces who were moving through East Jordan on their way to take up positions on the Israeli frontier. The plan devised by the new commander of the Jordanian front, the Egyptian General abd al-Munim Riad, was to concentrate four Iraqi brigades opposite Natanya for offensive operations. This would have represented the gravest threat to the Israelis, with the bulk of their army tied down in Sinai. But the Iraqis never reached their destination. Repeated air strikes played havoc with their columns and by the time they reached the river Jordan, the West Bank was entirely in Israeli hands.

The Jordanians had offensive plans of their own. Although the deployment of their troops was defensive in nature, Jordanian documents which fell into Israel hands reveal that they had plans for capturing Mount Scopus, Kibbutz Ramat Rahel to the south of Jerusalem, the range of the Gilboa hills, Bir Main and Kibbutz Shaalavim in the Latrun area, and Government House in Jerusalem—the former residence of British High Commissioners which now served as the UN Truce Supervision Headquarters. King Hussein scrapped the plan at the last minute, and decided to go for the Government House only.

The occupation of Government House by the Jordanians posed a threat to the entire southern part of Jewish Jerusalem, and General Narkiss with the approval of General Headquarters ordered one of his units to dislodge the Jordanians. No less a cause for concern for the Israelis was the concentration of Jordanian troops around Mount Scopus, a tiny enclave of Jewish territory behind Jordanian lines, an anomaly from the days of the 1948 war. As the Jordanian shelling and shooting in the Jerusalem area intensified towards midday of 5 June the Israeli armoured brigade which served as a general reserve for the central front received orders to move up towards Jerusalem from its rear positions near Tel Aviv in order to break through and relieve the garrison which had been isolated on Mount Scopus for the last 19 years. It started moving in the early afternoon of 5 June and, after five hours on the road, went immediately into the attack on two of the most dominating hills to the north-west of Jerusalem. Throughout the night the brigade advanced under heavy fire across difficult terrain which had been liberally mined, but by midnight it had broken through the range of hills to the north of Jerusalem and a secondary road leading to the

G

Jerusalem–Ramallah highway was virtually opened for the Israeli tanks. These moved slowly and carefully, aided by flares and by air strikes made repeatedly and precisely by Israeli-assembled Fouga Magistère jet training planes. By early morning the brigade had taken the village of Nebi Samuel, perched on a steep escarpment overlooking Jerusalem, had crossed the Ramallah road near Sharafat and was in battle with the Jordanians in the last hills before contacting Mount Scopus. This last battle cost the brigade heavy casualties, but long before noon Mount Scopus was relieved from its 19-year siege. Meanwhile, inside Jerusalem itself, the most dramatic encounter of the war was unfolding as the paratroop brigade fought for the city in a pitched battle which lasted for just over thirty hours, from 2 a.m. on Tuesday morning until the final capture of the Old City of Jerusalem on Wednesday morning, 7 June, at 10 o'clock. Both this action, and that of the armoured brigade, had been initially approved by GHQ as local attacks only, with the limited objective of linking up with Mount Scopus. The paratroops had, at first, been given orders to break through the Jordanian-held Jerusalem suburb of Sheikh Jarrah, which was the shortest route to Mount Scopus. There was, at the beginning of the fighting, no decision to capture all of Jerusalem, let alone the entire West Bank. The paratroop brigade, commanded by Colonel Gur, had initially been assigned to the Sinai front, and were bivouacked near an air base in the south of Israel, when, in the early afternoon of Monday, 5 June, they were ordered to pack up and move in buses to Jerusalem, where they arrived in the early evening. The senior officers, already at headquarters in Jerusalem, were studying the maps, for they were totally unprepared for their new assignment in Sheikh Jarrah. Most of the men in this crack brigade, which was largely made up of reservists, had no experience of fighting in a built-up area and had no knowledge of the topography of Jerusalem. But they were experts at night fighting. Their commander decided, therefore, to begin their attack immediately rather than wait for air cover early the following morning. For various reasons it took the brigade longer than anticipated to spread out along the northern area of Jerusalem to the east and west of the Mandelbaum Gate, and the actual attack began only at 0200 hours on Tuesday, 6 June, by which time the armoured brigade was already known to have broken through the Jordanian defences to the north-west of Jerusalem. Night fighting in built-up areas against a well-entrenched enemy is a complicated matter, which can well lead to many casualties, and in which the commanders can easily lose contact with the larger part of their units. This was the case in the fighting for Sheikh Jarrah, which, trench by trench, bunker by bunker, was cleared by the paratroops, who were having far more casualties than they admitted. The line of communication remained open, but little information as to the extent of the casualties was given. All they would say was, everything is going according to plan. In the early morning they had penetrated into the fortified police school which was used as an UNWRA building and were in the American Colony on the way to Rockefeller Museum. The men were not acquainted with the roads in the new part of East Jerusalem and started pushing towards the Old City instead of northwards towards the Rockefeller Museum. At the same time, the units that had taken the UNWRA building moved through Sheikh Jarrah on to Mount Scopus. After the link-up with Mount Scopus was completed, General Narkiss appealed to the Minister of Defence, Moshe Dayan, to be given permission to attack the Old City. General Dayan is reported to have hesitated, saying, "We will never be forgiven if we fail", to which General Narkiss is said to have replied: "History will never forgive you if you don't exploit this chance." General Dayan agreed and brought the matter to the Government for urgent approval.

Fighting slowed down towards the afternoon in Jerusalem although it persisted around the Mount of Olives where efforts were made by the paratroopers to take the strongholds around Victoria Augusta. There were further casualties there, too. At the same time other troops were closing in on Jerusalem from

the west in anticipation of taking the Old City. By the evening
the Old City was virtually encircled. In the morning of Wednesday, almost all resistance broke down, although sniping continued, and at 1000 the paratroopers broke into the Old City
and speedily overcame all resistance. This, as far as the Israelis
were concerned, was the high point of the war. All else, including the spectacular victories in Sinai, paled into insignificance
compared to the fact that the Temple area was once more, after
two thousand years, in Israeli hands.

Meanwhile, the Armoured Brigade had occupied the town of
Ramallah on Tuesday evening and continued down towards the
Dead Sea and Jericho, which it captured without any dificulty.
Once more events in the battlefield were preceding decisions at
General Headquarters. The Brigade had swept through Jericho
when it was ordered back because GHQ still feared that the
Iraqis might bring in armour in force in the central sector facing
Israel's narrow waistline at Natanya. With the armour down in
Jericho and the northern forces still occupied with the capture
of Jenin, such a move could be dangerous. The advance on
Jericho was only permitted the following afternoon,Wednesday
7 June, when it became plain that the Jordanian front had
collapsed and there was nothing more to fear in the central
sector.

The Jerusalem Brigade advanced southwards and took
Bethlehem and Hebron with hardly a shot being fired. But farther
to the north Jordanian resistance was much tougher and the
Israelis suffered heavy casualties in the battle for the town of
Jenin. Here again the Israeli advance had not been intially
planned, but was undertaken in reaction to moves by the Jordanians. General Elazar, commander of the northern front,
asked for permission from GHQ to attack Jenin, claiming that
Jordanian artillery in its vicinity was shelling a vital air base in
central Israel. Permission to silence the Jordanian guns was
granted, on the understanding that the action would be a limited
one. But once more the battle extended beyond initial intentions.
The Israelis, however, were operating on a flexible plan of

action. There was a great deal of improvization. Plans of attack existed for virtually every possible eventuality and the commanders had learnt these plans at staff colleges and in army exercises. Thus when it came to the real thing, the old plans were executed with hardly a hitch. And once the Jordanian front began to cave in, the Israelis went through in hot pursuit.

With the fall of Jerusalem, the resistance of the Jordanian army crumbled. By Wednesday afternoon, all shooting had stopped and by the night of Wednesday, the whole West Bank was virtually in Israeli hands—the last of the bridges over the Jordan still in Jordanian hands fell to the Israelis at 06 25 on Thursday morning, 8 June. For the first twenty-four hours the Jordanians had fought well and then they had just broken up. One of the major reasons for this was the peculair behaviour of King Hussein himself. Throughout the fighting he displayed extreme nervousness and lack of confidence. He was constantly in touch with President Nasser; he continually asked for advice and opinions, and changed his mind repeatedly. All this was, perhaps, understandable, considering the circumstances. But what caused irrevocable damage to the ability of the Jordanians to withstand the Israeli onslaught was the fact that within twenty-four hours he gave the order to retreat from the West Bank three times; each time he changed his mind and rescinded the order shortly afterwards, but after the withdrawal had already got under way. These orders and counter-orders created tremendous confusion. Troops left their posts and concentrated in the army camps ready for crossing the Jordan, only to be told to return to their posts. By the third time confusion reigned supreme. King Hussein's culpability on this score is one of the best-kept secrets in Jordan today. The army officers who know the truth do not dare make it public. But Jordanian prisoners of war were not so reticent. The reason for the King's inconsistency was that his desire to defend the West Bank was counter-balanced by his wish to save his army for another day. He could not allow its destruction. He, therefore, vacillated between the two, to the detriment of both.

Another reason for the quick collapse of the Jordanians was the poor deployment of the Jordanian army. In the days of General Glubb, the British conception of a proper defence deployment was to keep the main forces in the hill region, with the outlying villages in the frontier area only sparsely defended. In this manner, General Glubb had argued, the Israelis could be blocked from gaining a foothold in the hills of Judea and Samaria, while reinforcements could always be sent to any of the frontier villages in case of an Israeli attack. This defence concept was scrapped in 1962 when the National Guards were established for the prime purpose of defending the forward positions. In March 1965 the National Guards were disbanded. It had been an almost totally Palestinian formation, and its loyalty to the régime could not be assured. It was also feared that with the strengthening of Ahmad Shuqairi's Palestine Liberation Organization the Arab countries would press Jordan to transfer the Palestinian National Guards to Shuqairi's command. The Jordanians decided, therefore, to create five new Jordanian brigades instead of the National Guards, but their establishment had not yet been completed in June 1967. The defence of the forward positions, however, was now maintained by the regular army in place of the disbanded National Guardsmen. Instead of being concentrated in key positions in the hills, as Glubb had envisaged, the regular forces were now largely dispersed along the border. But the army was hard put to fill the gap left by the departed National Guards. In the past, in the northern sector, six National Guard battalions had guarded the Jenin area with one infantry brigade as a general reserve, while another twelve National Guard battalions with an infantry brigade in reserve had been stationed in the Nablus sector. But in 1967 there were only six infantry battalions defending the front lines where before fifteen National Guard battalions had been stationed and now there were no reserves. One Jordanian battalion, the 20th, or "Tarik ben Ziad" as it was called, was spread out in squads and platoons along almost ten miles of the border, while a second battalion had three companies in the Yabad area and the fourth near Bir Asin. According to plan, these units, if attacked, should have retreated to an area about nine miles to the south of the border and regrouped. This could have been done if the Jordanians had had to deal only with enemy infantry. But the plan was unworkable because of Israeli air superiority which did not give the Jordanian infantry a chance to reorganize. As a result, when the Jenin area was attacked by the Israelis on Monday night, the fighting was heavy throughout the night but the following morning the Israeli air strikes foiled all Jordanian attempts to move over the mountain roads in order to regroup, and heavy casualties were inflicted as convoys were shot up and bombed. The heavy fighting that did take place the following morning in the Dotan Valley to the south of Jenin occurred when a Jordanian armoured brigade, which had moved up during the night from the Jordan Valley, made a strong counter-attack, which was, however, thrown back after a pitched battle.

Another reason for the quick collapse of the Jordanian front must be sought in the character of the Jordanian army. The Arab Legion under Brigadier Glubb had been by far the best fighting unit in the Arab world. The officers had been mostly British, the soldiers semi-literate Bedouin on long-term contracts, tough, independent, well-versed in field-craft and in desert warfare. With a rifle in their hands, they were formidable fighters. But times changed. The British officers were expelled. The character of Jordan's population was changed with the annexation of the rump of Palestine. The needs and the tasks of the army changed, too. On the one hand it was entrusted with policing the turbulent population of the West Bank. On the other it had to modernize, to jettison the camel for the tank. The semi-literate Bedouin, the backbone of the Arab Legion, were passed over for promotion in favour of more educated elements who were felt to be more suitable for the needs of a modern army, but who lacked the special qualities which had made the Bedouin such a fine soldier. Thus the Jordanian army gradually took on the characteristics of the other Arab armies, political appointments and all. One of these was the appointment of Major-General Muhammad Ahmad Salim al-Bataniya as commander of the West Bank. An affable man of very large proportions, the first thing that General al-Bataniya did when the war became imminent was to transfer himself and his household goods from the Jerusalem area to Jericho and later to the eastern bank of the Jordan, from where he directed the war. There were other cases of service officers deserting their posts, such as Major Shams ed-din Aref, the commander of a battalion of brand-new Patton tanks which were abandoned intact in the Hebron district. In fighting of infantry against infantry the Jordanians proved to be formidable and the Israelis suffered many casualties. But as soon as the armour moved in, their fighting resistance dropped considerably. A typical example was the case of the Jordanian 10th Battalion, which was rushed up to reinforce the Radar heights to the north-west of Jerusalem, a vital vantage point defending the Jerusalem–Ramallah highway. When the soldiers saw the advancing tanks of the Israeli armoured brigade they turned and fled.

All these reasons helped to bring about the speedy collapse of the Jordanians in the face of an enemy numerically weaker, whose best units were tied down in Sinai. But, as in Sinai, the overall mastery of the air proved to be the most important factor in Israel's quick victory. By the evening of the first day's fighting all of Jordan's first-line aircraft had been destroyed. Israeli aircraft were free to roam Jordanian airspace at will, and they wrought terrible destruction to military convoys caught in the narrow, winding mountain roads of the West Bank.

The battle against the Jordanians had been unexpected, and the Israelis had entered it reluctantly. They had hoped that the Jordanians would remain as peaceful as the Lebanese. Had they done so, the Old City of Jerusalem and Cis-Jordan would still be in Jordanian hands. The Lebanese themselves were only saved from a similar fate by the sagacity of their Chief of Staff,

General Bustani. After the war had continued for forty-eight hours, Lebanon's Prime Minister, Rashid Karame, decided that the Lebanon could not sit by idly when all the other Arab states bordering Israel were fighting their enemy. He had evidently not yet heard of the destruction of the Egyptian air force, nor of the rapid advance of the Israelis into Sinai. Karame thereupon ordered his Chief of Staff to commence offensive action and to advance across the frontier into Upper Galilee. General Bustani refused to comply, on the grounds that the Lebanese army was no match for the Israelis and that such a move would be tantamount to suicide. Greatly incensed, the Prime Minister called in the Military Police and ordered them to arrest the General. It was now their turn to refuse to obey an order of the Prime Minister. They were loyal to their general, they maintained, and refused to take any step against him. In the meantime, news of the Arab defeats began to percolate through to Beirut, and Karame evidently realized that General Bustani had been right. The incident was hastily hushed up, and the Lebanese came through the war unscathed.

But the Israelis had no illusions regarding their northern neighbour, Syria. It had been the Syrians who had caused the trouble which sparked off war. No one in Israel expected them to keep quiet once the war began and, in contrast to the situation with Jordan or the Lebanon, no one wished to see the Syrians go unpunished. Yet on the first day of the war the Syrian front was the quietest of all. While the Jordanian guns opened up all along the front, the Syrian artillery remained ominously quiet. For the Syrians first wanted to know what was happening to the Egyptians before risking their own forces. They ignored the Egyptian pleas to open a second front. As we have seen, the Syrians were incensed by the Egyptian–Jordanian Treaty, and by the fact that the Egyptians had taken this step without even informing them beforehand. Now they were not going to stick their necks out for the sake of Cairo.

They did, however, have their offensive plans ready in case all went well on the southern front. These plans later fell into

Israeli hands, together with many thousands of top-secret military and intelligence documents, which the Israelis found in the regional military headquarters at Quneitra. According to these documents, the Syrians intended launching a large-scale attack in their central sector facing Mishmar Hayarden. The offensive, to be mounted with a force above divisional strength, had been planned in accordance with classic Soviet military doctrine. After breaking through at Mishmar Hayarden, the major Syrian force intended to advance on Haifa, with two secondary thrusts southwards to Nazareth and Afula. A second Syrian force was to have advanced through Lebanese territory towards Acre, while a third force was scheduled to mount a diversionary attack on Tel Dan, Kibbutz Dan and Shear Yishuv.

The Syrians deployed their forces in order to be ready to implement this plan. An assault force, consisting of several infantry brigades, an armoured and a mechanized brigade and a special commando force, was assembled opposite Mishmar Hayarden. Additional armoured units took up positions on the road from Quneitra to the assembly point of the assault force. Deeper in the rear, two infantry brigades, the 32nd and the 90th, were placed to the south and the north of Quneitra. Three more brigades manned the fortified positions along the frontier. A total of 65,000 men, 350 tanks, 300 artillery pieces and 200 anti-aircraft guns were massed in the 40-miles stretch of territory facing Israel.

Against this concentration of troops the Israelis mustered a far weaker force, which, during the first three days of the war, was drawn up in defensive positions. The major objective of the Israelis during those first days was to minimize the extent of possible damage by firing on the Syrian batteries, and, to the extent that there might be a ground attack, to prevent the capture of any Israeli position or settlement.

Yet despite this superiority in numbers during the first days of the war, the Syrian offensive failed to materialize. The only part of the plan to be implemented was the diversionary attack on Tel Dan. In the central sector facing Mishmar Hayarden, the Syrian concentrations were heavily shelled and bombed on 6 June, with the result that their deployment was disrupted. By 7 June it had already become clear to the Syrians that the Egyptian front had collapsed, and they called off their offensive. As for their attack on Tel Dan, it was a desultory affair. It was mounted by the 243rd Battalion of the 11th Brigade, aided by two T-34 tank companies, with the 2nd National Guard Battalion giving supporting fire. The attack was to have taken place at 0545 in the morning of 6 June, but was then postponed for a full hour as the battalion was not ready. An artillery bombardment began early in the morning and the battalion moved from Han ed-Dvir at the foot of Tel Hamra towards Dan. The assault was repulsed by the kibbutz members, and at 0815 the brigade commander ordered the battalion commander to stop the attack and retreat. This turned into a rout which cost the Syrians many casualties. Six Syrian tanks were knocked out and remained in the battle area.

One of the points learnt by the Israelis from the prisoners taken from the 243rd and other battalions was that the officers followed their troops into the attack at a distance of at least 50 yards, a fact which did not encourage the fighting spirit of the soldiers. In the fighting that took place later, it was found that wherever the officers stood fast and gave encouragement to their troops, as at the battle for Tel Faq'r, the Syrians fought well. There were many cases, however, where the officers were the first to turn and flee, leaving the soldiers to extricate themselves from the fighting as best they could. In at least two cases the Israelis found Syrian soldiers chained to their guns to prevent them from fleeing.

By Wednesday, June 7, the Jordanians had been defeated, and the war in Sinai was nearing its end. The turn of Syria had come. The powerful kibbutz organizations were exerting heavy pressure on the Government to take action to free the kibbutzim along the Syrian border from the ever-present threat of Syrian guns. The Ministers of Ahdut Ha'avoda, the left-wing party

heavily dependent on the kibbutz movement, strongly urged the
Government to take an immediate decision. Yet despite this
pressure the Government hesitated, and, surprisingly enough,
leading the "doves" was the Minister of Defence, Moshe
Dayan. He strongly opposed any action against Syria as long as
Israeli troops were still engaged in the south. Such a step, he
asserted, would be one of extreme irresponsibility. The Syrian
front would be the hardest to break, the one that would cost
Israel the highest rate of casualties. Syria, moreover, was backed
to the hilt by the Soviet Union, and an attack on her could lead
to consequences over which Israel would not have any control.
No decision was taken on the Wednesday, though even if there
had been one, thick mists over the Syrian plateau on Thursday
would have made an attack virtually impossible. But in the
afternoon, as the mists cleared, the Syrian guns opened up with
renewed intensity. Dayan once more weighed the chances and
decided to act. He contacted General Elazar, commander of the
northern front, and ordered him to prepare for attack, and then
informed the Prime Minister of his recommendation to reply
in force to the Syrian barrage. Mr Eshkol agreed with alacrity.

Such an offensive, however, was no easy matter. The hills
of Syria rise in a steep escarpment 1,000 feet above the Israeli
plains below. The Syrians were sitting in a natural fortress,
strengthened by triple lines of defence, each as imposing and
formidable in their way as the Maginot Line or the Atlantic
Wall. Deep concrete-reinforced underground bunkers, 5-foot
thick concrete gun-emplacements, tunnelled communication
lines, a labyrinth of basalt-lined fire trenches, guarded by broad
belts of mines, wire entanglements and concrete dragon's-
teeth, blocked the access routes to the plateau above. The line
was studded with bunkered tanks and artillery. One Israeli
soldier, when he saw the profusion of artillery lining the plateau,
remarked: "They planted guns here in much the same way as
the Jewish National Fund planted trees in Israel!" It was against
this citadel of rock, concrete and steel that General Elazar
launched his forces on the morning of 9 June

His plan was to smash through a single point of the defences in one concentrated attack, and then spill out in flanking movements behind the Syrian lines. For the first hours the battle was touch-and-go. General Elazar had chosen as his major point of attack one of the most difficult sectors from the point of view of terrain, to the north of Kibbutz Kfar Szold, one at which the Syrians least expected an attack. As a result, a great deal depended in the first hours on the Engineering Corps, whose men had to clear a path for the tanks under gruelling fire from the Syrians. Behind the Sappers came a column of 35 Sherman tanks, in single file, easy targets for the 130 mm and 122 mm artillery and the bazookas and anti-tank guns which rained shells on them at the rate of ten tons a minute. By the time the column reached its objective, the fortified village of Kallah, only two Shermans were still moving. The column commander had been wounded, his second-in-command killed, and a third officer who assumed command was also killed. The remnants of the force were led by a wounded young lieutenant.

At the same time, the riflemen of the "Golani" brigade scaled the neighbouring hills of Tel Faq'r and Azaziat under merciless fire and, in a three-hour battle in the trenches, fought with fists, knives, teeth and rifle-butts to overcome the Syrians. By sundown the Israelis had attained their bridgehead on the heights, at the cost of heavy casualties. The Tel Faq'r battle alone had cost them 37 dead and 82 wounded. Among the dead were a battalion commander and three company commanders, an epic illustration of the Israeli army's mode of fighting in which the officers lead their troops into battle. The following morning the Israelis continued their onslaught against the fortified positions, breaking through in the central sector to take Aalleiga, a key point, from which the Israeli columns continued south to Boutmiye and north to Quneitra. In this northern sector their troops pushed on towards the Lebanese frontier, taking the large Druze village of Majdesh-Shams on the way, and their front caved in completely when, in an attempt to force the UN to speed a cease-fire decision, the

Syrians announced over Damascus Radio that Quneitra had fallen—six hours before Israeli troops entered that key town on the road to Damascus. This announcement so demoralized the Syrian troops that they broke up and fled, and by 1430 that day Quneitra was indeed in Israeli hands, twenty-seven hours after their assault on Syria had begun. The road to Damascus was now open, and, in General Elazar's words, the Israelis could have entered the Syrian capital within another nine hours if they had so wished. The attack against the Syrians had cost the Israelis 115 killed and 322 wounded, as against the 1,000 Syrians killed, 600 captured and thousands more wounded. An enclave of Syrian territory, stretching from the Yarmuk river northwards to Boutmiye, Quneitra, and the heights of Mount Hermon to the Lebanese border remained in Israeli hands.

With the fall of Quneitra the fighting came to a virtual stop. A few hours later, at 1800 hours on 10 June, the UN cease-fire came into effect. The June War had ended.

It had taken the UN six days to part the adversaries. The initial Russian demand to combine a demand for a cease-fire with a withdrawal of Israeli forces played into Israeli hands. For it was opposed by the Americans and thus any effective and speedy UN action was stalemated. At least during the first 24 hours this Russian stand was based to a large extent on a faulty reading of the battle. The Israelis remained deliberately silent regarding their advance; the Arabs, on the other hand, were loudly proclaiming imaginary victories. The Russians, therefore, had no idea how urgent it was to obtain a rapid cease-fire. By the time they realized the extent of the calamity, the Israelis were already forging ahead, and insisting on a full Arab agreement to a cease-fire before they would halt their forces. The fact that it took the Arabs so long to swallow their pride and agree to a cease-fire cost them dear indeed.

The United Nations had proved to be powerless to prevent the war. It had now to demonstrate that it could impose peace. As silence descended on the battlefields, the scene of action shifted to the conference rooms in the United Nations Building in New York. But before we turn to the political war which took over from the war of the guns, we must first examine the effects of the fighting on the contestants themselves, the Arab countries and Israel.

Part III: Aftermath

CHAPTER 11

Victory

The Israelis first heard that victory was theirs late at night on Monday, 5 June, when General Rabin and General Hod broke their self-imposed silence and informed Israel and the world of the magnitude of the defeat which had been inflicted that day on Egypt's armed forces. From then on Israel's radio broadcast further victories hourly—the fall of Gaza, Israelis at the Wailing Wall, the West Bank in Israeli hands, Israeli units at the Suez Canal, the Star of David hoisted on Mount Hermon, the road to Damascus open. To the beleaguered Israelis, who were only just emerging from the back-to-the-wall mood of "fight to the end" which had characterized the pre-war period, the news came as all too incredible. They had expected air raids, missiles, poison gas, wholesale destruction and heavy casualties. Instead they were handed a spectacular victory of a magnitude beyond the dreams of even the greatest optimists. The shock of victory had a traumatic effect on the Israelis in much the same way as the shock of defeat had on the Arabs. But there were no victory parades, no triumphal arches in honour of the returning heroes. Beethoven and pop music were speedily restored to their rightful places on the radio programmes, in place of the martial music which had been played unceasingly during the war. Yet Israel was a transformed country after the war, politically, psychologically and geographically, and there was no turning the clock back to the days before the crisis.

Before 5 June, the Israeli Government would have been perfectly satisfied if the Egyptians had rescinded their decision to close the Gulf of Tiran and had reduced the tension along the Sinai border by a gradual return of their army to behind the Suez Canal. Now the targets were far greater. Israel was no more the poor man of the Middle East, with whom there was little need to negotiate, who had nothing to offer and whose only right of existence was purely moral—a most unimpressive factor in the present era of materialism. She had now become a power to be reckoned with. Her army had proved its worth. She now ruled over a million Arabs and occupied vast new territories. For the first time since the establishment of the state in 1948, Israel could negotiate from a position of strength. But she had been totally unprepared for the magnitude of her victory, had formed no plans how to translate it into political gains which would guarantee lasting peace. The Israeli political machine was not geared to make swift political decisions. The National Unity Government, composed of ten political parties covering the entire spectrum of political opinion, was far too cumbersome to allow for speedy action. One thing was certain. The scale of victory was such that there could be no question of Israel giving up her military gains in the manner she had been forced to do after the Suez War in 1956. For the situation this time was vastly different from 1956. Not only was the Arab defeat total but inexcusable. Israel could not this time be put in the dock as aggressor but enjoyed overwhelming international sympathy, with, above all, the US giving her firm support.

These differences go some way to explain the wave of facile optimism which swept over Israel immediately after the war. This time peace would be attained, was the general attitude. The Arabs would realize that they were no match for the Israeli army. They would cast aside their aggressive intentions, and a new era of prosperity would open in the Middle East. This feeling was exacerbated by the orgy of fraternization between Jews and Arabs in the occupied areas, and in particular in Jerusalem as the two halves of the city were once more cemented together.

But disillusionment soon set in. The miracle war was not going to lead to any magic peace. There was no sorcerer's wand to wipe away the implacable hostility of the Arab leaders towards the Jewish state. And with the disillusionment came a growing determination which embraced virtually the entire population: Israel's military victory would not be squandered cheaply; her terms for withdrawal from the newly occupied territories would be a peace settlement, and nothing short of that would induce her to budge. As the weeks passed and it became increasingly clear that the Arabs had no intention of making peace, the Israelis gradually grew accustomed to the idea that they would remain an occupying force in the new territories under their rule for a long time to come.

This realization gave birth to a wave of chauvinism which swept over Israel in the wake of the war. For was not the West Bank part of biblical Israel, the Land of the Fathers? Hebron, Jericho, Samaria and numerous other places in the newly conquered areas were biblical names which conjured up powerful emotions in the Bible-conscious people of Israel. The Government was soon being subjected to a growing pressure to annex the new territories outright. Large advertisements appeared in the Hebrew press proclaiming that "not an inch of our newly-won territory shall be relinquished". Public meetings were organized by "The Movement for the Territorial Unity of the Homeland". The entire country was being increasingly taken up in a great public debate on the future of the occupied territories. It was soon realized that there were no easy solutions. The Jewish nationalists who demanded annexation were countered by equally chauvinistic arguments which pointed to the demographic problems that would be created by annexation. Did not Zionism call for a Jewish state, they would argue. Should the Jews, for the sake of extra territory, dilute the Jewishness of their state by taking in a million extra Arabs, who, with their far higher birth-rate, would become a majority in less than a generation? The search for an ideal political solution led to a return to the grass roots of Jewish nationalism. Four major streams of thought found expression: there were the two contrasting nationalist schools of thought, one of which advocated an Israel in accordance with its biblical boundaries, while the other sought to maintain the "purity" of the Jewish state by admitting as few additional Arabs as possible. There was a pragmatic school of thought which put the accent on Israel's security: this school argued that the overriding aim of the Government should be to obtain borders which afforded maximum security for Israel's population, working on the assumption that the pre-June borders were impossible from the security point of view. The fourth major viewpoint reflected liberalism as opposed to chauvinism. The idea that Israelis should become a conquering people with their army controlling occupied territories was the very antithesis of traditional Jewish values, this line of thought insisted. The Israeli state could not exist on bayonets; this would be the negation of the basic tenets of Judaism on which the Jewish state was created.

Yet the arguments proved to be academic, devoid of reality. For all, even the liberals, were united in the conviction that Israel should remain in the occupied areas until the Arabs agreed to a political settlement which would, at the very least, provide assurance that there would be no recurrence of hostile acts such as those which had preceded the June war. The Government, therefore had no need to choose between the contrasting solutions, because the consensus of opinion in Israel agreed that it was up to the Arabs to make the first move. Thus, after several weeks of indecision, the Government agreed on a "do nothing" policy, which left all initiative for any change in the political aftermath of the war to the Arabs. The Government could hardly have acted otherwise, for the entire gamut of possible political solutions was represented within its ranks. The National Unity Government, so essential for the running of the war, was now proving to be increasingly unwieldy. The extremists in the Government were the former terrorist leader, Menahem Begin, and Yigal Alon and other Ministers of the left-leaning Ahdut Ha'avoda party. They favoured the speedy settlement of the Jews in the occupied areas, and the encouragement of Arab emigration with a view to the eventual annexation of the areas to Israel. The liberal approach was represented by the Foreign Minister, Abba Eban, who was a firm believer in a settlement with King Hussein, and by the Minister of Finance, Pinhas Sapir, who objected strongly to any idea of annexing large additional territories and opposed the idea of any fraternization with the Arabs. The religious Ministers advocated the need to defend the Jewishness of Israel, and were, therefore, opposed to adding to Israel territory heavily populated by Arabs, with the exception of eastern Jerusalem and the Etzion Hills. The left-wing Mapam Ministers were in favour of creating an independent Palestinian state in the West Bank. As for the two major figures in the Government, the Premier, Levi Eshkol, and the Minister of Defence, Moshe Dayan, both favoured the pragmatic approach of maximum security and minimal addition of Arabs to the population. Both were opposed to Alon's demands for settling the new areas with Jewish inhabitants, and both believed that there was no hurry to reach a settlement.

On one subject there was no divergence of opinion: the fate of Jerusalem. As of 7 June, the whole of Jerusalem was occupied by Israel, and it immediately became clear that, whatever the fate of the other areas occupied, Eastern Jerusalem would never be given up. Within a week the municipal boundaries of Jerusalem were redrawn to include the Old City, Mount Scopus and the Mount of Olives, Sheikh Jarrah and the suburb of Sharafat up to the airport in Kalandia (speedily renamed the Jerusalem Airport).* The Government met to decide the annexation of Jerusalem on Friday, 16 June, but the final legal form of the annexation and the possibility of international repercussions postponed the final act until 28 June when the Knesset approved the co-opting of the eastern part of Jerusalem

* There was criticism in Israel and abroad as to the size of greater Jerusalem. Possibly too big an area had been annexed. The new city boundaries left no area of land, no suburb of Jerusalem which could, in the future, in the event of settlement with the Arabs, form a base at which the capital for the Arab population living on the West Bank of the Jordan River could be established.

as part of Israel, guaranteeing the population of Arab Jerusalem full rights as citizens of Israel. In the previous three weeks, Teddy Kollek, the Mayor of Western Jerusalem, had been working round the clock, mobilizing bulldozers to tear down the wall separating the eastern and western parts of the city. He had called for all the sappers the army could give him to clear the no-man's-land of mines and booby traps. In co-operation with the municipality of the eastern part of the city, he had reactivated the municipal services of the Old City. On 29 June, the population of each side of the city were allowed to move freely to the other side. Towards the early afternoon there was hardly an Arab in the eastern part of Jerusalem, and hardly a Jew in the western part. Everyone was sightseeing, fascinated by this belated revolution in their lives. The same day the Israeli pound was declared to be the sole legal tender in greater Jerusalem. The members of the municipality of East Jerusalem declined to accept the offer of appointment as members of the greater Jerusalem municipality, although informally they were willing to co-operate as advisers to the mayor. The telephone lines in Jerusalem were connected to the Israeli lines, and within a very short time full tourist and other facilities were reopened to the public. Jerusalem was now the second largest city in Israel, with a population of over a quarter of a million people, as lively as it had been dormant in the two preceding decades. In the cafés, shops and cinemas, Jews and Arabs were fraternising in a manner which would have been considered impossible only a short while earlier. The Arab merchants enjoyed an unprecedented boom as wide-eyed Israeli bargain-hunters swarmed over their shops, buying up everything from Hebron glass to "Made in China" pencils, from damask silks to toilet soap. The annexation proved, up to a certain point, an economic success. But this was the sole unanimous decision the Government was able to take.

With such wide divergencies of opinion, it found itself unable to reach any other basic decisions of policy regarding the future of the occupied areas. The Ministers relied, instead,

on the formula of direct negotiations, and on Arab procrastination in coming to the conference table.

Yet although Israel was thus freed from laying down a basic policy regarding the future of the occupied territories, she did have to make countless day-to-day decisions regarding the current administration of the new territories she had gained so suddenly and unexpectedly. For on 12 June she found herself with more than a million Arabs to govern, and the question immediately arose of what policy she should adopt. For many Israelis the garb of conqueror made strange and uncomfortable clothing. Not since the days of Alexander Yanai, in the first century B.C., had the Jews been cast in such a role, and they entered into it diffidently at first, conscious of the unpleasant ring in the term "occupying force".

As for the Arabs of the West Bank and the Gaza Strip, the speed and completeness of the conquest had left them in a state of deep shock. The tanks which now rumbled through their streets, the troops who took up position at every street corner, were those of the enemy they had been taught to hate for the past nineteen years. Overcome with fear, they awaited the worst. They expected their women to be raped, the children to be butchered, and the menfolk to be rounded up in concentration camps. This is what they had been repeatedly told would happen if the Israelis ever succeeded in breaking into their homes.

Shortly after the occupation, one of the present authors visited a house in Tubas, a large village near Nablus. He was well received, but noticed the absence of women and children in the house. "We sent them to Amman immediately the fighting began," his host explained. After being questioned further, his host continued, hesitantly: "You see, when the Israelis approached Jenin, some Arabs from that town came here and told us that the Israeli troops were all equipped with knives which they would use to slit the throats of all women and children they found in the places they captured. Some of us managed to get our families out, but most of us didn't have the time." "And what happened to those that stayed?" he was asked. He replied, half in shame and half in wonder, "Not a single person in Tubas was harmed."

In those first hectic days during and immediately after the war, there were many excesses. There is no such thing as a war without people getting hurt, without property being destroyed, and without feelings running high. Private cars were commandeered, hotels were requisitioned to billet troops, valuables disappeared, "souvenirs" were taken, shops were raided. In this the Israelis behaved no worse than any victorious army throughout the ages, including the British and American armies in Europe in 1945. But the looting and pilfering were quickly stamped out. Within days the Israeli soldiers and civilians were paying for the food and trinkets which were passing in ever-increasing volumes from the West Bank to Israel. The excesses which the Arabs had been taught to fear—killing, raping, rounding up of men into concentration camps—never occurred.

We were visiting a house in eastern Jerusalem several days after the end of the war when there was a loud knocking on the door. Outside were ten soldiers, commanded by a young lieutenant. "We've come to search the house for arms," he told the owner of the house. "We're searching every house in the city." Outside, the occasional report of a sniper's rifle could be heard. The searches were, from the Israeli point of view, urgent and necessary. We watched the soldiers at their work. They opened every drawer and cupboard. They looked under the mattresses. They poked at the sofa and the armchairs. But nothing was broken or damaged, nothing taken, everything put back in its place. At the end of the search the young lieutenant, in halting English, offered his apologies to the Arab. "We have to do it," he said. "You should stop your snipers." They left, polite, restrained, correct, leaving the Arab completely bewildered. "I expected them to come in and smash everything," he murmured.

Not all the Israeli soldiers behaved well, but by and large the picture of the Israeli occupation which emerged in those first difficult weeks was a positive one. Even the most rabid extremists among the Palestinian Arabs had to admit that the hate propaganda had been proved wrong, and that the Israelis were doing their utmost to restore normal life as rapidly as possible. Crews of Israeli technicians worked overtime to repair the electric cables which had been torn down in the course of the fighting. Others worked on the water-pipe system. Within a fortnight of the occupation the essential services were working again, most private cars had been returned to their owners, the Arab bus lines were once more running and the shops had been reopened. The numbness began to thaw. People saw that they were still alive and that no harm would befall them.

But that first period of shock and panic had left its mark. Many thousands of inhabitants fled across the river to become refugees in Jordan. By the end of 1967 it was estimated that more than 200,000 Palestinians had preferred to become refugees rather than accept the rule of the Israeli Military Government. Very few of these, although given the option to return by the Israeli authorities, showed much interest in returning under the existing circumstances.

This flight into voluntary exile was attributed to various reasons. First there was the mass hysteria of the war itself. The most hard hit by this hysteria were the areas nearest to the border, especially Jericho and the 1948 refugee camps around it. The closeness to the border, the bitter memories of the war of 1948, the misery in which many of the refugees had been living since then, all provided fertile ground for those who first chose to cross the river into Jordan. We asked one of those who had stayed behind what had cause this mass exodus. "Panic," he replied, "and the psychosis of mass flight. We heard the explosions of bombs and rockets as the Israeli planes shot up our army vehicles on the Jerusalem–Jericho road. And the word went round: 'the Jews are coming'. Less than ten miles away is the river—and safety on the other side. Without thinking, the people collected their bundles and made their way to the bridge.

And those that wanted to stay saw the stream of people fleeing, and became frightened, and joined them. I myself", he added, "had great difficulty in persuading my wife and children that it was better to stay."

But this stream of refugees was to continue long after the first panic died down. There were many causes for it. Some were economic, as was the case with the families who lived off the earnings of their sons, brothers or husbands who were working in Kuwait, Saudi Arabia or the Persian Gulf principalities and who sent home remittances every month. Tens of thousands of Palestinians work in the Persian Gulf area, mainly in the oil fields, and many thousands more had gone farther afield, to North Africa, Europe and the Americas. The money they sent to their families in Cis-Jordan totalled more than £20 millions in 1966, a sizeable proportion of the entire West Bank income. These sums were now blocked in inaccessible bank accounts, and many families decided to cross over into Jordan where they could obtain this money and continue to receive their remittances. Others left because their husbands or sons were Jordan Government officials, or soldiers in the Jordanian army, and their economic future depended on their continued association with the Jordanian Government. There were those who believed that the Israeli rule would strangle the Palestinian economy and others who found themselves unemployed. The building trade in Nablus, the hotel and resort business in Ramallah and some of the local industry did not resume activity in the summer of 1967, and many of the newly unemployed chose to emigrate to other countries in the hope of finding employment there. Some departed because their homes had been destroyed, others because they feared arrest for extremist activity in the past. Many crossed the Jordan because they felt they had no future any more on the West Bank, and many others did so because they did not want to live under Israeli rule.

The Israeli Government did not actively encourage this emigration, but quite definitely did not object to it. In mid-June the army began regularizing the movement across the Jordan

River, and there were cases where buses were supplied by local military commanders for groups wishing to emigrate.* The movement eastward continued throughout the year, although it slowed down towards the end of the year to 500 a week.

World opinion convinced the Israeli Government that it should allow the return of the refugees. However, a surprisingly small number actually took up the offer made by the Israelis during the period given to them in August 1967. Although the quota agreed upon was over 30,000 and would probably have been substantially increased had the pressure of returnees been greater, only approximately 11,000 did, in fact, return to the West Bank. It is unclear why the number was so small, although it is attributed both to the lack of enthusiasm of the refugees and to the incompetence of the Jordanian Government.†

With the approach of winter, the existence of these refugees became a potent focal point for anti-Israeli opinion. They became the underdogs of 1967, and even the friends of Israel voiced their concern and indicated that it was up to the Israeli Government to make a gesture to help the refugees. Few expected any serious help from the Arab countries. The Israeli Government, while announcing that it had prepared plans for compensating the refugees, insisted that these could only be implemented as part of a general peace settlement, to be discussed in the peace negotiations.

Yet, despite the proportions of this mass exodus, the vast majority of Arabs preferred to stay where they were. Their old world had been destroyed; now they had to make the best of the new. And as contacts were made between them and Israelis— for the first time in nineteen years—many of them voiced

---

* Shortly after the occupation, the former Governor of Jerusalem, Anwar al-Khatib asked the Israeli Military Governor to supply transport for those wishing to leave. He explained that there were many who wished to rejoin their families in Jordan, and he begged the Jewish authorities to show good will. Anwar al-Khatib put his request in writing, and buses were accordingly supplied.

† During August the number of Palestinians actually emigrating was approximately 50% higher than those opting to return to the West Bank.

feelings and thoughts which had hitherto only rarely found expression in Arab countries. They were tired, they said, of living in an atmosphere of hate, of tension, of war. The time had come for peace, for an end to strife between Arab and Jew. The Arab leaders had proved themselves to be incapable of solving the Arab problem. Now providence had given them the opportunity to settle it by themselves. Some of the most in-fluential and representative of the Arabs in Cis-Jordan intimated that they would be willing to reach a peace settlement with Israel on the basis of an independent Palestinian state bound to Israel with economic ties, on the understanding that the refugee problem would be justly settled. "As for Jordan," some of them explained, "we are Palestinians and not Jordanians, and have never been treated as equal citizens by the Bedouin rulers in Amman. All government positions of influence on the West Bank were given to easterners, who are far less developed than we are; virtually all the economic development in the country, including nearly all industrial projects, was carried out at our expense on the East Bank. And the Jordanian army behaved here like an occupation force."

These thoughts were intimated to two Israeli officers who had been sent to the West Bank on 9 June on a mission which, in the words of *The Economist*, was "to test the response of well-known groups and personalities to the idea of creating an autonomous Palestinian State, having federal bonds with Israel." The re-sponse from West Bank leaders in those early days was definitely positive, although later, when the first shock of occupation was overcome, certain inner resistance grew. But in those early days after the war there had been a chance of a settlement between the Palestinians and the Israelis, establishing an autonomous state with close ties with Israel, defended by the Israeli army. In those first two weeks after the war, the majority of Arab leaders, with the exception of the hard-core Communists and extreme nationalists, would have accepted such a proposal at the time. This, in turn, would have had far-reaching reper-cussions on any talks of peace which could have eventually evolved between the Arab states and Israel. For such an agreement with the Palestinians would have knocked the bottom out of the Arab–Israel conflict, which revolves round the injustice which the Palestinians feel has been done them by the Israelis. However, the Israelis would not commit themselves so rapidly, and the opportunity was allowed to lapse.

Meanwhile, as the first period of shock gradually wore off, political activity among the Arabs was resumed. Contacts with Amman—albeit clandestine—were renewed. The Arab political leadership on the West Bank was taken up in a storm of introspective argument regarding its own future. There were the Palestinian nationalists who claimed that now was the time to press for an independent Palestinian entity, separate from Jordan. But there were many whose capital was tied up in the East Bank who, as the first shock of defeat wore off, declared increasingly that such talk was unrealistic, that an independent Palestine would be faced with economic catastrophe. They accused those calling for a settlement of treachery to the Arab cause. There were others still who pointed to the efforts of the Soviet Union at the United Nations General Assembly, and to the declarations of Nasser, Boumedienne and the other Arab leaders. "The Jews will soon be forced to withdraw from the occupied areas," they argued. "Let us be patient. Hussein will soon be back."

"Hussein will soon be back" was to become the overriding belief of the majority of the West Bank Arabs by mid-July. There were those who could tell you the exact date of his return; there were others who knew "from good sources" that the King was "at this very moment" negotiating with Israel. The rumour that there was about to be an under-the-table deal between the Israelis and King Hussein spread with the rapidity of a bush fire. Soon there was hardly an Arab who did not believe that the days of Israel's rule in the occupied areas were numbered. This being so, it well behoved the inhabitants to avoid two pitfalls, either of which could invoke the wrath of the returning Jordanians: one was the talk of an independent

Palestine, the other was any form of co-operation with the Israelis. The same Arab notables and intellectuals who only a week earlier had been loudest in their demand for a separate Palestine now piously called for a return of the King of Jordan as the only possible political solution. And the same officials who had previously been co-operating whole-heartedly with the Israeli authorities now had second thoughts, and the first signs of non-co-operation began to be seen in various parts of the West Bank.

At the same time the Jordanians stepped up their anti-Israel propaganda. Radio Amman daily called upon the people of the West Bank to stop co-operating with the Israeli authorities. "Government officials who continue working will have their pensions cancelled," it warned. Some of those who defied these warnings were threatened with reprisals.

This propaganda fell on fertile ground because of the uncertainty of the political future. This was one subject on which the Israelis, at that time, kept quiet. This atmosphere of uncertainty was ideal for extremist activity. The extreme nationalists pressurized the moderates into signing petitions protesting against the annexation of Jerusalem and calling for a return of the West Bank to Jordan. Meanwhile, in the handsome villas of Nablus some of the more extremist leaders of that town worked out their own strategy. It consisted of three stages: the first, to encourage King Hussein to reach a settlement with Israel and return to the West Bank; the second, after having got rid of the Jews in this manner, to revolt against Hussein on the grounds that he had betrayed the Arab people by reaching a settlement with the Jews; the third, to set up a Palestinian state on both banks of the Jordan.

The campaign of non-co-operation reached its height at the beginning of August with a one-day general strike of merchants in Eastern Jerusalem. By now the movement of non-co-operation included many of the teachers, who declared that they would refuse to use the revised textbooks (the hate propaganda, including numerous references to the Protocols of the Elders of

Zion, had been removed), the lawyers and many of the judges.

This growing volume of acts of defiance put the Israeli authorities in a difficult position. The policy they had been following had been one of maximum non-interference in the internal affairs of the Arabs. Considerable freedom of action was given to the Arab municipal authorities, while at the same time a number of projects were undertaken with the aim of speeding up the process of normalization. But now this policy was undermined by the action of the extremists. There were those in Israel who demanded a change in policy, with wholesale arrests of those signing the petitions, and reprisals against those refusing to co-operate.

The Arab extremists understood only too clearly the dilemma of the Israeli authorities. They saw that the Israelis wished to avoid using oppressive measures and their tactics throughout the month of August were largely designed to discover how far they needed to go to goad the Israelis into massive retaliation.

In this they did not succeed. The Israelis realized that a change of policy would mean playing into the hands of the extremists, and they reacted instead in a restrained manner. Some of the more active of the agitators were indeed arrested, but there were no wide-scale punitive actions. Indeed, the reaction to the extremist tactics was remarkably cool. Speaking at a rally of his Rafi party in mid-August, the Minister of Defence, General Moshe Dayan, stated his case simply and clearly: "If the Arabs of the West Bank decide not to co-operate with us, we'll run the region without them. If the bus drivers decide not to work, we'll put in Jewish drivers. If the lawyers or judges boycott the law courts, we have plenty of Jewish lawyers and judges who can replace them. If the teachers decide not to teach, the only sufferers will be the Arab children."

At the same time, the declarations of General Dayan and of other Israeli leaders that Israel intended to stay in the occupied areas until a peace settlement was reached with the Arab states began to have an effect. By the end of August there were signs of a growing realization by the Arabs that the Israelis were,

H

after all, in the West Bank to stay, and many of them began to have second thoughts about the campaign of non-co-operation. This change brought a revival of the concept of Palestinian entity, with several Arab leaders, notably from Ramallah, Jerusalem, Bethlehem and Hebron, pressing strongly for a separate settlement between Palestinians and Israelis.

But for the time being the Israelis were content to administer the occupied areas efficiently, without entering into political negotiations. The administration was executed by a Military Government which was subdivided into two districts, the North and the South, with seven districts under them, very similar in concept to the British Mandatory rule in Palestine between 1920 and 1948. As far as possible, former Jordanian government employees in the West Bank were retained, while Israelis were appointed to civilian posts only if no local inhabitant could be found to do the job. General Dayan, who, as Minister of Defence, was responsible for the administration of the occupied areas, was very explicit on this point. His instructions were: "Let the Arabs run their own affairs as much as possible, even if we have the people and the means to do it much better. There should be a minimum amount of friction between Arabs and Israelis."

The first budget of the Military Government for the month of July was of a relatively limited nature. It was approved on 30 June when the Israeli Finance Ministry allotted it £265,000. A more progressive, sophisticated budget for the eight months beginning 1 August until 31 March 1968, was approved by the end of July. By that time the Military Government was operating all the offices it considered necessary. There were, however, a number of outstanding problems which the Military Governor had to tackle in the first few weeks after the essential services were reactivated. The first and most pressing problem was that of unemployment. Building had come to a complete standstill; tourism, especially outside Jerusalem, had in the past been based largely on Arabs from the oil countries—from Iraq, Saudi Arabia, Kuwait and the Persian Gulf territories—and hotels in

Ramallah and Bethlehem were now closed or empty. There was less trade than in the past and there was danger of unemployment spiralling. The Military Governor was given authority to provide jobs in public works schemes, and by the end of August there were over 7,000 men working in different public works. Roads were repaired; work was continued on public buildings under construction; trees were planted; development projects, such as piping spring water to the village of Tubas, were implemented. The main problem was to maintain a minimum unemployment rate which would promote the mobility of Arab labourers on the West Bank.

A second problem was that of currency. The legal tender on the day of occupation of the West Bank was the Jordanian dinar, which was within the sterling bloc. The Israeli Government discovered, however, that most surplus liquid funds were automatically transferred to the Central Bank in Amman, and as a result, there were very few dinars on hand. It was anticipated that by the end of July the dinar reserves would run out and Israel was faced with the dilemma of either creating a new military "occupation dinar" or introducing the Israeli pound as legal tender on the West Bank. The first inclination was to introduce a military dinar and such a currency was printed abroad and sent to Israel during the month of July; but it was then felt that the local population would distrust the introduction of such a new currency, that, in fact, it had already been trading semi-officially in Israeli pounds, especially since the Palestinians were renewing their stocks and paying Israeli suppliers in pounds and selling merchandise to the Israeli tourists for pounds. It was then decided to use Israeli pounds, and as of 1 August there existed on the West Bank two legal tenders running parallel and reconvertibly—the Jordanian dinar and the Israeli pound.

But perhaps the biggest problem of all was the huge agricultural surplus expected from the middle of July until the end of September. The Palestinian farmer, although using primitive implements, was very diligent and the surpluses produced on the West Bank were usually sold to a number of Arab countries, especially to East Jordan, Kuwait and Saudi Arabia. The year 1967 promised to yield a bumper crop and the question was: how would these surpluses be dealt with? The advisers on agriculture to the Military Governor first arranged for a special budget guaranteeing minimum prices for dumping these surpluses and from then on, after obtaining this budget, looked for alternative ways not necessitating its use. The Israeli canning factories, the Israeli Army and the refugee camps consumed a part of these surpluses. But then, following suggestions made by some of the bigger Arab merchants, exports to Jordan were resumed. Trucks laden with merchandise, mainly agricultural produce, now began to ford the Jordan River at a shallow point to the east of Tubas and return empty several days later. The Jordanian Government agreed with alacrity to this trade, and at the height of the season over 1,000 tons of foodstuffs per day were transferred across the Jordan to be sold in the markets of Amman and Zarka, while some of the heavily laden trucks went as far as Kuwait. It was free trade and there was little supervision as to what the returns were, but the trade between the occupied Western Bank and the neighbouring Arab countries injected considerable sums into the West Bank and created a novel trading precedent between Israel and the Arab countries. For the first time since 1948 some slight unofficial economic relationship had been established between the Arab world and Israel.

For the first few weeks it had been the Government's economic policy to isolate the West Bank from both Israel and Jordan. The idea behind it was to establish a closed economy with a separate tariff system and customs and excise duties. The idea was probably not feasible from the beginning. The Israelis who could move almost freely into the West Bank and the Arabs who could move almost as freely in Israel were developing economic relations at a far faster pace than envisaged by the Government. It could not possibly raise the number of personnel it would require to recreate a new boundary only for the purpose of closing it economically. Similarly, the Israeli Government had not originally been enthusiastic about trade between the West Bank and Jordan, but here again demand proved to be so great that exports flourished. The staff of the Military Government were instrumental in developing this trade and in convincing the Government that it should reverse its stand and permit free trade. They succeeded up to a point. For a time there existed hopes that an evolutionary pattern would be developed in which economic ties would be strengthened, creating a certain *de facto* recognition which would have political implications in the long run. However, at a certain point a stop was put to this gradualist approach. The issue was raised over the question of the commercial banks of the Hashemite Kingdom of Jordan. On 5 June, eight banks were operating over thirty branches in Jerusalem and in seven towns on the West Bank. These had been closed down by order of the Jordanian Government and by order of the Israeli Military Commander. The banking activities were a central aspect of the economic activity on the West Bank. Deposits amounted to over 15 million dinars and outstanding credits to over seven million dinars. However, approximately six million dinars consisted of liquid funds which had been deposited in Jordan and unless these funds were returned to the West Bank, or at least made available to them, the Arab banks there would automatically become insolvent while the British banks which were operating under Jordanian law would be in an embarrassing position. It was, however, in the interest of the Jordanians to show the inhabitants of the West Bank that their interests, including their financial affairs, were close to their hearts. The Arab and British banks were anxious to reopen their branches for business reasons. The Israelis, for their part, were interested in restoring normal conditions to the West Bank and therefore wished to come to some kind of operating settlement with the Arab bankers. A preliminary meeting on the subject, organized by the International Monetary Fund, at which David Horowitz, the Governor of the Bank of Israel,

met senior Arab officials, was inconclusive. And then on
16 August two bankers from Jordan, representing all the commercial banks in Jordan, arrived in Jerusalem to meet the
Israeli authorities for preliminary negotiations with a view
to reopening these branches in order to safeguard the interests
of the depositors and the banks, and to revive business interests
so as to promote the economic life of the West Bank. The
agreement initialled by both parties is unique in many ways.
Although later rejected by both Governments, a group of
technocrats had in principle agreed to co-operate in a very
intricate, complicated banking protocol, which guaranteed
respect to the Jordanian and Israeli banking institutions. The
twenty-nine-point agreement included permission for trading
between the East and West Bank, as well as trading between the
West Bank, Israel and the rest of the world. It recognized the
fact that Israeli law would prevail in Jerusalem and that the
banks would operate according to instructions from the Head
Office in Amman on condition that these were compatible with
the Bank of Israel regulations. But this preliminary agreement
was not to be consummated, and following the Khartoum
Summit Conference, when it became plain that there would
not be a speedy settlement, a perceptible hardening of the
arteries could be felt concerning relations between Jordan and
Israel. This stiffening attitude on both sides coincided with the
recrudescence of Fatah terror activity. The Israeli Security
Services achieved remarkable results in minimizing the Fatah
operations. By the end of the year nearly 1300 members of
Fatah and other clandestine organizations had been apprehended and many more were killed in running figths with
Israeli army patrols. The organization of dedicated Arabs,
on the pattern of the FLN in Algeria or the Viet Cong, was
still far off. The vast majority of the population of the West
Bank was opposed to acts of violence. And experiments in
passive resistance by and large proved to be a failure, after the
local population realized that the Israeli authorities would take
strong measures against such acts.

Thus by the year's end the inhabitants of the West Bank had settled down to their new conditions, and the majority of the population was co-operating fully with the Israeli authorities. In the Gaza Strip, however, conditions were vastly different. Here the hatred of the Jews was much more intense, and resistance to the occupying Israeli forces was much greater. There were two main reasons for this: the first was the large number of inhabitants who had been trained by the Egyptian army and by Ahmad Shuqairi's Palestine Liberation Organization to form a resistance movement in case of an Israeli occupation. They had caches of weapons hidden away and throughout the summer mines were placed in tracks used by Israeli army vehicles. The second reason for non-co-operation was due to the memory of 1956 when Israel had for the first time taken the Gaza Strip during the Sinai Campaign. Many of those who had then co-operated with the Israeli Military Government were severely punished when the Egyptians returned. They had been taught a lesson and they blamed the Israelis for having abandoned them.

The most formidable problem facing the Israelis in the Gaza Strip was, however, the concentration-camp mentality of the population. For almost twenty years the majority of the 350,000 people in the Gaza Strip were unemployed refugees,* living in camps with limited rights of movement, surrounded to the north and east by Israel and to the south by the Sinai Desert. The Egyptian Government did not permit them to move freely out of the Strip, even into Egypt. They were not given Egyptian nationality and rarely an Egyptian *laissez-passer*. The refugees in Jordan, the Lebanon and Syria were all, after some time, given citizenship and relative freedom to move around. But in the Gaza Strip there had been little development in the past 19 years. The United Nations Works and Relief Agency supplied food, and the men had become accustomed to doing

* According to the census carried out by the Israelis after the war there were 220,000 refugees in the Gaza Strip, of whom 175,000 lived in refugee camps.

nothing. But these were largely a passive people and once having accepted the fact that this time the Israeli army was, in all probability, there to stay, they gradually accepted the Israelis as the rulers of the Strip. For both the Israelis and the Arabs of Gaza realized that this time there was virtually no likelihood of the Strip being returned to Egypt; of all the concessions the Egyptians would be willing to make for a settlement, the loss of the Gaza Strip would be the easiest. But for the Israelis the Gaza Strip proved to be a mixed blessing. They were faced with the tremendous challenge of re-educating, rehabilitating and resettling at least part of the refugee population. For there was no question of being able to find a livelihood for the camp population within the narrow confines of the Gaza Strip. Some of the inhabitants took advantage of the liberty of movement which they now gained for the first time since 1948, and made their way to the West Bank from where they emigrated to more distant lands. But this was only a trickle; the mainstream of refugees remained in the camps in the Gaza plain, where they represented the greatest single challenge to the Israeli Government in the aftermath of the war.

If overpopulation was Israel's major headache in Gaza, she had next to nothing to worry about in the Syrian Heights. Virtually the entire civilian population had fled, together with the Syrian army, from that abandoned military arsenal. Only in the northern end of the occupied Heights approximately 6,500 Druze remained, and they speedily accustomed themselves to the Israeli occupation. Here again the Israel Government was confronted with the question of what to do with this newly won territory. There were various possible solutions: one was a partial resettlement of the Gaza Strip refugees, a move which could help solve the problem in the south but only at the expense of creating a new one in the north. A more popular, though Utopian, proposal was to establish a small Druze autonomous state which would include the Druze of the Heights and to which some or all of the Druze of Israel would be encouraged to emigrate and settle. There were many attractions to this proposed autonomous buffer state. The Druze had proved to be friendly to the Israel Government. Many of them have served in the Israeli army and, particularly, in the Israel Border Police. The occupied area is, moreover, close to the Jebel Druze, the heartland of the Druze sect in Syria, and the fact that an autonomous Druze region would be set up in the Golan Heights could well lead to the creation of bonds with Jebel Druze and thus possibly neutralize the Syrians from any infiltration in the future to the south or the south-west. Such a state, of course, would remain under the sphere of influence of the Israelis.

But in spite of the attractiveness of this suggestion, little was done to implement it. On the other hand, the Israeli kibbutzim in the Hula Valley were demanding the establishment of new Israeli villages on the Heights. They believe that only by this means can their future peace be guaranteed, for these settlements suffered from repeated shelling by the Syrian guns on the Heights above them. Largely for these reasons of the security of the northern settlements, it is generally considered in Israel that some sort of continued Israeli presence in the Heights is essential.

If, however, keeping the Golan Heights was accepted as a natural ambition of the Israelis, the question of the Sinai Desert was far more complicated. Sinai was considered expendable by Israel, but only within the fraemwork of a general settlement and on condition that a formula could be achieved which would guarantee the full demilitarization of the peninsula. In such conditions, the virtually uninhabited desert could become an ideal buffer between Israel and Egypt. But as the months passed and there were no signs of any speedy settlement, the same tendency emerged in Sinai as in the other territories: continued occupation was leading to signs of permanency. Apart from the security aspect of staying in Sinai, the Israelis were beginning to discuss the economic interests as well. Since July there had been a steady flow of oil from the oil-fields in western Sinai to Elath. But Israel was after larger oil challenges and the Government approved a project for increasing the potential in Elath by laying a forty-inch pipeline from Elath to the Mediterranean which could transfer 50 million tons of oil per annum. Such a pipeline would, for the first time, put Israel as a major factor on the oil map.

There were other attractions in Sinai. There were water reserves in the el-Arish region which made a plan for resettling refugees in that area feasible. There were manganese mines and, the Israelis suspected, other mineral wealth still undiscovered and untapped. By the year's end Israel's geologists had, with Government approval, planned a geological survey of Sinai which would take well over a year to complete, a sure indication that the Israelis were not thinking in terms of a hurried withdrawal. Thus Sinai, too, was being caught up in the dynamism of the Israelis and each month that passed was making it more difficult for a settlement to be reached involving an Israeli withdrawal.

Thus Israel, almost despite herself, was becoming accustomed to ruling over territories many times her own size. But were the Israelis great enough to grasp the new opportunities and challenges which now faced them? Was the policy of masterly inactivity the correct way of exploiting her military gains? This policy of sitting pretty in the occupied areas and proclaiming that Israel would not budge until the Arabs came forward to direct peace talks put the onus of continued deadlock entirely on the Arabs. The Israelis were sincerely convinced that the Arabs had no intention of making peace, that the moderation of King Hussein and their willingness to agree to a general formula of non-belligerency were only a smoke-screen behind which the Arabs would seek to take from Israel her military gains and to restore the pre-June situation of hostility and violence. Thus, from their point of view, this policy was a correct one. For they were certain that the only way to bring the Arabs to the conference table was to continue this tough line. The Israelis, however, made no move to settle the refugee problem, which, for the first time, was now largely in their hands. They did little to encourage the efforts of the Palestinians to reach a separate settlement with them, though a Palestinian state on the West Bank, closely allied to Israel, could have given the Israelis maximum security with a minimum addition of Arabs to the Jewish state, and could have provided a breach in the wall of Arab hostility surrounding Israel. The Israelis failed to do this not because it was against their policy to encourage a separate Palestinian entity but because the National Unity Government was incapable of taking any decision at all.

The Israelis were, in fact, in danger of going back to the old indecisiveness which had so characterized their actions before the war. Despite all forecasts the "old guard" leaders, Levi Eshkol, Golda Meir, Zalman Aranne, Pinhas Sapir, and others, remained as firmly entrenched in power as ever. There seemed nothing the second generation of Mapai leaders could do about it, except to accept the proposal made by Shimon Peres, Rafi's Secretary-General, on the eve of the war, that Rafi should merge with Mapai, the moderate, middle-of-the-road party which had ruled over Israel since its establishment. At stake behind this merger could be the question of inheritance to the Premiership. Mr Eshkol, who was 71 when the June War broke out, had been grooming Yigal Alon, the dynamic leader of the left-leaning Ahdut Ha'avoda party, as his successor. Ahdut Ha'avoda was already in close alignment with Mapai, and largely because of Mr Eshkol's choice the two parties had decided to unite. But after the war General Dayan had become a formidable contender for the succession and his candidature would enjoy considerable support within Mapai itself, for many of the party militants were none too pleased with the choice of Alon. Mr Peres's proposal of a three-way merger was thus enthusiastically supported by those Mapai members who preferred General Dayan to Alon, and determinedly opposed by Alon's friends. The former group enjoyed the support of the majority of Mapai's second-line echelon, as reflected in the voting on the subject in the various party organizations. The latter group was made up largely by the "old guard" headed by

Mr Eshkol and the Mapai Secretary, Mrs Meir, for whom the Rafi party remained anathema.

The discussions around this proposed merger of Mapai, Ahdut Ha'avoda and Rafi formed the backdrop to Israel's internal political scene during the six months following the war. There were no ideological issues to hold up the merger, only the clash of personalities, with Levi Eshkol and Golda Meir ranged on the one side and their mentor David Ben Gurion on the other, and with the Alon–Dayan contest always in the background. Yet the eventual reunification of the labour movement was an inevitable result of the war, and the old guard were doing no more than holding up the march of history. The three parties were finally united in January 1968, transforming the Israeli political scene. Mapai, the party which had dominated the Jewish state's political life since its establishment ceased to exist. In its place came the "Israel Labour Party", bringing together once more the rebels who had left the ranks of Mapai in the past. Only David Ben Gurion himself, the supreme dissident, refused to be drawn back to the ranks of his erstwhile colleagues, preferring to stay in the political wilderness.

The new party promised to inject new life into Israel's creaky political institutions. But this was a slow process. And decisions were being pressed on the Government. If Israel had all the time in the world after the war, the Arabs did not. They felt that time was working against them, and, encouraged by the Soviet Union, they were soon pressing hard on Israel once more. It is to the Arabs that we must now turn.

CHAPTER 12

Disaster

The guns were silenced. An uneasy and tense quiet descended over the battlefields. Death and destruction had taken their toll in six brutal, savage days. In the stunned aftermath that followed, the Arabs took stock of their situation. It transcended their worst fears. Their armies were broken; their territories lay virtually defenceless before the victorious Israelis. The Egyptian army had lost 10,000 troops, 1,500 officers and 40 pilots killed in the fighting,* with many thousands more wounded. Five thousand Egyptian soldiers, including eleven generals and brigadiers, and many more colonels, had been taken prisoner. Thousands more were walking accross the desert, trying to reach the Suez Canal. Of Egypt's seven divisions in Sinai, four had been completely shattered, and three rendered ineffective. Of the 1,000 tanks that the Egyptians had brought into Sinai, more than 500 had been destroyed and another 100 captured intact by the Israelis. This represented nearly 60% of Egypt's entire armoured force. The percentage of artillery lost was even higher. Egypt's air force had been virtually obliterated: 338 out of a total of 425 planes were destroyed. The four airfields in Sinai had been lost; three more airfields in the Canal Zone were within range of Israeli artillery. The air force had, therefore, to be regrouped in a small number of remaining air bases. The overall balance sheet was grim, indeed. Writing in *The Times* on 11 June, Charles Douglas-Home, the Defence

* According to Nasser himself. He gave these figures in his speech on 18 November 1967.

Correspondent, described the battlefield in the following terms: "There must be at least 10,000 vehicles abandoned in Sinai; some are total wrecks, others untouched. . . . In the Mitla Pass, two miles of vehicles, soft-skinned and armoured, nose to tail, had been wrecked and wrecked again by air attack. Other convoys lay like broken-backed snakes across the desert roads. At other times it was like flying over a sand-table exercise, with whole tank squadrons in formation knocked out."

The Jordanian army had fared hardly better. The nine Jordanian brigades which had fought in western Jordan were wrecked, two infantry and one armoured brigade were completely destroyed. Some 8,000 soldiers were killed or wounded, and a large part of the Jordanian armour, guns and equipment was destroyed or fell into Israeli hands, while the Jordanian air force was wiped out in its entirety. The Syrians had been less badly hit, but nevertheless, two brigades had been virtually destroyed and three were badly mauled, and 100 tanks and a large quantity of artillery and transport were destroyed or captured. Forty of the tanks fell virtually intact into Israeli hands.

Far worse, from the Arab point of view, than these losses was the territorial metamorphosis that had occurred during those six days of carnage. On 5 June one Arab army had been poised only eleven miles from Tel Aviv, a second was massed high above the fertile plains of Hula, threatening the settlements spread out far below, and a third force was prepared to cut across the narrow stretch of land dividing Egypt from Jordan and thus isolate the port of Elath from the rest of Israel. The Jewish state was hemmed in, beleaguered by three armies to her north, east and south. On 10 June these threats to Israel had not only been removed, but the victorious Israelis stood within easy striking distance of Damascus, Amman and Cairo itself. The tables had been turned in one of the swiftest, most effective and most dramatic military campaigns the world had ever witnessed.

The shock of defeat was all the greater because of the high expectations of victory which had engulfed the Arabs immediately before the war. No one who did not witness the scenes of tumultuous preparations, or who did not hear the pæans of hatred pouring forth from the Arab radio stations, can imagine the intensity of emotions unleashed immediately before the hostilities began. Cartoons in the Arab press depicted scurrilously a tiny Israel cowering before the might of the Arabs. Press and radio commentators repeated, time and time again, the overwhelming superiority in numbers which the Arabs enjoyed over their enemy. They described Israel as a nest of Zionist gangs, weak and cowardly, dependent on the United States, no match for the united Arab armies massing on her borders.

Immediately after the war we spoke to numerous Arabs on the West Bank of the Jordan, and to many of the Egyptian prisoners held by Israel. They had all been certain that this time it would be a walk-over for the Arabs; that Israel did not have a chance; that Tel Aviv would be taken in a matter of days. This was the outstanding impression throughout the Arab world at the beginning of June even if President Nasser and the Egyptian High Command had no such illusion. The radio, the press, the calls to "jihad" emanating from the mosques, the heady declarations and speeches of Arab leaders and above all of Nasser himself, all these contributed to the fervour of excitement which swept through the Arab world.

From these pinnacles of self-intoxication the Arabs were, in less than a week, dashed to the depths of despair. The shock of this sudden transformation was overwhelming. It was a traumatic experience, which, in the period immediately after the defeat, left the Arabs numb. But as the effects of the shock began to wear off, the Arabs turned into themselves. One thought, one question was now asked, time and again: Why did it happen? What caused the defeat? There was, of course, the official apologia. The belief that Israel's victory was due to help given by American and British planes is still widespread in the Arab world.* But increasingly the Arab leaders and intel-

* Despite Nasser's belated admission that this was not true.

lectuals began to search within themselves for their own
weaknesses as the real cause for their defeat. Muhammad
Hassanein Haikal, the perceptive editor of *al-Ahram*, bluntly
warned his readers that the Arabs would not be able to beat
Israel on the battlefield until they caught up with her in their
grasp of modern technology.* A colleague of his, the Egyptian
Ahmad Baha ad-Din, wrote similarly that the Arabs were not
capable of annihilating Israel, and the fact that they, nevertheless, continued "to bandy this slogan around" was causing
the Arabs great harm.† But the most remarkable document to
emerge in this post-war introversion was a lengthy treatise
written in the Lebanese newspaper *an-Nahar* by Cecil Hourani,
a former political adviser to President Bourguiba and one of
the leading political theorists in the Arab world today. Hourani
spelled out the lessons the war contained for the Arabs in one
of the most fearless and hard-hitting criticisms of the Arab
handling of their conflict with Israel ever to have been made by
an Arab. The Arabs must understand their errors in the past
in order to be able to build the new society of the future,
Hourani asserted. They must see the truth as it was, without
distortion or exaggeration: "For too long the field of publicity
and expression has been left in the hands of professional
demagogues, blackmailers and semi-educated factions. Our
silence on the one hand, their clamour on the other, have led
the Arab nation not merely to disaster, but to the brink of
disintegration." Turning to the question of the Arab conflict
with Israel, Hourani stated his belief that the Arabs should
have followed a policy of containment rather than conquest.
"As a policy of containment," he noted, "the moves of the
United Arab Republic until 5 June 1967, could have been
successful. But it had implicit dangers, the greatest of which
was that, in the minds of those who were practising it, it could
at any moment be transformed successfully into a policy of
conquest. By this confusion in their own minds about their

* *al-Ahram*, 20 October 1967.
† *al-Musawar*, Cairo, 23 June 1967.

aims, and by their misjudgements of their own strength, the Arab governments brought about the disaster of 5 June." But what the Arabs do not like they pretend does not exist. "What greater proof of our capacity for self-deception and moral cowardice than that Ahmad Shuqairi* still sits with our responsible leaders, or the claims of one Arab Head of State that we were not defeated because we did not use our full strength." Turning to the future, Hourani asks: "Shall we in one, or ten, or twenty years seek another 'victory' like the one we have just gained, and lose the other side of the Jordan, the fertile plains of Damascus and Hauran in Syria, and the Litani and Hasbani rivers in Lebanon? And shall we still have Ahmad Shuqairi with us to consecrate the final victory of stupidity over intelligence, of fanaticism over common sense, of dishonesty over truth?" Hourani answers his own questions: "The answer lies with us. What we do in reaction to the events of the last few weeks will determine the future of our people, not for ten or twenty years, but for centuries. This time there can be no second chance. . . . Our first effort must surely be to win a victory over ourselves: over defeatism on the one hand, extremism on the other. These two dangers are in fact intimately linked together. The real defeatists are not those who look facts in the face, but those who refuse to do this, who deny facts and who are thus preparing for new defeats. The extremists are those who argue that our concepts were correct, but that we did not implement them seriously; and that, therefore, we should continue along the same path, but with more violent methods. If, however, our concepts were wrong, then the use of the same methods even in a more violent form can lead us to another defeat. It is, therefore, essential to rethink our basic ideas in terms of reality rather than of wishes." Hourani believed that "the resort to military force as a basic element in Arab policy towards Israel is an error"; that "the best chance of containing Israel lies in international pressures either within

* He was forced to resign from the leadership of the Palestine Liberation Organization in mid-December 1967.

or outside the United Nations." Such a containment should be
one of the ultimate goals of Arab policy; a second goal should
be "the gradual transformation of Israel from a European-
dominated 'exclusive' Jewish state into a predominantly
Oriental Jewish–Arab State".

Hourani's article contained much that was unacceptable to
the Arab masses. But, in his forthright manner, he was pioneering a "New Look" in Arab thought. He, too, stressed the fact
that the Arabs do not yet have the scientific and technological
skills, nor the general level of education among the masses,
which make possible the waging of large-scale modern warfare.
This was one lesson of the Six-Day War that was increasingly
sinking home, especially in Egypt. For it was not just a question
of modernizing Arab society, in itself a superhuman task. The
wars of 1948, 1956 and 1967 had shown that the gap between
Israel and Arab society was actually growing larger, that the
Israelis were steadily outdistancing the Arabs in their knowledge
and use of technological and scientific skills. Moreover, warfare
itself was growing more sophisticated. In the 1948 Palestine
War, Arab soldiers, armed with rifles and machine-guns, were
only with difficulty beaten by the similarly armed Israelis, who
suffered far heavier losses than in either of the two wars that
were to follow. In 1956, and immeasurably more so in 1967,
the victory of the Israelis was overwhelming, since modern
weapons played a more decisive role.

As the shock of defeat gradually passed, this lesson made an
increasingly powerful impact. It influenced President Nasser's
policy, and it provided a solid foundation for those who called
for a new approach to the Israeli–Arab conflict. For in the wake
of the war, an increasing number of Arabs were reaching the
conclusion which Cecil Hourani set out so ruthlessly: that
further war was useless, that the overriding need of the Arabs
was to retrench, to root out the basic weaknesses in Arab
society which led to their defeat, to modernize. In the words of
an Egyptian colonel who was taken prisoner: "Perhaps we
should put aside the dogma of a war of annihilation with

Israel. Perhaps we shall learn that we can live together." This is the viewpoint of a group of Egyptian intellectuals, who have called for peace with Israel and an inward-looking Egyptian policy as distinct from the previous pan-Arab policy followed by the Egyptian Government. The importance of this dramatic change of views should not, however, be overrated, and the influence of Egypt's intellectuals on the Government is minimal.

But, paradoxically enough, the same consciousness of present Arab weaknesses has formed one of the arguments of the opposing school of thought which has crystallized in the Arab world since the war. These Arabs stress the humiliation of the June defeat. It is so great that the Arabs must wipe it out, no matter how long it will take, or what the consequences are. But the Arabs are too weak to go to war against Israel. They must, therefore, keep hatred and tension simmering. They must prevent any possibility of co-existence until such time as they gain sufficient strength to wipe Israel out. This must be done by conducting guerrilla warfare and terror attacks iaganst Israel. The argument is familiar. It forms the basis of the extremist approach, emanating from Damascus and Algeria, and provides the *raison d'être* for the recrudescence of Fatah terror activity against Israel. The Syrians hasten to point out that the thesis of guerrilla warfare is the most suitable form of struggle for a weak country. The Arab weakness has been demonstrated. It must be overcome. But in the meantime the enemy, Israel, must be harassed and weakened, and revolutionary fervour among the Arabs will at the same time be maintained by the development of armed struggle or popular warfare tactics.

Closely linked to this ideology is the return once more to the old rivalry between the Ba'th régime of Syria and the Nasserist régime. The gap between them after the war widened considerably. They were now farther apart than they had been before the war. But the Syrians were once more emerging as the purists who reject any compromise with the enemy, or, to quote Hassanein Haikal, as the revolutionaries who are not willing to face reality. This ideological rivalry between the two had in the past been one of the major causes for the disaster which befell the Arabs in June 1967. Now, within months of that disaster, that rivalry was once more becoming a factor in inter-Arab affairs.

These heart-searchings form the background to much that happened in the Arab world after the war. They provide the frame of reference for the discussions, the decisions and the resolutions, as well as for the new tensions which took hold of the Arab countries immediately after the fighting ground to a halt. We must now turn to these developments.

By 8 June, before the fighting had been halted, it had already become evident to the Egyptian High Command that the war was lost, and that Egypt had suffered a stunning defeat. And the question inevitably arose: who would be blamed for the defeat? Who would be made to pay for it? There were, very obviously, only two possible choices: either the High Command would succeed in pinning the blame on the political leadership, with Nasser at its head, for having created the conditions for Egypt's *débâcle*; or the political leadership would point the finger at the professionals—the army, air force and Intelligence officers—for having failed the country at such a crucial hour. Understandably enough, the army commanders were determined that it would not be they who would be made to bear the responsibility.

That same day, some of the top officers, together with Marshal abd al-Hakim Amer and the Minister of War, Shams ed-din Badran, met at General Headquarters and asked Nasser and Zakaria Muhi ed-Din to attend as well. A heated discussion ensued in which Nasser pleaded that, with the enemy at the door, this was not the time to look for scapegoats. But the officers were out for blood. Shams ed-din Badran demanded Nasser's immediate resignation. The others followed suit. It was Zakaria Muhi ed-Din who finally calmed them, stating that both the political leadership and the army were equally responsible and if one resigned, all should follow. And Nasser himself appeared to agree to the officers' demand, promising that he would make a speech to the nation the following day.*

The following evening, on 9 June, less than twenty-four hours after the cease-fire came into effect, Nasser made his famous resignation speech. In it he announced that he had asked Zakaria Muhi ed-Din to take over as President of the Republic; he himself would give up all official and political functions and would become a private citizen. The speech was a masterpiece. It contained the correct mixture of humble willingness to become the martyr of the defeated Egyptian people, of excuses to lessen the shame of defeat, and of Churchillian bravado and challenge for the future. The United Arab Republic, he declared, had suffered a grave setback, but "I tell you truthfully that I am ready to assume the entire responsibility". But Israel had struck a blow "much stronger than her resources allowed". Egypt had had precise knowledge of the enemy's strength. "It was such that it could have been repelled by the Egyptian armed forces. But the imperialists came to Israel's aid. American and British aircraft carriers helped her war effort." British aircraft raided in broad daylight positions on the Syrian and Egyptian fronts. But imperialism would be overcome, leaving Israel to fight alone. "The forces of imperialism imagine that abd al-Nasser is their enemy. I want it to be clear to them that it is the entire Arab nation and not Gamal abd al-Nasser. The forces hostile to the Arab nationalist movement always try to picture it as abd al-Nasser's empire. This is not true, for the hope of Arab unity began before Gamal abd al-Nasser. It will remain after Gamal abd al-Nasser." Martyrdom, excuses, challenge and hope. It had a tremendous effect. That at least part of the reaction to the speech was carefully organized by the Arab Socialist Union is beyond doubt. Crowds were already gathering in the main squares of Cairo bearing banners and placards calling on Nasser to with-

---

* The account of this meeting appeared in the pro-Egyptian press in the Lebanon shortly after Marshal Amer's suicide, and appears to have been deliberately leaked then.

draw his resignation a full half-hour before the resignation speech was made. And within minutes of the end of the speech long convoys of trucks, commandeered by the Arab Socialist Union, were already roaring down the streets of Cairo, packed with workers chanting "Nasser-Rais" and bearing large placards which must have taken hours to prepare. The general pandemonium was increased by the fact that the dozens of anti-aircraft guns ringing the city opened the fiercest and most prolonged barrage of shells the Cairenes had yet heard, despite the fact that there was not a plane in the sky. The order to fire had been given by Army GHQ, who wished, by this method, to disperse the crowds and prevent the popular acclaim for Nasser's return. It was the most blatant demonstration yet of the army's hostility to their President. But it was to no avail. The ASU cheerleaders had done their work well. But much of the outcry was genuine and sincere. Hundreds of thousands of people, many in tears, thronged the streets of Cairo, Alexandria and other Egyptian cities demonstrating in favour of President Nasser. Appeals that he withdraw his resignation poured into the Presidency, not only from Egypt, but from all countries of the Arab world. An overwhelming emotion gripped the Arabs. Its causes were complex in the extreme. Nasser's charismatic qualities which had dominated the Arab scene for the past fourteen years had a great deal to do with it. For he had become more than a leader. He symbolized to many the father-figure, embracing within him the dreams and aspirations of the Arab people. It was he who had striven for Arab unity, who had given voice to the Arab yearnings to restore their golden period of splendour and greatness, who had led them against their enemies—Great Britain, Israel and that undefinable bogey, imperialism. The departure of Nasser would entail the demise of the father-figure, and all that he stood for. And never did the Egyptian people need a guarding spirit, a leader whom they could blindly follow, more than on the morrow of the defeat in Sinai.

The Egyptians are, at the best of times, an obedient people, prone to give their unquestioning loyalty to their leader. Now they grasped eagerly at the excuses which Nasser had offered them for the defeat. They wanted desperately to keep their father-figure intact. In the depths of their despair and humiliation they needed it more than ever. Nasser may, or may not, have guessed what the reaction to his speech would be. He very probably had a good idea of what would happen, for he has, in his past actions and speeches, demonstrated that he has an excellent grasp of the psychology of his people. But to make sure, he saw to it that the cheerleaders of the Arab Socialist Union were sent to work on the masses. For there can be little doubt that Nasser had no intention of really stepping down. His resignation speech was a well-planned exercise played out by a master tactician in political one-upmanship. He needed this overwhelming vote of confidence from the people in order to be able to deal with his recalcitrant generals. He had seen the way the wind was blowing at the GHQ meeting on 8 June, and he evidently decided to fight back. Shortly after his resignation speech a second statement by the President was broadcast over Cairo Radio. Nasser was "profoundly moved" by the demonstrations, he said, and would defer a final decision on his resignation until the following day. But in the meantime, his two most outspoken critics at the GHQ meeting, the War Minister, Shams ed-din Badran and Marshal Amer, had also handed in their resignations together with Nasser. And when, on the following day, Nasser's hold on the Government was confirmed and the National Assembly unanimously requested him to remain in office as Head of State, he pounced on the other officers who had taken part at the meeting at the General Headquarters. On 11 June the commanders of the UAR land, naval and air forces, General abd el-Mohsen Mortagi, Admiral Soliman Izzat and Air-Marshal Sidki Mahmud, were cashiered. So were four major-generals and a score of other senior officers. Nasser had outsmarted his generals.

The officers did not take their defeat lightly. Some of the hot-headed among them tried to force their way to Nasser's residence in Manshiat al-Bakri, but the crowds stopped them and they were arrested. An atmosphere of purge now descended upon Egypt. Between 700 and 1,000 officers were cashiered from the army. The security services were activated in a manner unprecedented in Egypt. People were encouraged to come and inform on their friends and neighbours. Arrests were carried out in their hundreds, interrogations in their thousands. This new wave of repression, carried out against the backdrop of a wrecked economy and the military *débâcle*, increased the tension and depression which had taken hold of Egypt in the wake of the shock of defeat. But Nasser's main preoccupation in those crucial weeks after the war was to preserve the reins of power in his hands. This took precedence even over getting the Israelis out of Sinai. And he dared not take risks. His first orders were to tighten internal security, to prevent any organized opposition to his régime.

The most immediate threat to Nasser came from the armed forces. The army was the main prop of the régime, but it could also become the main danger to it. None of the civilian elements could attempt a *coup d'état* without support from the army. But, equally, the civilians could not rule for a day if that support were removed. The Egyptian army had undergone a series of sharp shocks. It had suffered defeat on the battlefield. Its popularity among the people had disappeared. It was broken, wounded, hurt. As such, it could be very dangerous.

The army was the prime consideration of President Nasser immediately after the war. On the one hand he wanted to set it on its feet again in the shortest time possible in order to bolster up his weakening régime and provide an effective defence for the country. On the other hand, he needed to remove the disgruntled elements, the officers who had witnessed the extent of the defeat, who had known that the army had not been ready for war, and who might blame their President for having, nevertheless, created the conditions which led to that war. These officers, who could no longer be trusted, included nearly the entire senior echelons: almost the whole GHQ staff, divisional and even many brigade commanders. And each of these senior officers had his own followers in the army, officers who owed their rise in rank to the "protection" or friendship of a senior officer. These, too, had to be sought out to be retired on pension or dismissed. The result was the most violent shake-up the army had experienced since the Revolution. Not even the 1956 Sinai defeat had led to any widespread changes. The air force and navy commanders, Air-Marshal Sidki and Admiral Izzat, had served in their posts since 1953. The abrupt dismissal of hundreds of senior officers shook the armed forces to their very foundations. The army was, in effect, eliminated as a dominant factor in the Egyptian political arena.

The purges widened the gap of distrust which now separated the officers from Nasser and the politicos. The only way for Nasser to overcome the danger that this growing gulf represented was by creating a new officer class as speedily as possible to replace the dismissed senior officers. This was the task given to the new commander in chief of the army, General Mahmud Fawzi, a staunch Nasser supporter. General Fawzi is a relative of Sami Sharf, one of Nasser's right-hand men at the Presidency, who, in turn, had been the leading antagonist of Shams ed-din Badran, the ousted War Minister and close confidant of Marshal Amer. Nasser, supported by General Fawzi and the new chief of staff, General abd al-Munim Riad, set about rebuilding the army, injecting a new spirit into it, reviving the old feelings of loyalty to him and to the Revolution.

The Russians supported him in this endeavour. The Soviet airlift of military equipment, which began almost immediately after the war, not only enabled the army to rebuild its shattered formations, but also gave a tremendous boost to army morale. The Russians responded to the Egyptian appeal for equipment with an alacrity and efficiency which astonished Western and Israeli observers. During June and July they kept up an aerial supply line, with more than 250 flights of giant Antonov transport planes, which brought in some 150 aircraft and between 200 and 250 tanks. In August, further supplies were sent by sea.

By October they had replaced virtually the entire losses in aircraft and had sent in close on 300 tanks, bringing Egypt's total number to 700 tanks. This was amply sufficient to enable the army to regroup. The Egyptian High Command gave the orders for the re-establishment of three infantry divisions, one armoured division, plus an additional armoured brigade and a battalion of commandos and paratroops.* But it would take a long time before these formations would become completely battle-worthy. And in the meantime the army still posed a threat to Nasser's régime. But the danger was minimized by the fact that the larger part of the forces was kept in the Canal Zone to face the Israeli army. The tension, the periodic artillery duels and the danger which the Israelis represented now stood the régime in good stead. It kept the army occupied. In Cairo itself, hardly a tank could be seen in the vast army bases at Huckstep or Abbasieh. Those units not at the Canal were kept out of the capital. They were frequently moved from one base to another, and their officers were often switched to different units. Nasser was taking no chances.

Nasser's main preoccupation, as we have seen, was to keep his head above water. But other problems were pressing strongly on him and were increasingly affecting the balance of power of internal forces within Egypt. The shadow of the Israeli army poised on the eastern bank of the Suez Canal was stretching ever longer across Egypt. The hopes of the Egyptian leaders that international action would ensure a speedy withdrawal of the Israelis—as had been the case in the wake of the 1956 war—were dashed with the failure of the Soviet moves in the emergency session of the General Assembly. With each week that passed it became increasingly clear—painfully so—that only by offering very tangible concessions could the Egyptians hope to obtain strong enough international backing which might succeed in pressuring Israel into withdrawing.

But offering concessions to Israel was very bitter medicine

---

* These figures include the seven brigades (four regular and three of reserves) which were serving in the Yemen in July 1967.

indeed. The alternative—to be prepared for a lengthy Israeli occupation of Sinai until the Egyptian army became strong enough to risk another round of fighting—was hardly more palatable. This was the great dilemma of the Egyptian Government in the aftermath of defeat. But the discussions which raged in Government offices and in select homes in Cairo were not taking place in a vacuum. There was the inter-Arab scene to take into account, and the fact that the Syrians and Algerians were already setting the tone with an intransigent, extremist line which brooked no talk of concessions. There was, on the other hand, the disastrous economic situation within Egypt itself, caused by the loss of revenue from the Suez Canal, the tourist trade and the oil of Sinai, which comprised a strong argument in favour of a more conciliatory approach. For the type of urgent, large-scale economic aid that Egypt needed to tide over disaster could only be obtained from two possible sources: the United States, and the conservative, oil-producing Arab régimes, none of which were in favour of the hard line propounded by Syria and Algeria. There was also the problem of the Great Powers. A conciliatory approach would, of necessity, entail an effort to improve relations with the Western Powers, and in particular with the United States. But a change of policy towards the West was anathema to the influential left-wing elements in Egypt. These doubts and arguments regarding Egypt's future path found expression in two opposing schools of thought. One was led by Ali Sabry and the left-leaning party leaders of the Arab Socialist Union—the only organized political grouping allowed in Egypt—who urged increased socialism and closer ties with the Soviet Union. The other, led by Zakaria Muhi ed-Din, called for more liberalization at home and a switch in foreign policy towards the West. Each had his followers, and both had organs of the press to express their opinions. Whereas the pro-Western tendency found expression in the writings of Hassanein Haikal in *al-Ahram*, the Ali Sabry line was forcefully expounded in *al-Gumhuriya*. But on the fringes of these two divergent approaches, both of which remained within the bounds of the Establishment and loyal to Nasser, lay the real extremists: the extreme left-wingers and near-Communists in the trade unions, in Cairo University and in the literary circles,* and, at the other end of the spectrum, the ultra-conservatives of the Muslim Brotherhood and other religious movements. In the wake of defeat fanaticism was on the upsurge, battering on the confusion of emotions and gathering strength at the expense of the weakened Establishment.

The ferment which had been unleashed after the war was crystallizing into a confused struggle for ascendency in which Ali Sabry's Arab Socialist Union, the army and Zakaria Muhi ed-Din and his liberals were all involved. The party was increasingly emerging as a key factor in defending the Nasserist régime against the army. Zakaria Muhi ed-Din, long regarded as Nasser's favourite and as his most likely successor, was, on the other hand, being cast as a brake to the sovietization of Egypt which the party stalwarts advocated, and as a sop for the army and the liberalists, who feared the growing strength of the party. But it was the party on which Nasser's stay in power was becoming increasingly dependent, and which was now being groomed to take over the army's preponderant role in Egypt's political life. It was the party Socialist Youth, backed by the 40,000 militants of the Cairo branch of the ASU, who had organized the demonstrations on 9 June, and engineered Nasser's dramatic come-back. Ranged against Ali Sabry and the party were Marshal Amer and his supporters, and above all, Salah Nasr, the relatively unknown colonel who had, in 1953, become head of the Mukhabarat al-Ama, the General Intelligence Service, and had since become one of the more powerful figures in Egypt. Salah Nasr originally owed his position to his friend and protector, Zakaria Muhi ed-Din. But during the first years of his appointment he had to contend with the rivalry of the Military Intelligence, which, at its outset, had

* Centred mainly around the *at-Talia*, the main organ of the extreme left-wing in Egypt.

been under the control of Ali Sabry.* A mutual antipathy developed between these two men. When Sabry organized the Arab Socialist Union, Nasr and his Mukhabarat kept it under close surveillance. When the leaders of the party's socialist youth, led by Muhammad al-Khafil, distributed arms to their members in 1966 Nasr had them arrested. They were later released after President Nasser himself intervened. Both Salah Nasr and the army were out to clip the wings of the ASU. They saw Sabry as the evil counsellor who had misled Nasser into disaster. Many of the top army officers were disillusioned with Soviet equipment and with the Soviet military doctrine, which they blamed for their defeat. And they now opposed Sabry's call for yet closer ties with the Soviet Union. Their criticism of the Arab Socialist Union was aimed indirectly against Nasser himself, who was the nominal head of the ASU. Nasser had obtained prior approval from the ASU executive for all his major decisions in the tense three-week period before the war. The President himself had revealed this fact in his speech to the Trade Union executive on 26 May when he declared that the decision to demand the withdrawal of the UN troops and the closing of the Gulf of Aqaba "was authorized by the supreme executive of the Arab Socialist Union confident in the know-ledge that we shall have to engage Israel in battle".

The army clearly had a case against the party. And they were demanding that its power be curbed. But in this contest Nasser came down clearly and heavily on the side of the party. Hundreds of officers were, as we have seen, cashiered or arrested. Among them was virtually the entire upper crust of the army which had for years represented Egypt's new aristocracy, highly paid, pampered, all-powerful. Nasser was encouraged, or perhaps prodded, into taking this move by the Russians, who openly accused the senior officers of having been responsible for

* Wing-Commander Ali Sabry had been appointed head of the Air Force Intelligence in the latter days of King Farouk. In this position he gave invaluable aid to the "Free Officers Movement" which brought about the downfall of the King.

criminal neglect and of having sold the country out to the imperialists.* They had their own candidates for the top military posts among the Egyptians who had trained in the Soviet Union, and they made no bones about making their wishes clear. And they also demanded more direct supervision over the reorganization of the army. In one of the meetings between Nasser and Marshal Zacharov, the Soviet Marshal produced a list of all the Egyptian officers who had undergone training in the Soviet Union and demanded to know what they were now doing. Many, it transpired, had been transferred from active service to executive posts in nationalized industries, companies or banks. Others held relatively junior posts. Under Soviet prodding, many of these were now given senior posts in the army to replace those dismissed. One of those recommended by the Russians was the new commander of the air force, Muhammad abd el-Ezz.†

The army was removed from Egypt's political élite. But the delicate balance between party radicals and liberals of the Zakaria Muhi ed-Din type was maintained. It was evident that Nasser did not want to become a mere figure-head of the extremists and of the Russians. He needed Muhi ed-Din to maintain his independence. For expediency was forcing him increasingly away from the uncompromising, extremist attitude of the left wing. Two factors decided the course Nasser was now to chart. One was his desperate need for economic aid. The other was his realization that the Soviet Union could not help him get the Israelis out of Sinai. Only the United States, with its close relations with Israel, could do that. It was these two considerations which guided Nasser's line of action, which he made public at the summit conference of Arab Heads of State

* See *Pravda*, 7 September 1967. The Russians put the main blame on Marshal Amer and on the officers of the "business soldier" class prevalent in Egypt's armed forces. See also *Za Rubezhom*, No. 27, 1967, pp. 7–8: "There came to the fore a type of officer-businessman, who was concerned more with business than the military training of soldiers and sergeants."

† He was, however, found to be unsuitable, and was replaced within a month.

which convened in the capital of the Sudan on 29 August 1967.

The Khartoum summit marked the culmination of intense efforts to reach a consensus of Arab opinion regarding the steps which should be taken to mitigate the disaster that had befallen the Arab countries. The most treasured weapon in the Arab arsenal—the oil embargo—had proved to be a dismal failure. The Arabs had held this threat over Western heads for more than twenty years. In 1946 they had held acrimonious discussions but failed to agree among themselves to implement their threat to stop the flow of Arab oil to the West.* But, twenty-one years later, on the eve of the Six-Day War, representatives of the Arab oil-producing countries had convened in Baghdad and had unanimously decided to cut off oil supplies to any state committing aggression against any Arab country or giving aid to Israel. This time the threat was carried out. But the elephant gave birth to a mouse. The move caused inconvenience and considerable financial loss to Great Britain, but little else. It certainly did not produce the political results that the Arabs had expected. But for the Arab oil-producing countries the stoppage of the oil flow was disastrous. On 30 June the Saudi Minister for Oil, Sheikh Ahmad Zaki Yamani, warned that the economies of the Arab states faced collapse. He revealed that Saudi Arabia had lost £11 million in lost oil royalties in the twenty-four days since the embargo had been put into effect. On the same day the Kuwaitis announced that their national income had been cut by 40% because of the

---

* One of the secret decisions of the Bludan conference of Arab rulers in June 1946 had been to stop all economic concessions to Great Britain and the United States if the recommendations of the Anglo-American Commission's report on Palestine were implemented. At a later conference, at Sofar, in September 1946, the Saudi Arabian delegate warned that implementation of this decision would expose the Arabs to the derision of a hostile world, to which the Iraqi Premier replied "Britain and the United States will hesitate to support the proposal to partition Palestine, and might even oppose it if they know that support for the Zionists may cost them their oil concessions in our countries. Neither the British nor the Americans will laugh if we cut off their Middle East oil." See Jon and David Kimche. *Both Sides of the Hill*, pp. 56–57.

embargo. When the Economic Ministers of the Arab Countries met in Baghdad in July, the oil-producing countries demanded that the embargo be lifted forthwith. The one exception was Iraq, whose leaders surprisingly sided with Syria in pressing demands for an indefinite stoppage of oil. The Iraqis were in a peculiar position. They were being harmed more than anyone by the embargo. Unlike the Saudis or Kuwaitis they could not draw upon vast bank reserves to tide over their difficulties. They needed the oil royalties to cover their current expenditures. Without them they would not be able to pay salaries or maintain essential services. They had already suffered badly during the dispute between Syria and the Iraqi Petroleum Company in the winter of 1966, when the Syrians closed the pipelines and shut off the flow of oil. Now they took an extremist line, more out of fear that if they opposed the embargo the Syrians would sabotage the pipelines than out of any desire to commit economic hara-kiri. And they were fairly certain that the other oil-producing countries would not accept the extremist proposals. As was to be expected, the Baghdad conference failed to reach any decision. The distance separating the extremist oil have-nots from the haves was too great. The subject was deferred to the forth-coming Arab Foreign Ministers Conference to be held in Khartoum at the beginning of August.

But it was not only over the question of oil that the lines were once more being drawn across the Arab world. The "unity of the defeated" which characterized the state of the Arab world just after the war began to melt away in the heat engendered by inter-Arab friction. In the weeks following the end of the war, the Heads of State of the "progressive" Arab countries converged on Cairo as their natural rallying point. President Atassi of Syria was one of the first to make this pilgrimage to Cairo. But he was soon followed by Presidents Boumedienne of Algeria, Aref of Iraq, al-Azhari of the Sudan, and briefly by King Hussein, who, since he had signed a defence pact with Egypt on the eve of the war, hung rather uncertainly between the progressive and conservative camps of Arabism. Thesemeetings

of the "progressives" in Cairo and the coming and goings of
Boumedienne, Atassi and Aref between Cairo and Moscow
aroused the suspicion and the ire of the so-called conservative
Arab Heads of State, who were not kept informed of the
content of all these consultations, and who suspected that the
revolutionary régimes were once more taking up the cudgels
against them. And this was, indeed, exactly what the Syrians
and the Algerians wanted to do. The Syrians in particular
refused to have anything to do with the reactionaries, including
King Hussein. They and the Algerians strongly opposed the
convening of another Arab summit, which had been proposed by
Hussein. There should, they said, be a summit of Arab revolutionaries only. "There are some Arabs with whom I have no
wish to sit at the same table," Colonel Boumedienne is reported
to have remarked.

Throughout the month of July it appeared as if the extremists
would have their way, and that unity of action would once more
be dissipated in internecine strife. King Hussein told foreign
journalists* that he had lost all hope for an Arab summit
conference. Nasser refused to commit himself. He was still
feeling his way cautiously on the home front, and he felt
unsure of his revolutionary allies. His antipathy to the Syrian
Ba'th was stronger than ever. He neither forgot nor forgave the
tardiness of Syrian action during the war. His attitude to
Boumedienne was correct but unfriendly, vastly different from
the warm relations that had existed between him and Ben Bella.
Moreover, the Algerian leader was, in none too subtle a way,
trying to steal a march over him. For the first time Nasser's
once undisputed leadership of the Arab progressives could be
challenged, and the Algerians hastened to set themselves up as
alternatives to that leadership.

For the Algerians, victors of a seven-year war with the
French, the idea that the combined Arab armies of Egypt,
Syria and Jordan could be beaten in six days was inconceivable.
They looked upon the Arabs of the Mashrak (the East) with

* In an interview with *Time* correspondents (*Time*, 28 July 1967).

I

little-disguised contempt. Moreover, Boumedienne had his own reasons for joining the Arab in-fighting with such zest and for posing as a leader of the Arab world. Quite apart from considerations of prestige, he was aiming at calming growing opposition to his régime within Algeria and at neutralizing the more nationalist and right-wing elements headed by his Minister of Finance, Kaid Ahmad, by the popular Cherif Belkacem and by his own chief of staff. He therefore beat the drums of nationalism and extremism with the utmost vigour, and exploited to the full the fact that he was sending Algerian troops, planes and tanks to bolster up the Egyptian front at the Suez Canal.*

The Algerians were fully supported by the Syrians, who were quite happy to see a serious challenge to Nasser's leadership. The Syrians made no bones of what they considered to be the correct Arab answer to the disaster that had befallen them. Arab action should be waged on two fronts: a call for war in the form of a popular people's struggle, as the only means to wipe out the results of the *débâcle*, and a continuation of the struggle against reactionary elements in the Arab world. "The struggle for the liberation of Palestine will be waged throughout the Arab homeland" was a pet phrase of the Syrian press.

But behind this pugnacious attitude the Syrian régime had its own problems to face. Never had the military leadership been so unpopular. It was an open secret in Syria that the two crack units of the army, the 50th and, in particular, the 70th Armoured Brigades, had been kept behind in their bases in Homs and Damascus during the war to protect the régime against any possible uprising.† And the military junta, which was composed of a complex juxtaposition of political shadings and rival racial allegiances, was becoming increasingly divided among itself. At the outbreak of the war there had been four

* Boumedienne's pan-Arab fervour abated somewhat after the abortive coup of his chief of staff.

† The 70th Armoured Brigade, known popularly in Syria as the "protector of the régime", is commanded by Izzet Jedid who, like so many of Syria's ruling Establishment, is an Alawi.

distinct groupings: the followers of the Alawi General Salah Jadid, generally considered the strong man of the régime and leader of the Ba'th faction in the armed forces; those of the Defence Minister and commander of the Air Force, General Asad, also of the Alawi minority; the Ismaili grouping, led by extreme left-wing Khaled Jundi and his armed workers, by abd al-Karim al-Jundi, head of Intelligence, and Brigadier Ahmad el-Mir, commander of the key southern front; and a fourth grouping, headed by the chief of staff, General Suweidani, a Sunni Muslim, who emerged as a vital balancing-point between General Jadid and General Asad. One of the first results of the war was the overthrow of the Ismailis. They had been the most militant of all the groupings. Khaled Jundi was known to be pro-Chinese, and his demand after the war for the immediate arming of the people in preparation for guerrilla warfare was looked upon in fear and distaste by the army generals. The Russians, too, were anxious to get him out of the way. Together with Jundi, Brigadier Ahmad el-Mir was removed from his position as commander of the southern front in an obvious move to pin the blame for the defeat on him. At the same time Jadid strengthened his hold on the Ba'th organization by stepping up the purges he had begun before the war.*
But by July these moves, coupled with the soaring prices and the stories of the army's ignominious role in the war that were doing the rounds of the bazaars, had created a mood that was close to general civil disobedience. The threat to the régime was

* As he was responsible for appointments and promotions within the army, General Jadid held the whip-hand. The main criterion for promotion had become loyalty to the Ba'th party. From December 1966 to May 1967 General Jadid confirmed the expulsion of some 120 officers from the ranks of the Ba'th. They were all supporters of rival factions. Jadid's influence in the Ba'th Party can be gauged from the fact that the heads of the Information and Propaganda Office, the Foreign Relations, Education, and Organization Offices are all known Jadid supporters. His position in the party branches was greatly strengthened at the end of 1966 when the party leadership set up committees to visit all branches, examine their activities and weed out undesirables. The committees were packed with supporters of General Jadid.

ever-present. There existed a real danger that the officers opposing General Jadid might band together and, with the backing of the majority Sunni elements, seek to topple his régime.* To appease the population, the General ordered the release of prisoners among the merchants and the Ulema (the Muslim clergy) who had been arrested in their hundreds during the May riots. He relaxed some of the harsh economic controls in a bid to co-opt private capital into the country's shaky economy. And he maintained the atmosphere of war hysteria in an effort to boost the moral of the people. A blackout was reimposed in Damascus in July, khaki uniforms were distributed to all civil servants, air-raid drills were initiated, all to the accompaniment of continuous high-pitched war propaganda.

Under such circumstances the Syrian leaders were in no mood to consider concessions or moderation. Thus both they and the Algerians sought to impose on Nasser an extremist policy of continued war against Israel, against the reactionary Arab régimes, and against the West.

From an ideological point of view, Nasser probably was sympathetic to these demands. He had no love either for the Arab conservative régimes or for the West. But Nasser must have realized that splitting the Arab world into two rival camps would not, at that stage, do him any good. The conservatives would castigate him for his military defeat while in the "progressive" camp he would have to contend with Boumedienne's challenge for the leadership. Moreover, it was the conservatives, and not the progressives, who now held the trump cards. It was they who possessed the oil, and who could help rehabilitate Nasser's shattered economy. He therefore turned his back on his revolutionary allies and joined King Hussein in his call for an Arab summit.

Nasser's decision was of extreme importance for King

---

* At the beginning of 1968 this danger had become so great that, in a bid to forestall a Sunni take-over, the Government dismissed the Sunni chief-of-staff, the powerful General Suweidani and purged the army of his supporters.

Hussein. Of all the Arab countries, his was the worst affected by the war, and his dilemma was the greatest. The King had felt confident after the war that his Western allies would stand by him and force the Israelis to give up the West Bank of the Jordan. But he was soon to become disenchanted. At his meeting with President Johnson in Washington at the end of June, he was told bluntly, with none too great finesse, that he could have no hope of getting his lost territories back unless he reached a settlement with Israel. The British Foreign Secretary, although he displayed much more sympathy for the plight of the King, said, in effect, similar things. The Italian Premier was much more outspoken; he told the King that he would have to sign a peace treaty with Israel if he wanted to obtain the sympathy of the Western world. Nor did the Pope have comforting words for him: the head of the Catholic Church was not convinced that the holy city of Jerusalem should be preserved in Jordanian hands.

The King returned from his voyage a sadder and a wiser man. He evidently was not going to get help from the West. The Soviet Union provided no alternative, for the Russians, even if they wanted to, could not restore the West Bank for him. There remained the same awful choice which was facing Nasser: either concessions to Israel, or the possibility of Israel staying in the territory it had conquered for an indefinite period. During the month of July the King put out tentative feelers, through the medium of a third party, to discover what concessions the Israelis would demand in return for their withdrawal from the West Bank.* The Israelis replied that they would be willing to reveal their conditions—at the negotiating table, facing the Jordanians. But Israeli Ministers made no secret of Israel's stand: nothing short of a peace treaty would satisfy them, and even after such a treaty, their withdrawal would not include Jerusalem.

* These unofficial contacts were hinted at by Mr Eshkol in his interview with the Tel Aviv afternoon paper, *Maariv*. The full story of these contacts cannot yet be told.

King Hussein, courageous as he is, did not dare to sue for peace. He feared the fate that befell his grandfather, King Abdullah. With no hope of a quick settlement, the outlook looked grim indeed, so grim as to bring a British journalist to write from Amman that "the present prospect that the Israelis will occupy the West Bank of the Jordan indefinitely means that in a matter of months the Kindgom of Jordan may cease to exist".*

The avenues of escape from his untenable position were being closed, one after the other. But even a stalemate, the prospect of marking time, was dangerous. The percentage of Palestinians on the East Bank of the Jordan had been steadily increasing over the years. Long before the Six-Day War there had been a steady trickle of immigrants passing over the bridges of the Jordan towards the east.† The large migration of Palestinians had completely changed the character of the towns of the East Bank. Zerqa, for example, which had a population of barely 10,000 in 1948, was now a thriving centre with well over 100,000 inhabitants, the vast majority Palestinians. Jordan, in fact, was well on its way to losing its Bedouin, East Bank character, and taking on a Palestinian identity. These Palestinians, who numbered well over half a million, would not accept the loss of the West Bank quietly. Hussein, who had all but lost a kingdom and become a popular patriot at the same time, would rapidly lose his hard-won prestige and popularity unless he acted quickly over the West Bank. Moreover, there existed

* Gavin Young, in the *Observer*, 23 July 1967.

† Since 1949 there has been an emigration of 250,000 Palestinians from the West to the East Bank of the Jordan; 80% of them were refugees. The population of the West Bank at the beginning of 1967 was only slightly higher than it had been in 1949, despite the abnormally high 4% natural increase. Another 200,000 Jordanians emigrated abroad during this period; again, approximately 80% of them were refugees. Thus the refugee problem was well on its way to liquidation by means of mobility. After completing their census, the Israelis reached the conclusion that there remained only 120,000 refugees in the West Bank, of whom 60,000 still lived in refugee camps. There were 220,000 refugees in the Gaza Strip, 175,000 of them living in camps.

a real danger that the Palestinians of the West Bank would opt out of their allegiance to Jordan and sue for a separate peace with Israel. The idea of a separate, independent Palestinian entity took root among West Bank Palestinians immediately after the war, as we have said. Such a development could undermine the rule of the Hashemite House over Jordan, and constituted the King's greatest fear in the aftermath of the war. And even if the idea of a separate entity did not take root, the mere fact that the Palestinians of the West Bank were once more developing political activity of their own meant that the population would be increasingly difficult to handle once it returned to the Jordanians' fold. It had taken many years to glue the sides of the river into one state. The glue had now come unstuck, and the longer the two parts remained separate, the more difficult it would be to glue them together again. But the one way he might hope to get back the lost territory, by coming to terms with Israel, was unacceptable to the extremists, both in his and in the other Arab countries. If Hussein had any doubts on this subject, they were dispelled by a trenchant article written on 6 September by Mahmud Sherif, the editor of the Government newspaper *al-Dustur*. Sherif attacked those Arabs who believed in a political solution of the Arab–Israeli conflict. The only way, he declared, was to go to war again. There remained only one hope for the King—concerted Arab action. Such action, however, could not be directed towards another war, for the June War had proved that the Arabs were in no position to beat Israel. The only hope lay in concerted political action. The summit conference therefore assumed new and added importance for Hussein, and Nasser's support for the summit was greatly welcomed by him.

We thus come to Khartoum, where the fourth summit conference of Arab Heads of State was opened with great pomp in the evening of 29 August. But from the very beginning of the conference, the shadows of failure hung over it. There were the last-minute refusals to attend by the Heads of State of Morocco, Algeria, Tunisia, Libya and Syria. There had been failure to reach agreement at a meeting of Arab Foreign Ministers in Khartoum several weeks earlier, and at the Baghdad conference of Economic Ministers. There were contrasting declarations on the eve of the conference, made by the President of Tunisia on the one hand and the President of Syria on the other. There was President Sallal's announcement that he would not accept a Sudanese compromise proposal for the ending of the war in the Yemen. There was the personal antipathy known to exist between President Nasser and King Faisal of Saudi Arabia, and the hostility between the Syrians and the Jordanians. Seldom had a conference of allies met under such strained circumstances.

And, indeed, during the first hours of the conference, it appeared that the gaps between the various camps were too wide to be bridged. Nasser deliberately snubbed Feisal at the airport. The Syrian delegation, led by their Foreign Minister, kept away from the conference hall, and at the end of the first day, left Khartoum altogether. The semi-official Algerian newspaper, *al-Mujahid*, sneeringly called the conference "a medium-summit" of no great consequence.

Yet the Khartoum conference was not a failure. Nor did it end in the stalemate between extremists and conservatives which many had prophesied. At Khartoum the first measured Arab reply to the Israeli victories was made; the first blueprint of action which had the backing of most of the Arab countries was formulated. Deadlock was averted by the Syrian decision to boycott the conference and by the sulky attitude of the Algerians, who, evidently realizing that they were in a minority, preferred to remain silent. The Syrians left for similar reasons. Their demands for guerrilla warfare against Israel and for a continuation of the oil embargo against the West were evidently not going to be accepted. By leaving, they wished to demonstrate their determination to adhere to their own extremist policy and their refusal to toe any Egyptian-led moderate line.

Their departure left the field open for Nasser. He had come to make a deal with the conservative régimes and there was now no one of consequence to interfere. He rejected the extremist proposals. He supported the demands of Saudi-Arabia, Kuwait and Libya that the oil embargo be lifted. He agreed to pull his troops out of the Yemen and to cease his attacks on the conservative régimes. But he had his price. He needed financial assistance, urgently. Egypt could not hold out without outside help for more than six months, he told the conference. This was probably an optimistic evaluation—three months would probably have been more accurate. He needed foreign currency for the current needs of the Egyptian economy. As for a continuation of the war, "if you want us to continue the struggle, you will have to give us half your total incomes", Nasser warned his audience. Without mincing words, he gave a sombre picture of Egypt's military and economic situation in the aftermath of the war. Yet, despite her hardships, Egypt would never make peace with Israel. She was prepared to suffer a prolonged occupation of Sinai. But a lengthy occupation of the West Bank of the Jordan was quite another matter. This was far more serious. Given time, the Israelis would create new political realities, based on their present boundary along the Jordan River. The Palestinian people would then be doomed. The only way of preventing the Israelis from taking such steps was by political action. An offer of a political settlement could tie the hands of the Israelis, and restore the Arabs to the position they had held before the June disaster, Nasser declared. To achieve this aim the Arabs must be prepared to put on at least a show of making concessions. What are these concessions, Nasser asked. Admitting the existence of Israel? The Arabs had done that already when they signed the armistice agreements with Israel in 1949. Non-belligerency? This would only put off the final annihilation of Israel until such time as the Arabs were ready to go to war again. Freedom of shipping? The Israelis already had it in the Gulf of Aqaba and, as for Suez, this could be a subject for bargaining. But Nasser stressed one point. He, Nasser, was not willing to renounce his struggle for the rights of the Palestinian people. He totally rejected the Tunisian and

Moroccan stand which advocated a real end to belligerency and direct peace talks with Israel. There could be neither direct negotiations nor Arab recognition of Israel. If such a solution proved impossible, the Arabs would have no choice other than to revert to the alternative of war, but if this were to be the case they would have to prepare themselves for many years before they could challenge Israel once more in the field of battle. Nasser intimated that a proposal such as the one put forward by his friend, Marshal Tito, might be acceptable. This called for an Israeli withdrawal in return for freedom of passage through the Aqaba Straits, a Great Power guarantee of the integrity of the borders of the Middle East, and Israeli goods, but not ships, to be allowed through the Suez Canal. The important thing, he insisted, was to reach a formula which would bring about an Israeli withdrawal. Once this was attained, the Arabs could revert to their pre-June position of hostility towards Israel. Nasser's plea was echoed by King Hussein, who, like Nasser, asked for a mandate to reach a settlement with Israel, so that "after the (Israeli) withdrawal we can return to our former ways and methods".

Nasser got what he wanted at Khartoum. Egypt emerged the richer by a promise of an annual payment of £95 million from the conference. One of the decisions of the summit was to set up a fund for the rehabilitation of those countries hit by the war. Saudi Arabia was to pay £50 million per year, Kuwait £55 million and Libya £30 million. These sums were to be distributed to Egypt, to Jordan and eventually to Syria. And Nasser also obtained the summit's agreement to his political proposals. The summit resolutions reaffirmed the need for united Arab action, though King Hussein was told that the Arab countries would not object if he reached a separate settlement, provided he did not make peace with Israel. It called for a combined political and diplomatic offensive on a world scale aimed at "annulling the effects of the aggression". But it maintained the principle of non-recognition of the State of Israel and no peace negotiations with Israel, and reaffirmed the right of the

Palestinians to their country. The resolutions marked a defeat for the extremists—the Syrians, the Algerians, and the Palestinian Liberation Organization of Ahmad Shuqairi—who opposed in principle any political settlement. But they were a far cry from the "decision to make peace" to which, according to *Le Monde*'s special correspondent, Eric Rouleau, Nasser had come on the eve of the conference.

Nasser emerged from the summit with enhanced stature. He re-established his position as the leader of a large part of the Arab world. It was his proposals, and not those of Boumedienne or Atassi, which had been accepted. And the financial settlement gave him a new lease of life.

But his position at home had reached a new point of high danger. The struggle for power inside Egypt had reached its climax. Marshal Amer and the ousted service officers had not been idle. They plotted their come-back, but their planning was as faulty as their preparations for the June War had been. On 27 August, only two days before Nasser left for Khartoum, Marshal Amer was, according to the plan, to have presented himself at Headquarters of the Eastern (Suez) front, and, with the aid of a forged Presidential decree restoring Amer to his former position as Deputy Commander in Chief, was to have taken over the command of the troops there. He was then to have addressed an ultimatum to the President demanding the return of all the deposed officers to their former positions. In the event of refusal, he was to have advanced on Cairo at the head of an armoured brigade. But the plot never reached the first stage. Someone tipped Nasser off and the plotters were rounded up. Nasser invited Amer, his old friend and relative by marriage, to dinner, and informed him that he was being placed under house arrest. While the meal was still in progress, picked troops raided Amer's house in Dokki. They found an arsenal of light arms and bundles of leaflets of a seditious nature stacked up in the house. In the house itself were several dozen officers, many of whom had been sought by the military police, who had taken refuge there.

Among those arrested then and in the days that followed were the former War Minister, Shams ed-Din Badran, ex-Minister of the Interior Abbas Radwan and some fifty officers and civilians. They included Salah Nasr, the head of the Intelligence Service, his deputy and many of the top Intelligence officers. Nasser was taking no chances. Severe repressive measures were taken to prevent an uprising in favour of the arrested men. Eric Rouleau described the situation in Cairo on the eve of the summit in a dispatch to *Le Monde* on 30 August. "Troops were confined to barracks," he wrote, "military police were patrolling the streets, a close guard was being mounted around official buildings and bridges by soldiers with helmets and automatic weapons."

Two weeks later, on 15 September, the people of Egypt were told that Marshal Amer had committed suicide. The news came as a profound shock, and in particular to the officer class which was still reeling from the harsh measures being taken against it. By no means a brilliant officer, Amer had jumped from the rank of Major to that of Field-Marshal because he had been Nasser's friend. From the purely professional point of view he had been no better a strategist or commander than any of a dozen or more senior officers. But Amer himself knew this. He never attempted to pull his rank on his friends. Instead he became their mouthpiece, their go-between with the President. Amer pulled strings, arranged matters, defended the rights of the officers, got them good jobs when they left the army. For all these reasons, he was very popular in the army, and most of the senior officers felt an intense loyalty to him. His death came as a crowning blow. It had a tremendous impact on all ranks of the army. On the night of Amer's death, a mysterious attempt was made on Nasser's life. The President had been staying in Alexandria. There were rumours that he was ill. As he was about to leave his place of residence, shots were fired at him. But the attempted assassination was hushed up.

Did Amer really commit suicide or was he killed? The world may never know the answer. But many people in Egypt, especially in the army, are convinced that Amer did not take his life by his own hand. And this belief has created an unbridgeable gap between Nasser and Amer's colleagues.

But on the face of it, Nasser was now in a strong position. His main opponents—the ones who had demanded his resignation and who had been in a position to back up their demand with tanks and troops—were now neutralized. But the danger of a coup was still ever-present. Nasser had overcome the immediate crisis period immediately after the war. His position in October was already much stronger than it had been in August. The economic collapse had been staved off by the contributions from the Arab countries, while his armed forces were being bolstered up by the massive Soviet arms consignments. But the régime as a whole had been struck an irrevocable blow by the June disaster. It had lost its popularity, its hold on the people. Despite repressive measures, the people of Egypt were openly voicing their criticism. At first they wished to exonerate Nasser, to put the blame on his advisers. But when they saw that he was still surrounded by the same ministers, their disillusionment deepened. Nasser's gamble was to pin all the blame on Amer and the ousted officers. But was this accepted? Did this automatically make the others guiltless in the eyes of the people? The demonstrations of workers and students in Cairo in February 1968 provided the answer.

But for the time being, Nasser could devote himself to the problem of getting the Israelis off his doorstep. Strengthened by the outcome of the Khartoum summit, he now unleashed his political offensive, in close conjunction with King Hussein and President Tito. It was designed to repair Egypt's relations with the Western world, which had reached their nadir with the outbreak of the war, and to convince the United States that a settlement could be reached with the Arabs provided that Israel could be induced to withdraw her forces to the pre-5 June demarcation line. The steps taken by the Egyptians to bring about a restoration of relations with Great Britain were one aspect of this policy. So was the prudent transfer of Ali Sabry to the Suez area. When it came to amelioration of relations with the West, Nasser preferred to have Zakaria Muhi ed-Din as the man around Cairo, and Sabry in the background. The voyages of King Hussein were another aspect of this policy. Even his trip to Moscow was designed more to pressure the West into being more accommodating than to gain aid from the East. The offer the Russians made to him during his Moscow trip, to supply him with all the arms he needed on condition that he jettisoned all his Western arms, could hardly have been enticing for him. Such an arrangement would have put him entirely in Soviet hands and would, in all probability, have meant that he would not get another penny or cent from the West.

King Hussein, indeed, played a key role in this political offensive. He is the most popular of all the Arab leaders in Western eyes. He and King Faisal of Saudi Arabia were the pillars on which Western policy in the Arab world had rested. He was eminently the most suitable spokesman for the new Arab policy of coaxing the West into a settlement calling for an Israeli withdrawal. His statements in Europe and the US after Khartoum were in full co-ordination with President Nasser. And even the Syrians and the Algerians promised not to sabotage the King's efforts. President Boumedienne is reported to have told the King, during his visit to Algeria in October, that he could do whatever he liked, as long as he did not ask for active Algerian support for his pro-Western policy. The Syrians likewise told President Nasser that they would not interfere. "Let the King break his head on a political solution. You will then come round to our way of thinking," was their attitude.

Were Nasser and King Hussein sincere in their efforts to reach a settlement, or were they, as the Israelis believed, putting on only a façade of moderation designed to gain Western support of their demand for an Israeli withdrawal without really intending to make any move towards permanent peaceful coexistence with Israel?

The answer is a complex one. There can be no doubt that both Nasser and Hussein were willing to come to some sort of a settlement with Israel. This in itself marked a tremendous change from their previous attitude of ignoring Israel's very existence. The sheer totality of the June defeat, the shambles to which their economies had been reduced, and the black outlook for the future all made them much more realistic in their outlook on the Israeli–Arab conflict. They already knew they would not be able to beat Israel in a war for a very long time. They now realized that they would not be able to recover their lost territories unless some sort of settlement was reached.

But what should the terms of such a settlement include? Would they entail only tactical concessions in order to bring about an Israeli withdrawal without altering the basic Arab objective of annihilating the State of Israel at some future date, or would they comprise a definite step towards lasting peace? It was around this question that the deadlock revolved. The Arabs were willing to make tactical concessions only. The Israelis, backed by the Americans, wanted more. They demanded a settlement which would remove the basic threat of future violence. And they insisted on guarantees to prevent such a settlement from becoming a worthless scrap of paper once the Israelis withdrew from the least part of the occupied territories.

These were the respective stands of the Egyptians and the Americans when the Egyptian Foreign Minister, Mahmud Riadh, met Arthur Goldberg in New York during the meeting of the General Assembly in October 1967. The series of talks between the two marks an important departure from the previous position taken by Egypt. It was the first high-level confrontation between Egypt and the United States since the war at which a political formula for the Middle East deadlock was sought by both sides. But after a week of discussions the two sides were nowhere nearer to understanding. Mahmud Riadh's opening tactic, based largely on Marshal Tito's proposals, was so far apart from the American demand for a permanent peace settlement that the two could make no headway.

The American stand put the Egyptians in an invidious

position. They had, after a period of agonizing heart-searching, reached the conclusion that they must make some concessions. They agreed to permit Israeli shipping in the Gulf of Aqaba. They would allow Israeli goods, though not the Israeli flag to pass through the Suez Canal. They were willing, though they never publicly said so, to give up the Gaza Strip. They would, if sufficiently pressed, in all probability, agree to the demilitarization of the Sinai Peninsula. They would accept a generally worded declaration of non-belligerence. But no more. Even these concessions were arrived at only after the most tortuous self-appraisal of their own situation. Considering the background of Arab–Israeli relations these concessions, if they were to be implemented, were, in themselves, remarkable. They were agreed upon only after the Egyptian leaders reached the conclusion that they had absolutely no chance of defeating Israel militarily in the foreseeable future and that they could not possibly begin to put Egypt's economy on its feet again as long as the Israeli army remained on the banks of the Suez Canal.

But this step forward to a settlement that the Egyptians were willing to make was still so far distant from the maximum Israeli demand for total peace that not only the Israelis, but also the Americans, were unwilling even to consider them.

Thus, by October, total deadlock was once more reached. For the Egyptian leaders, and in particular for President Nasser himself, the granting of further concessions was well-nigh inconceivable. It would be a negation of all that Nasser had stood for throughout the years of his rule; it would be tantamount to political suicide. But to break off the dialogue with the Americans, to turn his back on the search for a political solution and return instead to the fold of the extremists, to the hard line of no concessions and continued warfare, was equally unthinkable. For that would entail continued Israeli occupation of the Sinai Peninsula, increased tension with the West, and no possibility of staving off economic collapse.

Two weeks after the failure of these talks came the sinking

of the *Elath*. From the Egyptian point of view, it was an act of folly comparable to the irrational deeds of 23 May which had led to the June War. Was the sinking connected with the failure of the New York talks? Were the Egyptians trying to show the Americans that they were down but not yet out, that they were still a force that was not be to trifled with? The timing of the event appears to indicate some interconnection. But Government decisions are very often complex affairs, even if they are taken by one man. They very rarely operate on the principle of deed and consequence. They are usually the sum total of many components, some of which might be quite irrational or even irrelevant to the final decision. The attack on the *Elath*, one would suspect, was a decision of this nature. The *Elath*, patrolling up and down on the fringe of Egypt's territorial waters, was to the Egyptians as a fly that buzzes round the nose of a nervous and irritable man; there comes a moment when he loses his temper and swats the fly, even if he might break something in the process of swatting. The Egyptian navy commanders had reported to Nasser the course taken regularly by the *Elath*. They asked for permission to attack it. At first Nasser refused. But the reports continued. The fly was still buzzing. And finally Nasser gave his approval. He evidently believed he could explain the attack away by his claim that the Israeli destroyer had been within territorial waters, which it was not. The Egyptians believed that the Israelis would bombard Port Said in retaliation. Fantastic though it seems, they failed to take into account that the Suez refineries had been a sitting target for Israeli guns since the June War. It was one of the crassest and most expensive oversights Nasser ever made.

That the attack on the *Elath* had been carefully planned beforehand was as much as revealed in the stories appearing in the Cairo press. But it was not only the *Elath* which disappeared into the deep blue sea. With it went the hopes that Egyptians and Israelis might, despite all, find a speedy solution to the impasse. Once more the vicious circle of violence and counter-violence was begun. The Israeli counter-blow was swift and heavy. The destruction of the giant oil refineries at Suez was a catastrophic blow for Egypt's reeling economy. They could have attacked the refineries at any time after the June War. They desisted. But the *Elath* sinking, and the attendant loss of lives, washed away Israeli scruples. Yet in the anger and bitterness which the action and counter-action provoked there was born one small seed of hope: the blows had been so cruel and senseless for both sides that perhaps they would restore some vestige of sanity before it was too late. It was a tiny, faint hope, but it provided the only glimmer of light in the darkening gloom which, together with the smoke billowing out of the burning Suez refineries, enveloped the Sinai battlefront in the last days of October.

In the meantime, the Syrians had been busy putting their theories of guerrilla warfare into practice. We have already seen the effect which the June War had on the Fatah terror organization. Hundreds of Palestinian students had left their studies to volunteer for military training in Algeria. Only a few of them reached the Middle East before the war had ended. But in the aftermath of the fighting the Syrians once more took the Fatah in hand. The Fatah activists from Europe and Algeria were called to Damascus, and a plan for an overall terror offensive was decided upon. The conclusions they reached were significant:* no Arab country could possibly be a match for Israel for at least five to six years. This being so, there was no point in continuing the pre-war policy of forcing a war on the Arab countries by means of escalation through terror. Their actions should now take on a different purpose: not to implicate Arab countries in hostilities, but as guerrilla warfare to be directed within Israeli-held territory itself. Instead of the hit-and-run raids of pre-war vintage, Fatah would now reorganize, with Syrian help, in Viet Cong manner, in the towns and villages of the West Bank of Palestine. The discussions at Damascus, at which Yasir Arafat, the chief of the Fatah, and General Suweidani, the Syrian Chief of Staff, were the main participants,

---

* They were revealed by senior Fatah members captured by the Israelis.

laid the foundation for the new Fatah.* In the wake of the Damascus meeting dozens of senior Fatah activists, from among the veterans of the German branch, infiltrated through Jordan to the West Bank. Their aim, as prescribed by Arafat, was to establish Fatah cells in every village, to set up arms caches and to organize and train guerrilla bands in the hills, where their members would hide out in the caves which have been used for similar purposes since the days of the Bible. The organizers brought with them quantities of arms and Arabic translations of Viet Cong training manuals. At the same time the Syrians, by none-too-gentle means, carried out large-scale recruitment of Palestinian refugees living in Syria, who were pressed into Fatah training camps which had been established in the vicinity of Damascus.

In a bid to transform Fatah into a mass underground movement, hundreds of Palestinians were sent to these camps, and from there through the underground route to the West Bank. They were helped along this route by men of the 421st Battalion of the Iraqi army. This battalion had been formed from Palestinian recruits and had been infiltrated by the Fatah as a means for obtaining military training for its members. Now it formed part of the Iraqi Expeditionary Forces stationed in Jordan and the battalion was used to transfer men, arms and equipment in their Iraqi army trucks from the Syrian border through Jordan to the Jordan River, where they would be led across into Israeli-held territory in the dead of night. Some of the Fatah bands began operating. A bomb was placed in a Jerusalem cinema, another in the USIS library in Tel Aviv. Both were

---

* The rivalry existing between Syrian leaders found expression in their contacts with Palestinian underground movements. From documents captured by the Israelis it became clear that the Syrian Head of Intelligence, General Jundi, had, before the war, taken the Palestine Liberation Front under his protective wing, while General Suweidani was associated with the Fatah. Shortly before the war, when complete control over the terror organizations became imperative, General Suweidani extended his hold and placed one of his men, Major Suhil, as co-ordinator of all the Palestinian movements operating from Syria. He continued this close control through the Major after the war, until his own dismissal.

discovered and removed before they could do any harm. Explosive charges were laid in kibbutz factories, in villages and on railway tracks. But the damage was not great. And the Israeli security services soon had the terror campaign under control. By the end of November the vast majority of Fatah members in the West Bank had been rounded up. They were often given away by West Bank Arabs, who feared the trouble and the reprisals their actions would cause.

Thus, as the year 1967 drew to an end, both the violent approach of the Syrians and the Palestinian terrorists and the political formula advocated by the Egyptians had reached a dead end. Neither was successful. The Syrians and the Fatah failed because the conditions were not suitable for a Viet Cong or Algerian FLN variety of warfare. The vast majority of the Palestinians themselves wanted none of it. And the Israelis, with their efficient intelligence and security organizations, were easily able to prevent any mass movement from taking root. The Egyptians failed because they had still been thinking in half-measures. They had not yet grasped the fact that the Israelis were in no mood to surrender their gains unless they received tangible guarantees of future peace in return. And this time the Israelis could persevere in their demands because they enjoyed the solid support of the United States. None the less, Nasser was not yet inclined to make peace, despite the catastrophic conditions of Egypt's economy. Disastrous as the economic situation of Egypt was, this in itself was not sufficient to make Nasser change his attitude. This situation was indeed steadily worsening. Unemployment was growing. A quarter of a million evacuees from the Canal Zone crowded the shanty-towns in Cairo and Alexandria. Factories were standing idle for want of raw materials. Development projects were abandoned. Prices were soaring. Yet Egypt still stood firm in her decision not to make peace. Thus the year ended on the note of unclear vistas and unanswered questions: would the deadlock bring both the Egyptians and the Israelis to soften their attitudes in order to make a political settlement feasible? Or would the Egyptians, in the face of Israeli demands for peace, which they were not willing to grant, go over to the camp of violence and join the Syrians and Algerians in their extremist approach? Or would the simmering discontent in the Arab lands sweep away existing régimes and lay the foundations for a new future? And, above all, there was one question on whose answer the peace of the world could well depend: had the world witnessed one more round in an unfinished war, or had it seen the formation of an embryo of peace in the oldest trouble spot in the universe? It was around this question that the activities of the Great Powers revolved in the aftermath of the war, and it is to these activities that we must now turn.

CHAPTER 13

The Political War

The relationship between the United States and Israel on the one hand, and the Soviet Union and Egypt on the other, both immediately before and after the June War, could be likened to that of partners in a game of solo whist. None of the players knew what cards his partner possessed or what card he was going to throw down next; each played independently, yet in partnership. There were no orders given, no undercover comparing of hands. But the partnership with the stronger hands tended to collect the tricks.

Throughout the crisis period leading up to the war the Americans had no way of knowing what Israel was planning, and the Israelis, on their part, were in the dark regarding possible American reaction. This, indeed, was one of the cardinal reasons for the indecision of Israel's leaders. The Americans scrupulously followed their self-imposed injunction of no collusion. They continued this policy after the war. But by then they had realized that the outcome of the war was a victory not only for Israel, but for them too. The new situation which had emerged in the Middle East by mid-June was ideal for them. Not since the Cuban confrontation had the Russians been so discomfited. The defeat of the Egyptians showed up, for all the world to see and ponder over, the limitations of Soviet aid and support. Moreover, at a time when the Russians had, to a very large extent, the whip hand over the US in Vietnam, the Americans sorely needed a counter-balance, and they now found it in the Middle East. This was, indeed, the only region in the world where the cold war had been fluid enough to allow for such a delicate and dangerous game of political one-upmanship. But the Americans had come out on top, thanks to the Israeli army, and they intended to stay that way. This meant supporting Israel's demands, for any setback inflicted on Israel would be a gain for the opposing side, not only for Egypt, but also for the Soviet Union. Thus, for the first time in the Middle East, there emerged an almost complete identity of interests between the United States and Israel, and this fact made all the difference to the ability of Israel to stand firm in its demands. It was a far cry from the situation after the 1956 Sinai Campaign, when the US had withheld her support from Israel. She was then forced to withdraw from the territories she had gained within six months of the end of the war.

This identity of interests forms one of the central features of the war's aftermath. Most of the political moves revolved around it. For all the parties concerned—the Arabs, the Russians, the French, the British, the Yugoslavs, *et al.*—came to realize that Israel could not be budged from the position she had taken as long as she enjoyed American support. In the words of one of the senior Egyptian officers interned in Israel, who was discussing the political situation, Israel could not be moved by a frontal assault, but only by an attack on the flanks. But as long as the Americans were guarding her flanks, Israel's position was virtually impregnable.

And because the United States played such a vital role, those wishing to change Israel's stand were forced to try to come to terms with the Americans in the hope either of driving a wedge between them and the Israelis, or of persuading them to pressurize Israel into altering her stand. And the harder the American line became, the more accommodating the Egyptians —and the other Arabs—sought to be. This was the most complete vindication of those who had always opposed the "Arab" lobby which had advocated that it was in the West's vital interests to appease the Arabs, even if necessary at the expense of Israel. The fathers of this school of thought could be found in the Arabists of the British Foreign Office from the days of Brigadier Clayton down to Sir Harold Beeley. But they were equally well entrenched in the State Department and had in the past received weighty support from the influential oil lobby. Support for Israel would, in their opinion, estrange the Arabs and endanger the vital interests of the West in the Middle East, including, above all else, the flow of oil. But now, in the war's aftermath, the Western Powers were finding that the opposite was happening. The oil embargo was lifted after a bare two months. Within a month of Nasser's speech in which he accused British airmen of bombing Syrian and Egyptian targets during the war, Hassanein Haikal was hinting, in an article in the *Sunday Times*, at Egyptian willingness to improve relations with Great Britain. And despite the United States' unequivocal stand in support of Israel, the Egyptian Government sought the return path to better relations with Washington. The unbridled attacks on the US on Radio Cairo and in the Egyptian press were abruptly stopped. The accusation that the US and Great Britain had participated in the fighting on Israel's side was dropped. And all this despite, or maybe because of, a progressively stiffening attitude on the part of Washington during the months following the war.

The Arabs were not the only ones to get no change out of the Americans. When the British Foreign Secretary complained that the closure of the Suez Canal was costing Britain £20 million a month, the American Secretary of State, Dean Rusk, replied frostily that the Canal closure did not represent a problem for the American economy. And the Russians, who maintained constant contact with the Americans over the Middle East crisis, found them as firm as a rock. With both the Americans and the Israelis maintaining their hard, inflexible attitude, which rested on the new facts created in the Middle East by the conquering Israeli army, the onus of seeking a settlement was placed fairly and squarely on the Arabs and the Russians. For now the boot was on the other foot. Whereas during the crisis period the Americans and Israelis had sought to change the *status quo* created by Nasser's closing of the Gulf of Aqaba, now it was the Russians and the Egyptians who were striving to change the new realities and revert to the *status quo ante*.

But both the Americans and the Israelis demanded a price for any change. The American stand was summarized in the five points which President Johnson laid down on 19 June:

1. The fundamental right of every nation in the Middle East to live, and have this right respected by its neighbours.

2. Justice for the refugees.

3. Full maritime rights for all nations. "Our nation has long been committed to free maritime passage through international waterways, and we, along with other nations, were taking the necessary steps to implement this principle when hostilities exploded."

4. Curtailment of the arms race.

5. A peace settlement. ". . . the crisis underlines the critical importance of respect for political independence and territorial integrity of all the states in the area. . . . This principle can be effective in the Middle East only on the basis of peace between the parties."

These five principles formed the basis of American policy in the Middle East after the June War. Implicit in them was support for the Israeli stand which stated clearly that there would be no withdrawal from the occupied territories without hard and fast guarantees for peace. The Israelis added the provision that such guarantees could only be given in the framework of direct peace talks between the Arab states and Israel, without intervention of a third party. The Americans were more elastic in their definition of guarantees for peace, and the greatest fear of the Israelis during the post-war period was that the Americans and the Russians would come to an agreement concerning peace guarantees which would be considered insufficient, and thus unacceptable to the Israelis.

And this was exactly what appeared to happen in mid-July after the emergency session of the General Assembly, which had been convened at the behest of the Soviet Union, which failed to adopt any of the four resolutions seeking a solution to the Middle East impasse. After a week of intensive behind-the-scenes negotiations between Mr Rusk and Mr Goldberg on the one hand and Mr Gromyko and his aides on the other, the United States and the Soviet Union reached agreement on a compromise resolution which would have linked an Israeli withdrawal with the ending of the state of belligerency between Israel and the Arab states. The Egyptians, after much heart-searching, were willing to accept the proposal, and, with considerably more alacrity, so were the Jordanians. But the Syrians and the Algerians refused categorically to agree to any solution which involved Arab acceptance of the State of Israel, and insisted on an immediate and unconditional Israeli withdrawal from occupied territories. Under their pressure, the Egyptians and Jordanians rescinded their acceptance and the Gromyko–Rusk compromise agreement, which was never made public, was abandoned before it had the chance of seeing the light of day.

The Israelis, who had remained prudently quiet, were relieved at this demise of joint-power efforts. They had been saved from a difficult situation by Arab intransigence. For they considered that a general renunciation of the state of belligerency on the part of the Arabs was not a sufficiently binding guarantee of peace to justify their withdrawal. They wanted something with teeth in it, not, as they put it, a vaguely worded document which could be torn to shreds when the Arabs saw fit to do so. The Americans, as we shall see, gradually came round to their point of view.

But for the time being there was complete deadlock. The emergency session of the United Nations General Assembly had ended in failure. None of the four resolutions obtained the two-thirds majority needed for adoption: a resolution put forward by eighteen Latin-American and Caribbean nations which linked Israeli withdrawal to the ending of the state of belligerency, and which was the most favourable to Israel, obtained 57 votes in favour and 43 against, with 20 abstentions; a Yugoslav resolution, co-sponsored by Cyprus and thirteen Afro-Asian countries, calling for unconditional withdrawal of Israeli forces, obtained 53 votes in favour and 46 against, with 20 abstentions; a Soviet resolution demanding withdrawal, restitution by Israel to the Arabs for damage caused, and condemnation of Israeli aggression was defeated on a paragraph-to-paragraph vote; and an even more strongly worded resolution put forward by Albania received only 22 votes in favour, with 71 against and 27 abstentions. The Americans had given their support to the Latin-American resolution, while the Russians backed the Yugoslav one in addition to their own.

This failure marked a tremendous blow to the Arabs and a severe setback for the Russians, who had in the first place called for the convening of the emergency session over and against American opposition. For the Arabs the disappointment was particularly great. They had been convinced that their losses in the battlefield would be made good by political action, in the same way that they had regained their lost territory after the Suez War of 1965. They had powerful and influential friends: the Communist bloc, Yugoslavia, India, the Muslim countries, the militants of Africa and Asia. They felt confident that these friends would produce a formula favourable to them, and this confidence was strengthened by the fact that of the two traditional friends of Israel who had sided with her in 1956 in the Suez War, one, France, had come over entirely to the Arab side, and the other, Britain, was wavering under the effects of the oil embargo and the closing of the Suez Canal. The fact that such a strong constellation of friends and allies proved impotent in the face of American steadfastness had a greatly demoralizing effect on the Arabs. This defeat, more than anything else, dispelled the last remaining doubts of President Nasser regarding the need for an Arab summit conference, and it also pushed him into the decision to discard his virulent anti-American policy and to try, instead, to mend his fences with the all-powerful United States.

For the Arabs, unlike the Israelis, could not afford to allow the stalemate to continue indefinitely. The Israelis were sitting pretty. Their new borders, on the banks of the Suez Canal and the Jordan River, and on the heights of Golan, were ideal for defence. They were in no hurry to reach a settlement. But the Arabs were. The economic, political and psychological consequences of Israel's gains were catastrophic for them. Both President Nasser and King Hussein desperately needed to regain their lost territories, and they had no time to lose.

It was this desperation, spurred on by the defeat at the UN, which gave birth to the Khartoum formula of the political settlement and to the Arab overtures to the West. This radical shift of policy on the part of the Arabs was made possible primarily because the Russians did not oppose it. In fact, the Russians gave President Nasser every encouragement to improve his relations with the West—within limits.

For, by August, when the Arabs went to Khartoum, the Russians must have fully realized their own limitations in the face of American and Israeli intransigence. They had tried, at the end of the fighting, to threaten Israel into withdrawing. On 9 June leaders of the Soviet Union, Bulgaria, Czechoslovakia, East Germany, Hungary, Poland, Rumania and Yugoslavia convened in Moscow to discuss the situation in the Middle East. In a joint statement* the Communist leaders denounced Israeli aggression, and warned Israel that if it did not withdraw, "the Socialist States which sign this statement will do everything necessary to help the people of the Arab countries to administer a resolute rebuff to the aggressors. . . ." The following day the Soviet Union severed diplomatic relations with Israel, to be followed by the other signatories of the joint statement. In the Note handed to the Israeli Ambassador in Moscow on 10 June, the Russian threat was put in much more explicit form: "Unless Israel immediately halts its military actions, the Soviet Union, jointly with other peace-loving States, will adopt sanctions

---

* The Rumanians, who throughout the Middle East crisis had taken an attitude independent from the other Communist countries, objected to the strong denunciation of Israel, and refused to put their signature to the joint statement.

against Israel, with all the consequences flowing therefrom."

These threats caused considerable apprehension in Israel. Some sort of Soviet action against Israel was half-expected. But, in contrast to the aftermath of the Suez War, when Soviet threats had been largely instrumental in obtaining an Israeli withdrawal, this time Israel decided to ignore them.* And the Russian threats proved to be hollow. For they had no means of carrying them out without risking confrontation with the United States. And this they were not prepared to do.

Their next attempt was at the United Nations. But this, as we have seen, proved no more successful. Mr Kosygin's famous meeting with President Johnson at Glassboro on June 23 and 24 evidently confirmed his belief that the Americans would on no account call for an Israeli withdrawal unless the Arabs offered concessions. The Russians, by this time, were every bit as anxious as the Arabs to reach a settlement of the Middle East impasse. The war had been an unnerving experience for them. It had uncovered their weaknesses vis-à-vis the United States. It had brought them near the abyss of direct confrontation with the Americans. They had, moreover, lost something like £400 million worth of military hardware, and a great deal of prestige and political capital to boot. They had no desire to see a repeat performance. And, like the Americans, they had no wish to see the Middle East becoming the jumping-off point for a third world war.

The settlement that the Russians were working for, however, was very different in nature from the one the Americans wanted. For whereas the primary aim of the United States was to reach a formula which would remove from the Middle East the state of perpetual tension, hostility and belligerency which had existed before 5 June, the Russians wanted the exact opposite. The settlement that they were striving for was one which would

---

* Israeli leaders have declared that their fear of Great Power sanctions after the 1956 Suez War was a gross miscalculation on their part. They are now convinced that the Russians were bluffing then as they were later in 1967.

bring an Israeli withdrawal from the occupied territories with
minimal Arab concessions, in order that the pre-June state of
tension between Arabs and Jews could be perpetuated. For the
Russians had realized that their continued presence in the Arab
countries of the Middle East depended largely on the perpetua-
tion of the Arab–Israeli conflict. Without that conflict the Arabs
would have no need of the Russians, and the greater potential
of the United States to provide economic aid would eject the
Russians from the positions they had won in much the same
way as had happened in other parts of the world.

The Russians, therefore, needed the Arab–Israeli conflict.
They had no wish to see a lasting peace between the two
adversaries. But equally, they could not allow the conflict to
explode once more into open war, with all the attendant dangers
of a further defeat for their client states, and, much worse, of a
possible escalation into a Soviet–American confrontation.

They therefore counselled moderation. They urged the Arab
leaders to come to terms with Israel, which would lead to an
Israeli withdrawal without removing the basic hostility and
tension which the Russians wished to preserve. A general
declaration of non-belligerency which could, in time, be revoked
or ignored, plus certain tactical concessions, such as freedom
of shipping in the Gulf of Aqaba and the Suez Canal, would
suit this purpose of the Russians. But even such mild proposals
constituted unpleasant advice for a people smarting under the
terrible humiliation of the sort the Arabs had just suffered.
The Russians had to be careful not to incur the wrath of their
Arab friends. They therefore sought to assure the Arabs of their
continued support and friendship by waging an all-out war of
words in which their heaviest guns, from President Podgorny
and Premier Kosygin through UN Ambassador Fedorenko
down to *Pravda* and *Izvestia*, fired salvo after salvo of vituperation against Israel. At the United Nations the Russian representative spared no word with which to castigate the Jewish
state, likening her to "Hitlerite masters", while Kosygin, in his
speech at the General Assembly, compared Israeli actions "to

the heinous crimes perpetrated by the Fascists during the Second World War".

Behind this Soviet verbal violence against Israel lay a dramatic struggle for power within the Soviet Union itself, the details of which are still shrouded in the mists of secrecy which usually envelop Soviet in-fighting. But enough information has filtered through to reveal that there were severe differences of opinion inside the Kremlin over Soviet Middle Eastern policy, with the Red Army commanders, backed by the more dogmatic elements in the Communist Party leadership, led by Alexander Shelepin, demanding a much tougher line against Israel and the West than the political leadership was willing to risk. The Red Army leaders saw in the Middle East set-back an opportunity which could be exploited. For paradoxically, whereas the Arab defeat was construed as a severe blow for the Soviet Union in the world as a whole, in the Middle East itself the Russian position was greatly strengthened. The Egyptians and the Syrians were now totally dependent on the Soviet Union in order to overcome their losses and rebuild their armies. The Russians could, therefore, dictate their terms. The militant faction in the Soviet leadership, and in particular in the defence establishment, were clear in their minds as to what these terms should be. They should include Soviet bases in Alexandria, Port Said and Latakia, greater political dependence of the Arabs on the Soviet Union, and the expulsion of remaining Western interests from the Arab world with the active help of the pro-Soviet Arab countries. The Soviet political leadership—Brezhnev, Podgorny and Kosygin—were in complete agreement with these aims of Soviet policy in the Middle East, but saw them as secondary to the prime Soviet aim of maintaining their policy of peaceful co-existence with the West and preventing a Soviet–American confrontation. They were not willing to sacrifice these basic tenets of Soviet foreign policy for the sake of a Soviet adventure in the Middle East. On the other hand, they could not risk a collapse of Soviet positions in the Arab world which could be immediately used against them by Shelepin and the army

Marshals. They could not have wanted a failure in Egypt to be put at their door in the same manner that Indonesia and the Cuban missile episode had been blamed on Khrushchev.

The Soviet leaders, therefore, far from taking the line that they might be throwing good money after bad, instead made every effort to strengthen their hold on the Arab world by pouring in military aid and by working for an Israeli withdrawal, which they considered an essential precondition for a strengthened Soviet presence in the Middle East. Hence their attitude at the UN, where they urged the Arabs to accept the joint American–Soviet compromise solution which called for an Israeli withdrawal in return for an Arab declaration of non-belligerency.

The Arab rejection of this proposal forced the Russians to realize that too great an insistence by them on major concessions could cost them Arab friendship. There were already rumblings in the Arab world, after the Gromyko–Rusk proposal, that the Russians were selling out on the Arabs.

The Russians, therefore, changed their tactics. They gave their blessing to the political offensive unleashed by President Nasser after the Khartoum summit conference, which was designed to prod the West into putting pressure on Israel to withdraw to the pre-June demarcation lines. They accepted the toning down of Arab attacks on the West which this offensive necessitated. For the Russians had evidently come to the conclusion that there could be no lessening of the danger which the Middle Eastern situation held for them until the Israelis withdrew, and there could be no method of obtaining Israeli withdrawal without Western pressure. And if the West, or to put it more simply, the United States, succeeded in persuading the Israelis to withdraw at the cost of Arab concessions, it would be better that the Americans rather than the Russians force these concessions out of the Arabs.

Moreover, the prospect of the Arabs softening their approach to the West could not have caused the Russians much alarm. For they must have known that their position, in Egypt and

Syria at least, was so strongly entrenched that no amount of wooing of the West could bring these countries under their present régimes back entirely in the Western fold. President Nasser and the Arab Socialist Union of Egypt, and the Ba'th régime of Syria, would always prefer the Soviet Union to the West; their entire political *aison d'être* was based on this attitude. And there was the massive arms lift to back up this reasoning.

The Russians, therefore, did not stand to lose much by this new Arab tactic. We thus see them, from August, playing a deliberately muted role in the search for a political settlement in the Middle East. The Arabs, with Marshal Tito as an enthusiastic supporting actor, were playing to an American audience, while the Russians stood in the wings, with bouquets ready if the play succeeded. The climax to this play came at the beginning of October, with the series of talks between the Egyptian Foreign Minister, Mahmud Riadh, and the American Ambassador to the UN, Arthur Goldberg, which we mentioned in the previous chapter. These talks were to have produced the formula leading to an Israeli withdrawal in return for Arab concessions.

But the talks failed. The concessions the Egyptians had to offer, based on Marshal Tito's proposals and limited by the Khartoum injunction of no direct talks, no recognition and no peace with Israel, were insufficient. The Americans were unimpressed by the performance. In the course of the talks the Egyptian Foreign Minister went so far as to give his agreement to the Gromyko–Rusk proposals of July: a declaration of non-belligerency in return for an Israeli withdrawal. But the American attitude had hardened. What had been good in July was no longer suitable in October. They now demanded much more precise terms for a settlement. They wanted a clear definition of the meaning of non-belligerency, with guarantees that the situation before 5 June could never return. And they insisted on full maritime rights for all nations, including the use of the Suez Canal by Israeli vessels, and not only for the passage

K

of Israeli goods in foreign ships, which was the furthest the Egyptians were willing to go on this subject.

For the Americans had reached the converse conclusion to that of the Russians. If, in Russian eyes, the Arab-Israeli conflict was a necessary precondition for Soviet penetration of the Middle East, the removal of that conflict became a vital American interest, purely within the cold war context. The Americans, therefore, had every reason to prevent the very thing that the Russians and the Arabs were seeking to attain, namely the return to the pre-June conditions of tension and violence in the Middle East. Moreover, by the autumn of 1967 they had begun to see through the political offensive of the Arabs, and to understand that the declaration of non-belligerency, as it stood, meant in reality hardly anything. Hence the hardening attitude of the Americans in October, an attitude which made it clear that neither tactical concessions nor a general formula of non-belligerency would be sufficient.

There were other factors which influenced the American stand. Quite apart from political considerations, President Johnson felt a sincere friendship for the State of Israel, and considered himself duty bound to give her every help he could. And there were also political undertones. President Johnson, more than most American Presidents, was dependent on the votes of the big cities. It was, however, in the large centres of population that his Vietnam policy was meeting most opposition. Conversely, it was in the cities and, understandably enough, among the Jews, that his tough line with the Arabs was most enthusiastically applauded. This fact could not have escaped the President in an eve-of-elections year.

The Americans repeated their demands to King Hussein during his visit to the United States in November. The King was increasingly taking over the leading role in the political offensive the Arabs were waging. In a series of lightning visits which brought him to half a dozen European capitals and finally to the United States, he succeeded in winning for the Arab world a great deal of sympathy and support which had previously been reserved for Israel. The King handled his public relations with the utmost skill and dexterity. In public appearances he was the epitome of moderation. It was not the Israelis whose existence needed guaranteeing, he would declare, but that of the Arabs, for since 1948 Israel had been steadily expanding at the Arab's expense. The Jews had created another tremendous refugee problem, and had, moreover, imprisoned a million Arabs within one vast concentration camp. "We are willing to live in peace with our Jewish neighbours," he repeatedly declared, but he would not grant the right of existence to the State of Israel. "There are Jews and Zionists, just as there were Germans and Nazis." The Arabs had nothing against the Jews living in peace, but not within the framework of a Zionist state which had usurped the land of the Palestinians and was now threatening to include new Arab territories within its boundaries. Privately, in his talks with Western leaders, the Jordanian monarch spelt out concessions the Arabs were willing to make in order to obtain an Israeli withdrawal. These included: complete termination of the state of belligerency; a declaration on the rights of all *peoples* of the region to live in peace and security; freedom of shipping in the Gulf of Aqaba and in the Suez Canal; demilitarization of the Sinai and the West Bank of the Jordan; freedom of access for the Jews to their holy places in the Old City of Jerusalem. In return the King demanded a complete withdrawal to behind the 5 June demarcation lines (except in the case of the Gaza Strip, which Nasser was, according to Hussein, willing to surrender) and a settlement of the refugee problem with international help.

These conditions, however, were completely unacceptable to the Americans, and President Johnson made this plain to the King during their meeting in November 1967. For there was nothing to prevent the Arabs ignoring the declaration of non-belligerency, nothing to guarantee that the Middle East was on the way to a lasting peace. They proposed instead that a UN mediator be appointed whose task it would be to bring the two sides to a permanent peace settlement by noting all the points in dispute which could then be settled by negotiations one after the other.

The Americans put extreme pressure on the King and the Egyptian Foreign Minister to accept this formula. They reminded the Arabs that previous intransigence had cost them dear; if they refused, American proposals in the future might be considerably tougher for the Arabs. King Hussein wavered. He was inclined to accept. But the Egyptians refused. Instead, encouraged by the Russians, they summoned the Security Council to discuss the entire Middle East crisis, and successfully blocked the American proposal with an Indian counter-proposal.

The Security Council debate on the Middle East in the latter half of November 1967 developed into one of the most dramatic political tugs-of-war that that august body had witnessed in many a year. The Americans could barely suppress their anger and disappointment at the fact that the Council was meeting at all. A week earlier they had been more optimistic than ever before that a political formula was at last in the offing. They had felt that they could succeed in convincing the Arabs to agree to their formula of negotiations with the Israelis through the mediation of the UN. Once the Arabs agreed, they believed they could also persuade the Israelis to co-operate. And then came the Egyptian decision to convene the Security Council. Behind this decision were the Russians, who wished to prevent at all costs a settlement made at American bidding and on American terms. By putting forward a proposal similar to the one the Latin Americans had proposed in the General Assembly in July, the Arabs and the Russians hoped to gain a majority in the Security Council for a call to Israel to withdraw in return for a declaration of non-belligerency. They very nearly succeeded in their ploy. But in the ensuing deadlock between the two opposing Powers, the British stepped in, and, for the first time since the beginning of the Middle East crisis, were able to influence events in a region in which, not so long ago, Britain had reigned supreme. Lord Caradon, the British representative at the

Security Council, presented his compromise resolution which was unanimously accepted, thus saving the world from another interminable debate on the Middle East in the General Assembly.

The British proposal called for a withdrawal of Israeli forces from occupied areas—the Arabs tried without success to persuade Lord Caradon to add the word "the" before the word "occupied"—and linked that withdrawal to a declaration of non-belligerency. But it also called for the definition of permanent and safe boundaries for all countries in the region, the demilitarization of certain zones, for freedom of shipping and for a just solution to the refugee problem. Above all, it cleared the way for a UN mediator—Gunnar Jarring, of Sweden, was chosen—to leave almost immediately for the Middle East.

The British had a special interest of their own in solving the crisis. Of all the countries of the West, Great Britain was the hardest hit by the Middle East fighting. The oil embargo had affected her more than any other country. The closing of the Suez Canal was costing her some £20 million monthly. And the accusations of her collusion with Israel during the war had led the Governments of Iraq, Syria and the Sudan to break off diplomatic relations with her; Algeria and Egypt had already taken this step previously over the Rhodesian issue. The British were, therefore, understandably more anxious that a settlement be attained than most other countries. Their overriding concern was to ensure the continued flow of oil from the Middle East and to obtain the speedy reopening of the Suez Canal. But their efforts in this direction were based on a number of misconceptions. They had not grasped the significance of the Arab change of tactics towards the US caused by the hardening American approach. George Brown, the Foreign Secretary, still followed the old Arabist formula that, in order to guard British oil interests in the Middle East, it was essential to maintain friendly relations with the Arabs. Mr Brown ignored the lessons to be learnt from the lifting of the oil embargo, which was rescinded not because of British overtures but because the Arabs realized that the embargo was hurting them more than its intended victims and because they were anxious to appease the West. The tiger in the Arab oil tank was a paper one, but the British Foreign Office chose to ignore this fact. It shunned the revolutionary concept of guarding the oil interests by means of instilling in the Arabs the fear that they might lose the income from their oil if they used it as a lever for political blackmail. But Mr Brown was guilty of further miscalculations. He did not realize that after the war King Hussein had become expendable as far as the Israelis were concerned. This led him to the mistaken belief that Israel could be persuaded into giving up the West Bank of the Jordan in order to prevent the collapse of King Hussein's kingdom. British efforts in this direction were soundly rebuffed by the Israelis. He also failed to take into account the depth of feeling existing in Israel over the uniting of Jerusalem. In July 1967 the official policy of the British Government was still that the whole of Jerusalem, including the Jewish sector, should be internationalized. For the Israelis such a solution was so ridiculous that the popular Israeli press, at least, ceased to take Mr Brown seriously.

There was another miscalculation on the Foreign Secretary's part which was to cause trouble for him at home. For Mr Brown did not take sufficiently into account the extent which his policy could be taken to task in Parliament and in the British press. This point was underscored when he returned to London from the emergency session of the United Nations. His handling of the Middle East issue was one of the causes for the drop in popularity which the Foreign Secretary suffered in the latter part of 1967. Mr Brown, in his speech at the UN, put strong emphasis on the need for an Israeli withdrawal. He did not link such a withdrawal with guarantees for Israel's security, as many other speakers did. "War should not lead to territorial aggrandizement," he stressed. And he warned Israel that any step taken to annex Jerusalem would "not only isolate them from world opinion, but will also lose them the sympathy that they have." These stern words were somewhat offset by Mr Brown's call for "free and innocent passage through international waterways for all ships of all nations", but observers construed the British Foreign Secretary's speech as being markedly unfavourable to Israel. Israeli public opinion hastened to compare Mr Brown with his predecessor, Ernest Bevin, whose name is still anathema in Israel. Mr Brown's main point in his General Assembly speech was that a new form of UN presence would be necessary in the area in the future, and a special representative of the Secretary-General should be nominated in order to advise on the role the UN should take to maintain peace in the region. This attitude, again, fell far short of Israeli hopes of translating their victory into a permanent peace settlement, for the UN, in their eyes, could at best freeze the existing hostile coexistence as it had done for the previous twenty years.

Thus British efforts were suspect in Israeli eyes even before the dispatch of Sir Dingle Foot and, later, of Sir Harold Beeley to Cairo for talks on the resumption of diplomatic relations. Israeli public opinion jumped to the conclusion that the British were preparing to sell them out, despite assurances that any resumption of relations with Cairo would not be at the expense of Israel. Much more pertinent was the constant pressure the British maintained on the Israeli Government over the question of accepting back refugees from the West Bank who had fled to Jordan, and whose plight was pitiful. The British Ambassador in Tel Aviv, Michael Haddow, made repeated *démarches* on this subject to the Israeli Government, which may well have been instrumental in bringing about certain concessions on the part of the Israelis.

Mr Brown did succeed, however, in improving Britain's relations with the Arabs, and in particular with Egypt. His tireless efforts to restore relations found an answering call in Cairo. The Egyptians had, as we have seen, realized that only by improving their relations with the West could they hope to reach a solution which would lead to an Israeli withdrawal to the pre-June demarcation lines. But to mend fences with the US, which was openly following a pro-Israel policy, was no easy matter for the Egyptians. It was far easier to influence the US by means of Great Britain, especially in view of the stand the Foreign Secretary had taken. Mr Brown's efforts thus fell on fertile ground, and they were crowned with success in December 1967 when the two countries once more exchanged Ambassadors. The Israelis had believed that the British, in their eagerness to see the Suez Canal reopened, would agree to present the Arab case before the Americans. But their suspicions were allayed by Lord Caradon's last-minute effort at the Security Council, which had saved the Israelis from a severe diplomatic defeat. Mr Eban, the Israeli Foreign Minister, subsequently held a number of talks with Mr Brown, and the misunderstandings between Britain and Israel were finally cleared up when Mr Eshkol met Mr Wilson in London on 17 January 1968.

Thus, by February 1968, it looked as if the British were on the way to achieving the remarkable feat of gaining the confidence of both Cairo and Jerusalem. But the influence that Britain could bring to bear on events in the Middle East was negligible; it declined even more after Mr Wilson's announcement on 16 January of Britain's abdication of her East-of-Suez role, and her virtual demise as a world power.

Hardly more effective were the moves of the French, though the Israelis, at least, were more concerned with French policy in the Middle East than with that of the British. France had for years been considered Israel's special ally. That this ally should have deserted them in their most difficult hour left the Israelis disappointed and angry. But the blow was offset by Israel's new relationship with the US; the damage was limited to the embargo on the supply of French planes, of which the Israelis were informed as early as 9 June, at the height of the war. Thus the ability of the French to influence Israel's actions was much less than President de Gaulle had evidently envisaged in May 1967 when he received Israel's Foreign Minister at the Elysée before his visit to the US. The President's stern warning to Mr Eban not to go to war over the Gulf of Aqaba and to rely on the Great Powers to find a solution to the Middle East crisis was ignored by the Israelis, and this in turn led to the steadily

worsening relations between France and Israel which reached
their climax on 27 November 1967, when President de Gaulle
castigated Israel in his half-yearly press conference and made
remarks about the Jewish people which were interpreted in Tel
Aviv and elsewhere as being anti-Semitic. President de Gaulle's
silence over the blockading of the Gulf of Aqaba in May, his
hard words to Mr Eban, the imposition of the embargo, his
accusations that Israel had acted in an aggressive manner, his
instructions to the French delegation at the UN to vote against
Israel, and finally his disparaging remarks on the Jews and on
Israel at his press conference—all these were treated by the
Israelis as solid evidence of the hostile attitude of the French
Government towards Israel.

Yet the picture as not so simple. Israel continued to receive,
right up to the outbreak of the war, vital military supplies from
France. These supplies were resumed immediately after the war.
France, in fact, remained the single most important supplier of
military equipment to the Israel defence forces, and was more
than willing to supply everything the Israelis needed, including
the most modern weapons—everything except the fifty Mirage 5
planes that the Israelis had ordered. The stand taken by President
de Gaulle against Israel was severely criticized in many quarters
in France. The powerful French aircraft industry was up in
arms against the embargo. Not only was it in danger of losing
an excellent customer—for the Israelis had always paid in hard
cash for their aircraft—but the embargo was frightening off
other prospective customers, who feared that the French might
subject them at some future date to similar pressure.

This criticism of the President's policy in official quarters on
the one hand, coupled with the public outcry caused by his
remarks on the Jews who, *inter alia*, he called a 'domineering
race', led President de Gaulle to take what was, for him, a rare
step: he retreated from his outspokenly hostile attitude towards
Israel, and reiterated the friendship he felt towards the Jewish
state. The President was given this opportunity when, in the last
days of 1967, Ben Gurion addressed a long personal letter to

him, repudiating the remarks he had made about the Jewish people and outlining the special relationship which had existed between Israel and France. President de Gaulle hastened to reply to the former Israeli Premier, and took the unusual step of publishing the exchange of letters after obtaining Ben Gurion's agreement. In his reply, de Gaulle reaffirmed that he considered Israel "a friend and an ally", and that France would oppose any attempt to annihilate the Jewish state. He blamed the Egyptians for blockading the Gulf of Aqaba, but he reiterated his belief that Israel had "overstepped the bounds of moderation when she ignored the warnings of the Government of the French Republic and waged battle, and by force of arms occupied Jerusalem, and Jordanian, Egyptian and Syrian territory, and followed a policy of suppression and deportation".

It was this ignoring of the French warning, as much as the closer relations between Israel and the US, which rankled with the French President. But French policy was not so much aimed at "punishing" Israel as at regaining influence in the Arab world. And the French saw results. President de Gaulle's stand was warmly praised in the Arab press. French oil interests in Algeria were untouched, while important oil concessions were gained by the French in Iraq after a high-ranking Iraqi delegation visited France in December 1967. Discreet negotiations were begun by French bankers with the Kuwaiti Government with a view to syphoning off some of the Kuwaiti reserves from Great Britain to France. French interest in Iraq and the Persian Gulf area was heightened by Mr Wilson's declaration that Britain would pull her troops out of the Persian Gulf area by 1971. The Iraqi President was invited to Paris and was received with great pomp in the French capital in February 1968. In Cairo the French Ambassador let it be known that President de Gaulle might, under certain circumstances, agree to act as mediator in the Arab–Israeli dispute.

But such a possibility remained unlikely in the extreme. For neither French nor British deeds could appreciably affect or alter the situation in the Middle East. In 1968, more than ever before, the region had become dependent on acts and decisions taken by the two super-powers.

By the beginning of 1968, the Soviet comeback into the Middle East had become the dominant factor in the political aftermath of the Six-Day War. The Russians had, within six months, covered all the losses in military equipment suffered by the Syrians, and replaced more than 75% of the planes and tanks lost by the Egyptians. This alone put the Syrians and the Egyptians into a position of dependence on the Russians to an extent far beyond their pre-June connections with the Soviet Union. And in addition there was the political support of the Russians for the Arab case, and, of far greater importance, the physical presence of Soviet power, as demonstrated by the Soviet naval flotilla and by the squadron of Russian bombers which flew into Cairo airport in December 1967 for a lengthy stay. This appearance of Soviet military might in the Middle East had a profound effect on political and military developments. Its mere presence restored confidence to the Arabs, and enabled them to hasten their preparation for another round of combat with Israel without fear of an Israeli pre-emptive strike aimed at preventing these preparations reaching dangerous proportions. Thus the Soviet moves had the effect of giving a new lease of life to the Arab aspirations of annihilating Israel, even if this was not the Russian intention. The Russians had shown them that all was not yet lost, that there was an alternative to a political settlement, and that if they bound themselves entirely to the Soviet Union they would obtain sufficient military aid to enable them to fight yet another day. Their half-hearted willingness to come to terms with Israel was, by the end of 1967, fast melting away under the warmth of Soviet benevolence.

The Russians were after high stakes. A Russian-oriented Middle East would be the fulfilment of age-long Russian aspirations. The Middle East could serve as a window looking out towards the Indian Ocean to one side and the African continent to the other. Russian entrenchment in this vital area— and not least in its southernmost tip, in the Yemen—would be a fitting milestone to mark the fiftieth anniversary of the Soviet Union. Moreover, the possibility of using the Arab countries as forward bases opened up new vistas for Soviet moves in the cold war. The Russians had never previously thought in terms of Soviet intervention in localized conventional wars. But one of the characteristics of the 1967 manœuvres of the Warsaw Pact armies was the emphasis placed on marine assault troops and naval landing craft, both of which are used for offensive purposes in conventional warfare. The Russians also began building aircraft carriers for the first time in 1967; with the facilities offered to them in Latakia, Port Said, Alexandria, Algiers and Aden, such vessels could upset the power structure existing in the Mediterranean area, and eventually also in the Indian Ocean. By 1968 the Soviet Mediterranean fleet had already become a force to be reckoned with, with an estimated forty-five vessels in the area with crews numbering close to 25,000. At the same time, they had at least 6,000 military "advisers" in five Middle Eastern countries, and Soviet pilots were believed to be flying aircraft against the royalists in Yemen's civil war.

Thus the Russian penetration of the Middle East had succeeded more than any other similar operation in other parts of the world, and they had every interest in deepening this penetration. The key was the Arab–Israeli conflict, and its continuation became a vital factor in Russian foreign policy. When a high Russian official was asked why the Soviet Union did not employ the Tashkent spirit for the Middle East as she had done over the Indian–Pakistan crisis he replied that the Tashkent peace formula had been used in a dispute between two equal peoples, but in the Middle East there was a struggle between the forces of imperialism as represented by Israel which sought to overthrow the progressive forces of the socialist régimes of Egypt and Syria, and there could be no "Tashkent" between imperialism and socialism. Thus the Arab–Israeli conflict was reset in the terminology of the cold war, with both the Arabs and the Jews being drawn against their will into the vortex of Great Power rivalry.

The powerful Soviet build-up in the Middle East increased internal strains within the American establishment in a manner reminiscent of the pre-June days. Now, as then, two schools of thought crystallized, with the "appeasers", led by some of the top State Department officials, demanding a halt to US support of Israel as a means to wean the Arabs away from the Soviet grasp, as opposed to those who believed that the new arms build-up in the Arab states was all the more reason for the US to increase its support for Israel, in order to prevent a Soviet-backed Arab victory over Israel which would be construed throughout the world as a defeat for the US.

But despite the doubters, President Johnson maintained his firm pro-Israel policy, and he went out of his way to demonstrate this fact when Mr Eshkol visited the US on 8 January and spent two days as President Johnson's guest at his Texas ranch. Although the Israelis did not obtain the Phantom aircraft they had hoped for, the declaration after the talks made it plain that the US was standing by its commitments to Israel, and would review the question of arms supplies if the Russians continued to arm the Arabs.

One of the points which emerged from the Johnson–Eshkol talks, which threw a ray of light on an otherwise sombre picture, was the guarded optimism of both leaders regarding the mission of Gunnar Jarring, the Swedish diplomat who had been appointed special UN representative in the Middle East. The Americans, President Johnson stressed, placed great importance on his mission. They were willing to back him to the hilt. And they had reason to believe that the Arabs were also willing to co-operate with him. His mission represented, in their opinion, a great opportunity which should not be missed. Mr Eshkol replied by greatly complimenting the Swedish diplomat, and assured his American host that Israel would do everything possible to make his mission a success.

The mission was by no means easy. Both the Arab and the Israeli press were unsparing in their criticism. Yet the quiet diplomacy and supreme patience practised by the Swede showed results. He succeeded in bringing about an exchange of prisoners between Egypt and Israel, though he was less fortunate over the freeing of fifteen ships trapped in the Suez Canal since the June War: the Israelis agreed to their departure via the southern exit of the Canal, but refused to agree to the Egyptians clearing both the northern and southern ends without receiving prior guarantees that Israeli ships would have the same rights to use the Canal as the ships of every other nation.

Yet these were side issues. Jarring's main efforts were directed to bringing the Arabs and the Israelis together, either in direct or, preferably, indirect talks, with Jarring acting as "go-between". By February 1968 it appeared as if Jarring's persistence was proving justified. In an important policy statement, Israel's Foreign Minister, Abba Eban, declared that Israel would agree to a form of negotiations with the Arabs, based on past precedent. This was taken to refer to the procedure used at the 1949 Rhodes armistice talks after the Palestine War where Israelis and Arabs negotiated under the chairmanship of a UN mediator, Dr Ralph Bunche. Mr Eban's statement was construed as a willingness on the part of Israel to forgo her demand for direct negotiations, and an acceptance of Jarring's proposals that Israelis and Arabs send delegates to Nicosia, where, without meeting directly, they would nevertheless conduct negotiations through the medium of Gunnar Jarring himself.

In the capitals of the West the political pundits predicted a major breakthrough in the political impasse of the Middle East. Mr Eban's declaration had shown a way out, and it was now up to the Arabs to make the most of it. There was, at first, no response from the Arab capitals. This, in itself, was an encouraging sign. Unofficially, Egyptian diplomats let it be known that they welcomed the Jarring proposal for separate but simultaneous talks in Nicosia, but they wished to have minimum publicity for any talks that might take place. Mr Jarring himself was called post-haste back to New York for consultations with U Thant. The stage was set for a new, and possibly crucial, phase in his mission.

But the optimism was short-lived. Once more the unexpected took a hand in the Middle East. As the Jarring proposals were being studied in Jerusalem and in Cairo, a military tribunal in Cairo pronounced sentence on the commanders of the Egyptian Air Force and Army who had been accused of "negligence, which marred the victory of the Egyptian forces" in the June War. General Sidki Mahmud, former commander of the Air Force, was sentenced to fifteen years in prison; others received lighter sentences.

The publication of these sentences provoked a wave of unrest in Egypt. Matters came to a head on 21 February, when workers in the giant military factories in the Helwan region downed tools and held a stormy protest meeting in which they condemned the leniency of the military judges and demanded the death penalty for the accused. Encouraged by the local branch of the Arab Socialist Union, the workers then surged out into the streets, intending to call on other factories to gain mass support for their demands. But demonstrations and protest marches were strictly forbidden in Egypt. For years the only demonstrations that had taken place were those organized or encouraged by the Government. This one very evidently did not fall under that category. Despite the involvement of the Arab Socialist Union, the Minister of the Interior gave orders to restrict the protest meeting to the confines of one factory only. But as the workers filled the streets of Helwan, the police panicked. The order to open fire was given. Workers were wounded, and the rumour went round Cairo like wildfire that at least fifteen had been killed by the bullets of the police.

The situation now rapidly worsened. Tension rose; a revolutionary atmosphere could be sensed in the city as anger against the police, the army and the Government mounted. The storm burst on Saturday 24 February as tens of thousands of students and workers converged on the National Assembly, in the centre of Cairo. Another group made for the offices of *al-Ahram*, smashing windows, overturning cars and setting fire to buses on the way. The cries of the students, which had at first been confined to chants of "death penalty for the guilty", soon changed tone and content. They were now directed against the Government and against President Nasser himself. Not since 1952 had Cairo witnessed such scenes.

Despite a Government warning that demonstrators would be heavily punished the students continued their violent wave of protest. On Sunday 25 February pitched battles between students and police took place in the vicinity of the University buildings and outside *al Ahram*, once more a target for the students' wrath. A students' delegation was received at the National Assembly and demanded, *inter alia*, total liberty of expression and thought, and withdrawal of the secret police from the universities. Outside the Parliament building, students paraded with banners proclaiming "We demand liberty and democracy". Inside the building of the National Assembly, Members of Parliament were conducting a bitter auto-critique of the régime to a degree unique since the overthrow of the monarchy in 1952.

Faced with this open rebellion of students and workers, the Government was forced to make concessions. A hastily worded announcement declared that the Minister of War had not confirmed the sentences passed by the military tribunal, and General Mahmud and the other accused would consequently be re-tried. Another announcement, directed at the students, declared that their grievances would be studied; later they were told that the sixty students arrested would be released. But all this was not enough. The people wanted to hear their leader, whose silence throughout that tumultuous week had been more expressive than any speech. Finally, on 3 March, Nasser appeared before a mass gathering of workers at Helwan, organized by the Federation of Trade Unions.

The tone adopted by the Egyptian President at Helwan was both paternal and placatory. The demonstrations and the bloody encounters with the police had been the result of a series of misunderstandings, he averred. They had been exploited by counter-revolutionary elements in order to demand the "suppression of the Arab Socialist Union, the dissolution of the

National Assembly, the liquidation of the youth movements and the establishment of democracy and liberty of expression". Egypt must not grant any liberty to the enemies of the revolution, Nasser declared, for reaction wished to profit from her defeat.

Nasser was defending the revolution from the enemies within —the counter-revolutionary elements, as he called the Muslim Brotherhood. Yet in such circumstances it was imperative for him to make a strongly worded statement regarding the enemy at the gates, the Israelis entrenched on the eastern bank of the Suez Canal. A particularly thoughtless and ill-timed administrative decree, issued by the Israeli Minister of Interior at the request of the Minister of Justice, gave him this opportunity. The Israelis had abolished the status of "enemy territory" which had existed hitherto in the areas occupied by them in the June War. The reasons for this decree had been administrative and juridical, but the Arabs seized on it as proof that the Israelis intended to annex the territories outright. Referring to this decree in his Helwan speech, Nasser declared that it supplied a new stimulus for the Arabs to liberate their territories, foot by foot, no matter how great the sacrifice would be. The inference was plain: the Arabs would have to go to war again, though he was careful not to say so in so many words.

Moderation was thus once more thrown to the winds. In the face of internal unrest, Nasser, as so many other leaders had done before him, called for the "sacred unity" of the people with the army in order to overcome the dangers besetting the nation. That week the Jarring proposals were rejected out of hand by the Egyptians, and, later that month, in a major reshuffle of the Egyptian Government, the leading moderate who had advocated a more liberal foreign policy, Zakaria Muhi ed-Din, was dismissed.

The hopes that had been pinned on a settlement between Jordan and Israel fared no better. We have seen, in the beginning of this book, how a relatively small group of extremists, banded together in the Fatah, played a major role in bringing the Middle East to war. Now the play had come full circle. The cycle was beginning again. Yet once more the Fatah was creating an escalation of violence. King Hussein appeared powerless to prevent their actions, which in the early months of 1968 were becoming increasingly frequent and daring. Their plans for establishing themselves in Cis-Jordan, and creating there a mass underground movement had, indeed, been foiled by the efficiency of Israel's security services and by the refusal of the local inhabitants to co-operate with the Fatah guerrillas. Instead, the Fatah set up camp on the eastern bank of the Jordan, making almost daily forays across the river into Israeli-held territory. Matters reached a head when, on 18 March a bus taking Tel Aviv high-school pupils on a trip to the Negev hit a Fatah mine; two were killed and twenty-eight pupils were wounded. This was too much for the Israelis. Public opinion demanded action. It came on 21 March, in the form of a massive attack across the Jordan, in which two Israeli brigades participated. The Israelis were out to wreak vengeance on the Fatah; their main objective was their main base at Kerameh, which they destroyed after bitter fighting. One hundred and fifty members of Fatah were killed and an equal number taken prisoner; the Israelis lost twenty-nine soldiers killed and some seventy wounded, a high price to pay for such a raid.* Foremost among the casualties of this raid were the plans of Gunnar Jarring for an early meeting between Jordanian and Israeli representatives through his mediation. Terror and violence had killed the hopes of a speedy settlement. Moderation and good

---

* The high number of casualties among the Israelis was largely due to the manner in which the raid was carried out. The Israelis had hoped to limit their action to the Fatah only. They warned the Jordanians beforehand not to intervene, and dropped leaflets on the forward villages warning the inhabitants not to leave their homes. The Israeli soldiers were under strict orders not to harm civilians and not to fire on houses unless fired upon. The Israelis, hampered by these orders, thus advanced on an enemy who was awaiting them and who had had time to prepare for the attack. The Israelis claimed that the raid was not punitive but rather a pre-emptive strike aimed at preventing a massive terror offensive which the Fatah had planned. The Kerameh raid disrupted the Fatah plans, though small-scale Fatah forays continued unabated.

sense were once more in full retreat in the Middle East, and it seemed that the Fatah were once more succeeding in embroiling the Arabs and the Jews in battle, against the will of the majority, as it had done in May 1967. Once more the prospects of a peaceful settlement faded, one more mirage in the wake of a sandstorm.

But was peace in the Middle East a mirage? Were the Arab and Jewish peoples destined to fight, and fight again, until such time when the use of new and terrible weapons would bring a bloody stalemate, annihilating the hopes and aspirations of both Arabs and Jews? At first sight this indeed appeared to be the trend. Both in Israel and in the Arab countries the winds of chauvinism and intransigence were blowing strongly. The Israelis who demanded an outright annexation of the territories they had conquered were encouraged in their attitude by the extremist declarations of the Arab leaders, who called either for a popular war and armed struggle "*à la* Vietcong", or for a holy war, a "Jihad", to exterminate the Jewish state. Could the Israeli contention that there would be no withdrawal without peace and security be condemned in view of these threats of the Arabs? The Israelis, moreover, pointed to the last time they had withdrawn from conquered territory in return for guarantees: that had been in 1957, after the Suez War. Neither the guarantees of the Great Powers nor the presence of the United Nations Emergency Force had been sufficient to prevent the escalation leading to the June War. and the Israelis were not prepared to withdraw once more solely in order to gain another ten years' respite. This time they wanted something more tangible in exchange for a withdrawal, and on this point the entire nation, except those demanding annexation, was united. But what the Israelis wanted—recognition, fixed and recognized boundaries, peace—were the very things the Arab leaders, at the Khartoum summit conference, had committed themselves to withholding. Neither Nasser (as the events of February 1968 showed) nor even Hussein dared to compromise on these points. The only way out of this deadlock, so it seemed a year after the war, was a hostile co-existence lasting three, five, ten or fifteen years until a new escalation, triggered off by hotheads or extemists, would once more set the Middle East aflame.

It was a sombre picture, made all the more so because of the probability that in any future war in the Middle East non-conventional weapons would be used, with resulting loss of life and with attendant political consequences for the entire world. Yet such a path was not inevitable. The June War had unleashed new emotions and new forces in the Middle East, which, one year later, had still not taken shape. There was, as yet, no clear picture, but there were signs pointing the way. In Egypt, the February riots had demonstrated that the politically conscious section of the population had lost confidence in the President and in the régime. The remnants of the Military Junta, backed by police and security services, no longer held the country in an iron grip. An increasing power vacuum was opening up, and forces of both the left wing and the right were preparing themselves for the political struggle that lay ahead. In Jordan, King Hussein's inability to keep the extremists in check was giving the Palestinians the opportunity they had been waiting for since the Palestine War of 1948. The Bedoui "Establishment" was fast losing its dominant position to the more modern, sophisticated Palestinians. Jordan was, in fact, becoming Palestinized, with a Palestinian population swollen by a quarter of a million inhabitants from Cis-Jordan and the Gaza Strip who had crossed over to the East Bank since the outbreak of hostilities in June 1967. The established patterns were changing, and in the shambles of the June War a new future was being born in the Middle East.

Will these changes lead to peace? A year after the war the Middle East was still in a state of turmoil, and peace was still as far off as ever. The Arabs had conceded defeat in battle but not in war. In their eyes the June fighting had been one more phase in a war which had begun fifty years earlier when Lord Balfour dispatched his famous letter to Chaim Weitzmann through Lord Rothschild, and which would continue until the State of Israel was annihilated. The June defeat had, they admitted, been disastrous for them, but it would only cause a postponment of their final victory. Some of the Arabs even developed a form of inverted Zionism, patterned on the Jewish "Return to Zion". "The Jews waited 2000 years until they succeeded in returning. We are patient. We will, if necessary, wait as long as that." The more extremist among the Arabs applied the Maoist theory of "fight, lose, fight, lose, until in the end you win" to the Palestine situation. This was the attitude adopted by the Governments of Syria and Algeria.

For the Arab objective has been nothing less than the complete destruction of Israel as an independent political entity, and their propaganda does not cease to preach the need to bring this about. But how deep does this propaganda really go? Do the Arabs really believe in the call for "Jihad" against the Jews? Has it penetrated deep into the masses, or is it only a "transistor Jihad", exciting the emotions but failing to create the real fervour associated with a holy war?

Hatred, like love, is a sentiment which is difficult to measure. If official pronouncements, written media or conversations with gullible journalists are the yardstick, then Arab hatred for Israel is beyond measure. There can be no doubt that, indeed, the constant propaganda has had a profound effect on the Arab masses. It has introduced certain stereotypes into the mainstream of Arab thought which will be very difficult to eradicate. Thus Israel is presented as a cancer in the body of Arabism which must be removed at all costs. She is the incarnation of evil. She is a base for imperialism, which established her with the aim of destroying Arab nationalism. The evil force behind Israel is the power of world Zionism, for whom all means are justified, as the Protocols of the Elders of Zion prove. The danger to the Arabs lies in the coalition of the forces of evil: Israel, World Zionism and imperialism.

This hate propaganda, conducted by the official organs of the Arab world, has continued unabated throughout the years. The reviling of Israel has become almost a ritual, without which no speech or article is complete. Every accusation or denunciation, no matter on what subject, must perforce include Israel or World Zionism.

Yet if the approach of the Egyptian prisoners who were in Israel, and of that of the million Arabs in Cis-Jordan, is anything to go by, this hatred did not percolate into the Arab consciousness as deeply as might have been expected. The degree of fraternization and co-operation between Israeli and Arab in Jerusalem and in Cis-Jordan is amazing when this constant hate propaganda is remembered. There have, as in every war, been many ugly incidents. The Israelis have, in many cases, been too heavy-handed. They have at times meted out punishment to the innocent for the hostile acts committed against them by the Fatah terrorists. Yet the Fatah terror campaign against Israel after the war has failed largely because the Arab population in Cis-Jordan refused to give the Fatah members aid. Indeed, of the hundreds of Fatah members apprehended by the Israeli security forces since the war, the large majority were caught on the strength of information supplied by the Arab population. Similarly, very few of the Egyptian prisoners voiced opinions of unadulterated hatred. They had been affected by the stereotypes of propaganda but very many believed that Israel and the Arabs could eventually live together provided the refugee problem was honourably settled and that Israel gave suitable guarantees that she had no expansionist aims. Most of the officers insisted that the Egyptian *fellah*, who makes up the vast majority of the Egyptian population, has no idea what Israel is and what the Israeli question is really about.

Thus, despite the official hate propaganda, voices of reason are being heard. These are, it is true, still isolated cases. But compared with the impermeable wall of hostility before the war, the change is startling. We have already mentioned the theories of Cecil Hourani and of President Bourguiba. Among the Palestinians, the movement for an independent Palestine, at peace with Israel, comprising at first Cis-Jordan only but eventually to include the East Bank of the Jordan, is steadily gaining ground. In February 1968 a leaflet entitled "Palestine for the Palestinians" was distributed in its thousands in Cis-Jordan. It was signed by the "Preparatory Committee for the Congress for a Palestinian State". Among those who believe in the need to bring to an end the strife between Arab and Jew, based on the creation of a Palestinian state and an honourable settlement of the refugee problem, are some of the most influential Palestinians in Cis-Jordan, men like Dr Taji Faruki and Aziz Shehade in Ramallah, Elias Bandak, the Mayor of Bethlehem, Sheikh Muhammad Ali al-Jaaberi, Mayor of Hebron, and other leading figures in Jerusalem and Nablus. Aziz Shehade is a case in point. One of the leading lawyers in Palestine, he had fought tenaciously for years for the rights of the Palestine refugees, acting as their unofficial adviser and spokesman. Now he believes that the cause of the Palestinians —and especially the refugees—can best be served by peace on honourable and favourable terms for the Palestine Arabs, and he has worked courageously to foster this belief. His views are being repeated in ever-widening circles among the Palestinians. One of the leading left-wing lawyers in Nablus told the present authors that he, and many like him, had lost all confidence in the Arab leaders to win back the rights of the refugees. "They are using us as a political football, and don't care a damn if we live or die." The only way, in his opinion, was to reach a settlement with Israel. "The two countries, Palestine and Israel, aligned together, could become a veritable Garden of Eden in the Middle East," he declared. Similar ideas were being increasingly expressed in Israel, and there was the example of Teddy Kollek, Mayor of Jerusalem, who worked tirelessly to bring the Arabs and the Jews of Jerusalem together on an equal footing.

Such opinions are not limited to Palestine and Israel. In Egypt there is an increasing realization that some sort of a peace settlement is the only way to bring Egypt out of its present state of near-bankruptcy. Some Arabs have openly begun to agitate against the militarism which has swallowed up so much of Arab wealth during the past years. A group calling itself the "Union of Free Arabs" distributed a pamphlet, which was published in full by the Tunisian weekly *Jeune Afrique*,* which revealed that since 1950 eight Arab countries had spent nearly ten thousand million dollars on their armies. Since 1955 military equipment to the value of $4,300,000,000 had been bought from the Soviet Union, $2,400,000,000 from Great Britain and $1,350,000,000 from the USA. This money, the authors of the pamphlet claim, could have been used to transform social and political conditions in the Arab world. "What does the future hold in store for us?" they ask. "More fantastic dreams, or constructive enterprises? The complete frittering away of our national potential, or the building of a progressive Arab society living in dignity and security?"

This was the question which an increasing number of Arabs were asking themselves in the wake of the war. But for the present the Arab leaders were committed to the policy that the June War was one more battle in an unfinished war. They were being encouraged in this belief by the Russians, who, as we have seen, considered continued tension between Arabs and Jews to be vital for their own aspirations in the Middle East.

The extremism of the present Arab leaders, fed by political expediency and encouraged by the Russians, stands in the way of any peaceful settlement of the Middle East crisis. Peace can only come about when new leaders take over and when the Middle East is removed from the grip of the cold war. But as long as the Arab–Israel conflict remains enmeshed in cold-war politics, the prospects for peace are poor indeed, and there can be little hope that swords will be turned into ploughshares in the land of the Bible.

* *Jeune Afrique*, 17 December 1967.

Index